"In an age of abundant digital texts, we need to go back to the manuscripts, their materiality and aesthetics, and their surprising features to get a realistic sense of the time in which biblical texts were created and first transmitted. Based on several major research projects, Garrick Allen presents fascinating insights into the changing design of biblical manuscripts, their layout and paratexts, titles, prefaces, prologues, cross-references. The book is well written and entertaining, and may change the way readers see the Bible."

—JÖRG FREY
University of Zurich

"In *Words Are Not Enough*, Garrick Allen brings the thrilling results of manuscript studies to a broad audience of students and scholars. As he shows, the New Testament is a material object that human communities continuously make and remake. With clarity and grace, he teaches readers what attending to manuscripts and their paratexts can offer while also showing, step by step, how to go about this work. This book performs a valuable service that will benefit anyone interested in the New Testament, early Christian history, and the history of the book. Highly recommended."

—JENNIFER WRIGHT KNUST
Duke University

"The increased attention given in recent decades to the documents that convey the text of the New Testament is most welcome. In this book, one of the leaders in this area of research makes clear the significance of paratextual features of manuscripts for a better understanding of the history of both text and canon of the New Testament."

—MICHAEL HOLMES
Bethel University

"Brimming with knowledge, this invaluable introduction will intrigue, surprise, and—most importantly—educate anyone who wants to understand the manuscripts and physical reality of the New Testament."

—CANDIDA MOSS
mingham, UK

"In this compelling and significant contribution, Garrick Allen provides an accessible guide to the fascinating materials that survive in New Testament manuscripts but that are systematically left out of modern critical editions. Allen's three-dimensional approach to the texts of the New Testament reconnects the texts with the world of the manuscripts. Get acquainted with the gems hiding in the critical apparatus, learn about the features that frame the text, and catch glimpses of the lives of readers who pondered the New Testament before you. Your reading of the New Testament will never be the same again."

—LIV INGEBORG LIED
Norwegian School of Theology

"This book is a game changer! As exegetes we are mainly interested in what we call the New Testament text(s). But a Bible is so much more—material, binding, titles, introductions, images, and marginalia—and all this influences our reading and understanding. It is time to change the field of biblical studies. Garrick Allen's fascinating and very readable book opens the door."

—TOBIAS NICKLAS
University of Regensburg

"The Bible is often imagined as a kind of monument, a fixed point in an ever-changing world. In his new book, Garrick Allen argues persuasively that this model overlooks the Bible's materiality: the Bible is always more than the sum of its texts, and—precisely because it is valued so highly—it changes constantly as its formatting and packaging changes."

—FRANCIS WATSON
Durham University

"This important and engaging book draws our attention to everything that is usually left unscrutinized on the pages of a Bible or manuscript. Allen shows us, through his sensitive analysis, how paratexts shape biblical interpretation in profound and unexpected ways."

—YII-JAN LIN
Yale Divinity School

WORDS ARE NOT ENOUGH

Paratexts, Manuscripts, and the Real New Testament

Garrick V. Allen

WILLIAM B. EERDMANS PUBLISHING COMPANY
GRAND RAPIDS, MICHIGAN

Wm. B. Eerdmans Publishing Co.
4035 Park East Court SE, Grand Rapids, Michigan 49546
www.eerdmans.com

© 2024 Garrick V. Allen
All rights reserved
Published 2024

Book design by Lydia Hall

Printed in the United States of America

30 29 28 27 26 25 24   1 2 3 4 5 6 7

ISBN 978-0-8028-8335-3

Library of Congress Cataloging-in-Publication Data

A catalog record for this book is available from the Library of Congress.

This publication was made possible through the support of a grant from Templeton Religion Trust. The opinions expressed in this publication are those of the author and do not necessarily reflect the views of Templeton Religion Trust.

To Eloise and Ivy

Contents

List of Figures and Tables ix

Preface xiii

FRAMING THE NEW TESTAMENT — 1

1. The Bible as Change — 5
2. Materiality, Layout, and Paratext — 8
3. Matthew in the Scofield Bible — 17
4. Matthew in the Green Bible — 27

TITLES — 35

5. The Titles of the New Testament — 39
6. Titles in Revelation and the Catholic Epistles — 46

CROSS-REFERENCES — 57

7. Eusebius and His Paratextual System — 63
8. Exploring the Euthalian Tradition — 76

CONTENTS

PREFACES	91
9. Prologues and Division in Acts	101
10. Making Lists Out of Acts	110

TRACES OF USE	123
11. Corrections and the Curious Case of Codex Montfortianus	131
12. Daydreaming and Learning with the New Testament	145
13. The Margins and Biblical Scholarship	161

Bibliography	171
Index of Subjects	191
Index of Manuscripts	194
Index of Scripture and Other Ancient Sources	196

Figures and Tables

Figures

Figure 2.1. The end of Hebrews and start of 1 Corinthians with multiple paratexts (P46, Dublin, Chester Beatty, CBL BP II, 38r) — 14

Figure 2.2. Gospel of Mark, starting at 1:10, surrounded by many different paratexts (GA 2604, Dublin, Chester Beatty, CBL W 139, 124r) — 15

Figure 4.1. Matthew 24:29–32 with catena, text division, and one Eusebian cross-reference in the left margin (GA 2604, Dublin, CBL W 139, 101r) — 30

Figure 4.2. Canon Table 2 showing texts shared by Matthew, Mark and Luke (GA 2604, Dublin, CBL W 139, 6r) — 31

Figure 6.1. Subscription to the Catholic Epistles (GA 307, Paris, BnF, Coislin grec 25, 254v) — 52

Figure 7.1. Canon Table 1: passages shared by all four gospels (GA 2604, Dublin, CBL W 139, 5r) — 65

Figure 7.2. Matthew 166_1 in the left margin between main text and outer margin commentary (GA 2604, Dublin, CBL W 139, 75v) — 70

Figure 8.1. Chapter list to Romans in margins of the *hypothesis* to Romans (GA 250, Paris, BnF, Coislin grec 224, 159v) — 82

Figure 8.2. Chapter 4 in Romans according to the Euthalian system with marginal commentary (GA 250, Paris, BnF, Coislin grec 224, 167r) — 84

Figure 9.1. Title to the prologue to Acts (GA 1162, Patmos, St. John the Theologian Monastery, 15, 1r) — 102

FIGURES AND TABLES

Figure 9.2. Start of the lection list (GA 1162, Patmos, St. John
the Theologian Monastery, 15, 2v)   106
Figure 10.1. Short quotation list (GA 1162, Patmos, St. John the
Theologian Monastery, 15, 3v)   112
Figure 11.1. Later insertion of the Johannine Comma in the
upper margin, with corresponding location marker (dash)
in the right margin (GA 177, Munich, BSB, Cod. graec. 211, 74r)   133
Figure 11.2. The Johannine Comma in Codex Montfortianus
(GA 61, Dublin, TCD MS 30, 439r)   134
Figure 11.3. Owner's note (GA 61, Dublin, TCD MS 30, 12v)   135
Figure 11.4. Complex correction in Matt 7:8–10 (GA 61, Dublin,
TCD MS 30, 16r)   141
Figure 12.1. Triangle guy with two little friends in the lower left
margin (GA 1175, Patmos, St. John the Theologian Monastery, 16, 6r)   148
Figure 12.2. A battle in the margins (GA 1175, Patmos, St. John
the Theologian Monastery, 16, 98r)   148
Figure 12.3. Angel, foot, underbite man in profile (GA 2049,
Athens, Hellenic Parliament Library, 45, 254r)   149
Figure 12.4. Sea-going ship (GA 497, London, British Library,
Add. 16943, 58r)   150
Figure 12.5. Jesus with tiny little hands (GA 1735, Mt. Athos,
Great Lavra Monastery, B42, 192v)   151
Figure 12.6. Prayer by Peter the Shoemaker (GA 2604, Dublin,
CBL W 139, 310v)   153
Figure 12.7. Practice writing in the lower margin at start of
Acts (GA 1277, Cambridge, Cambridge University Library,
Ms. Add. 3046, 1r, 4v, and 114r)   156
Figure 12.8. Additions to an eleventh-century copy of the Praxapostolos and Paul's letters (GA 1270, Modena, Biblioteca
Estense Universitaria, α. W. 2. 07, 7v)   158

TABLES

Table 7.1. Parallels presented in each canon table   67
Table 7.2. Comparison between four passages in Canon Table 1   68

Figures and Tables

Table 8.1. Number of chapters in the Euthalian tradition	80
Table 8.2. Synopsis of chapter titles whose topics relate to Romans *kephalaion* 4	85
Table 9.1. Division of Acts according to the lection list in GA 1162	107
Table 10.1. Short quotation list in GA 1162	111
Table 10.2. List of miracles in the Acts hypothesis	117

Preface

My goal for this book is to show the value of returning to the most basic sources that we have for the New Testament: the manuscripts, their texts, and their other features. The new questions that arise when we work to get behind our printed Bibles and critical editions are important for both scholars and those who are interested in Bibles for any number of other reasons. For scholars, I argue that we must utilize our critical editions to get at the materials they represent, to use editions as tools to understand our complex tradition, not only as proxies for the texts of the authors (or something close to it). The truly interesting evidence for many emerging questions in biblical studies is buried in the critical apparatus and in the manuscripts represented in that space. The dense mass of sigla and numbers that comprise the apparatus contain multitudes, worlds unto themselves, most of which remain unexplored. Expanding access to manuscript images and the underlying data that make up our editions has enabled us to begin to ask new questions and look for answers in new places.

For students and other people who think carefully about the Bible and its effects, I argue that engaging the manuscripts shows us that the New Testament is not necessarily what we tend to think it is. The consistency presented by the Bible as a reproducible, monolithic printed book obscures the underlying intricacies and idiosyncrasies of human effort that has made the New Testament what it is today. When we look at the manuscripts and the things they do, we gain a deeper understanding of the significance of this collection of letters and narratives (and one apocalypse for good measure). We only have the New Testament today because thousands of mostly anonymous people preserved, transmitted, thought about, cared for, and engaged with these literary works that were important for their own lives in one way or another. As Mary Wellesley notes, "Manuscripts hold stories and snapshots of the lives of people whom we otherwise might not encounter—anonymous scribes, artists and writers... it is through manuscripts that we can try to access something of their lives."[1] When we are able to empathetically think about Bibles in conversation with people from the past, we can start to rethink our own interactions with sacred texts.

This book grew organically out of my research on the New Testament's Greek manuscripts over the past five years or so. It was first conceived as part of a project entitled *Paratextual Understanding: A Cognitivist Approach to the Aesthetic Features of Manuscripts,* funded by the Templeton Religion Trust, in which I worked to connect the study of manuscripts and their features to larger philosophical discussions surrounding a theory of artistic value known as aesthetic cognitivism. Working closely with a manuscript at the Chester Beatty in Dublin, I explored the ways that the features of manuscripts we tend to overlook—many of which I examine in this book—might transmit knowledge to readers about the text and instill understanding about things beyond the text itself. Working closely with researcher Anthony Royle, I was interested to see how reading in manuscript cultures might change how people view the world and their place in it. This book is one result of this research; it is my attempt to argue for the effects of some of these features on readers and to begin exploring the larger consequences for these realities in biblical studies and the humanities writ large. Although it's focused on ancient sacred texts, and the New Testament in particular, this book is shaped by my reading of philosophical literature on aesthetics, and it works to set an agenda for the research at the boundaries of biblical studies, philosophy, and even the empirical sciences.

Work on this book has also been informed by the ongoing project *Titles of the New Testament: A New Approach to Manuscripts and the History of Interpretation* (TiNT), funded by the European Research Council. In collaboration with a team of researchers here in Glasgow, we are in

---

1. Mary Wellesley, *Hidden Hands: The Lives of Manuscripts and Their Makers* (London: Riverrun, 2021), 281.

Preface

the process of digitally editing every form of every title in every Greek manuscript that transmits part of the New Testament.[2] This work has given me the opportunity to spend hours and hours reading hundreds of manuscripts, all the while paying special attention to all the features that frame the text. The chapters on titles in this book are facilitated by this project and the data we've gathered thus far. I'm grateful to my team, Kelsie Rodenbiker, Martina Vercesi, Kimberley Fowler, Maxim Venetskov, and Lily Su, for their work on this project.

The final ongoing collaborative research that informed this book is the *Annotating the New Testament: Codex H, Euthalian Traditions, and the Humanities* project funded by the Arts and Humanities Research Council (UK) and undertaken in partnership with Kimberley Fowler, now at the University of Groningen. This project focuses on the Euthalian apparatus, a complicated and overlooked collection of lists, prefaces, and cross-references attached to most of the New Testament. We are currently working with researcher Emanuele Scieri to catalogue the diffusion of these features in the manuscripts and to make a new edition of GA 015, the earliest witness to this tradition. Like the TiNT project, this initiative has afforded me the opportunity to sit and read manuscripts—a rare thing in the modern university context. This project has especially informed chapters 10 and 12.

I wrote this book because I wanted to connect my work on these projects to larger critical questions about what constitutes the Bible, the New Testament, and sacred scripture. The book works to make these collaborative research projects accessible by offering something to scholars, students, and others interested in the Bible alike. It is not the final word on any issues I raise in it; instead, I hope that it brings us new questions about the fundamental substance of the New Testament and how we should engage it, pointing to new evidence that helps us think about both old and new questions. For students and other readers, I hope that this book begins to show that there is much work to be done on a corpus many of us know so well and that our own practices of reading are part

---

2. See Garrick V. Allen and Kelsie G. Rodenbiker, "Titles of the New Testament (TiNT): A New Approach to Manuscripts and the History of Interpretation," *Early Christianity* 11 (2020): 265–80.

PREFACE

of a long and interesting story of how people in the past have engaged these works. There is much more fruitful research to be carried out on the New Testament's manuscripts and their texts.

Before moving on to the book itself, there are some housekeeping issues that need to be mentioned here. Because manuscript study has some technical aspects and terminological issues, I want to clarify a few things about how I speak about the manuscripts in what follows. First, I want to discuss the concept of a "New Testament manuscript." In his book *Textual Scholarship and the Making of the New Testament*, David Parker argues that this concept is not very helpful because the manuscripts are so diverse in the works they preserve, their order, their texts, and their other features that calling something a "New Testament manuscript" doesn't really tell us much about it.[3] The phrase "New Testament manuscript" unintentionally reflects a theological idea about a fixed canon, even though very few Greek manuscripts reflect this canonical ideology. I agree with Parker that this phrase has limited utility in some discussions. However, when I use it in this book, the phrase refers to any manuscript that preserves at least part of a work that is now viewed as part of the New Testament without making any theological judgments about canon and recognizing that the spectrum of what we describe as "New Testament manuscripts" is quite broad and heterogeneous.

It's also important at this stage to clarify three distinct but related terms: text, work, and manuscript. A *manuscript* is a physical, handwritten reading object, like a codex or roll, that makes a text accessible to readers. I use the word *text* to refer to the specific instantiation of a *work* on a given manuscript, while *work* refers to the combination of *texts* that represent it. Put more simply, a *manuscript* is the physical object that is inscribed with a *text* of, say, the Gospel of Matthew. But the Gospel of Matthew is a literary *work*, crafted from each form of its *text* as it exists in the *manuscripts*. Traditionally, interpreters or exegetes are interested in the work, textual critics are concerned with the work's texts as they appear in the manuscripts, and art historians or codicologists are interested in the manuscripts as objects.[4] While I carefully distinguish

---

3. David C. Parker, *Textual Scholarship and the Making of the New Testament* (Oxford: Oxford University Press, 2012), 32–64.
4. See Parker, *Textual Scholarship*, 10–31.

Preface

these various levels of engagement in this book, I point out how each are interconnected, relevant, and legitimate for the study of the New Testament. It is not only the work and texts of the New Testament that matter; how the texts are presented in the manuscripts should shape the ways we view the works.

Finally, I want to clarify how I refer to manuscripts in this book, especially for the uninitiated. Because this book is concerned primarily with the New Testament, I start by describing each manuscript according to its Gregory-Aland (GA) number. GA numbers are keyed to the *Kurzgefasste Liste*, or abbreviated list, a catalogue that enumerates manuscripts that preserve any part of the Greek New Testament, managed by the Institut für Neutestamentliche Textforschung in Münster. The *Liste* exists in a print form, last published in 1994, and in a digital form that is regularly updated by the institute.[5] The *Liste* is an important tool for the study of these manuscripts, offering information on the holding institution, the layout, contents, and dates of each manuscript, and access to other resources like catalogues and bibliographies.[6] In addition to the GA numbers, I give the holding institution and call numbers for each manuscript and the diktyon number. The library information enables you to locate the current (or sometimes last known) physical location of the manuscript. The diktyon numbers are labels that are given to all Greek manuscripts inscribed on parchment and paper and serve as the basis for the Pinakes database of medieval Greek manuscripts, of which most of the items in the *Liste* are a part.[7] Together, the *Liste* and Pinakes are good places to start understanding the historical context of any given manuscript. So, for example, I might introduce a manuscript like this: "In GA

---

5. Kurt Aland, ed., *Kurzgefasste Liste der griechischen Handschriften des Neuen Testaments* (Berlin: de Gruyter, 1994). The digital version may be found on the website https://ntvmr.uni-muenster.de/liste.

6. See my discussion in Garrick V. Allen, "Digital Tools for Working with New Testament Manuscripts," *Open Theology* 5 (2019): 13–28. See also the overview of useful tools for manuscript study in David C. Parker, *An Introduction to the New Testament Manuscripts and Their Texts* (Cambridge: Cambridge University Press, 2008), 35–57.

7. "Pinakes: Textes et manuscrits grecs," https://pinakes.irht.cnrs.fr/ [accessed 9 August 2023]. See André Binggeli and Matthieu Cassin, "Le project *Diktyon*: Mettre en lien les ressources électroniques sur les manuscrits grecs," in *Greek Manuscript Cataloguing: Past, Present and Future*, ed. P. Degni, P. Eleuteri, and M. Maniaci (Turnhout: Brepols, 2018), 202–6.

xvii

PREFACE

2604 (Dublin, Chester Beatty, CBL W 139, diktyon 13571), a twelfth-century illuminated gospel manuscript, there are multiple prefaces." From this information you can see its number in the *Liste* (2604), its location (Dublin), its call numbers (W 139 at the Chester Beatty), and its diktyon entry (13571).[8] This is enough information to clearly identify the manuscript and to give you the tools to investigate it further if you wish. Where possible, I give links to places where images can be found online, although not every manuscript is always accessible, and the links will probably cease to work within five years or so. In terms of accents and breathing marks for Greek text, I follow the presentation of these features as they appear in the manuscripts, which means the accentuation of texts taken directly from manuscripts will often differ from standard convention.[9]

I want to conclude this preface by acknowledging the many people that shaped this book and made it possible for me to write it. Multiple people read drafts of the book, in part or in whole, helping me to avoid many serious pitfalls. (Those that remain are of course very much my own.) Many thanks are due to Christopher Brewer, Liv Ingeborg Lied, Jennifer Knust, Kelsie Rodenbiker, Andrea Stevens, Lily Su, Maxim Venetskov, Martina Vercesi, and Christopher Willard-Kyle. My mother, Julie Grantham, also read very early drafts. The only place I've previewed any part of this book was at the Nils Dahl Seminar at the University of Oslo in October 2022. This was a very encouraging experience and I'm grateful especially to Hugo Lundhaug, Blossom Stefaniw, and Gregory Fewster for their comments and reassurance. One of the things I enjoy most about my job is that I get to interact with so many talented and thoughtful people in so many places. This book is dedicated to my daughters, Eloise and Ivy, who are mostly baffled by why I care so much about "old books."

---

8. In instances when I refer to multiple manuscripts that share a particular feature or reading, I often give only the GA numbers in order to keep things readable.

9. For a clear introduction to working with manuscripts and some of the technical terminology often used by scholars, I highly recommend reading Liv Ingeborg Lied and Brent Nongbri, *Working with Manuscripts: A Guide for Textual Scholars* (New Haven: Yale University Press, 2024).

FRAMING THE NEW TESTAMENT

The first time I remember leafing through a Bible, I was probably ten years old. Snooping through my grandparents' house looking for the stash of Werther's Originals and peppermint gum that seemed in endless supply, I came across a fat book in the main cubby of a dusty rolltop desk in the basement covered in typical grandparent detritus. I flicked aside the pencil nubs, floral framed sticky notes, old greeting cards, a crossword dictionary, and return address stickers. Deadlifting the book from the desk, I flipped it open. I didn't know anything about the Bible. I couldn't name a prophet or any of the books in the collection. I had a vague notion of why Jesus might be relevant, supplied secondhand (and unsolicited) by a devout kid in the neighborhood who told me that I had to love Jesus more than baseball. (I still find this idea hard to swallow.)

But this volume was different from other books I had read. Not only was it exceedingly heavy, but it seemed to have a special kind of thin paper edged with gold that only showed when the covers were pressed together. Its text was in two columns with lots of numbers mixed among the words, and it had several pastel paintings of people and scenes I couldn't recognize. It also had lots of other writings at the front that made it seem more like a calendar or family archive of some sort; things like lists of deaths, births, marriages, baptisms, and confirmations, and a place to describe these important events. And, jammed between the pages were countless mementos: funeral and wedding programs, family pictures, postcards of the pope, ticket stubs, and handwritten notes. The book surely had significance, but I couldn't articulate what it was.

I had, of course, picked up my grandparents' family Bible, an encounter that left me with the impression that the Bible was something monumental, something unchanging and authoritative by dint of its sheer girth, if nothing else. But looking back, I see now that it showed me that the Bible was something else, too—a place of memory where the highs and lows of our family could be collected in a kind of sacred space alongside a text of some assumed authority. For me, at ten, this one random copy was *the* Bible, even if its contents were at least partly defined by the births and deaths of my extended family, my grandmother acting as a sort of scribe, an arbiter of memory.[1]

Now, as someone who reads and writes about the New Testament for a living, I'm acutely aware that *the* Bible can't be equated with any one of its copies. After all, there are thousands of manuscripts of the New Testament in Greek (the language it was initially written in), alongside thousands of manuscripts copied in other languages, and millions of printed copies produced in hundreds of languages, not to mention the proliferation of digital Bibles. Bibles are everywhere, and the differences between any two copies can be significant (or not) for any number of reasons. It's best to think of the Bible not as a monolith but as a diverse set of ancient works whose texts and materials are subject to constant change. Change has been central to the New Testament from the first time these works were first copied through to the

---

1. The tradition of the family Bible goes back at least to the seventeenth century and is closely tied to emerging consumer culture. They became especially popular in the United States after the Civil War. See Mary Wilson Carpenter, *Imperial Bibles, Domestic Bodies: Women, Sexuality, and Religion in the Victorian Market* (Athens: Ohio University Press, 2003), 3–31; and Ruth B. Bottigheimer, "Family Bibles," in *The Oxford Encyclopedia of the Bible and the Arts*, ed. T. Beal (Oxford: Oxford University Press, 2015), 313–19.

modern publishing industry, which underwrites new translations and repackages old ones to appeal to more niche audiences. The book I encountered in my grandparents' basement is only one of the many modern versions of the Bible that exist in numerous translations and modern languages, not to mention the many thousands of manuscripts that have parts of the New Testament, in dozens of languages, dating back to the second century CE.

Chapter 1

THE BIBLE AS CHANGE

This book explores the significance of the ways that the New Testament has changed and what this means for how we think about scripture. It's an invitation to see scripture as something more than static words on a page, to see it as the product of a long and ongoing tradition of writing, reading, and interpretation by mostly unknown people from the ancient world through to today. Words are not enough because Bibles have never been just words; it is a continuous process that stretches back to antiquity, perpetrated by scribes and readers and, today, printers and software developers.[1] We participate in this process when we read it and consider the other things that make up the Bibles we read.[2] Change generates new ideas, reshapes the scriptural past, and enables us to empathize with the many people who have helped shape Bibles as we encounter them today. Change is a basic fact of life, and Bibles cannot escape this reality. Change has the potential to be revelatory.

We can see the Bible as a process when we compare any two copies, especially those with different translations and target audiences. But the constant change that defines the New Testament is especially obvious

---

1. On the processes of manuscript production and the main actors involved in the Byzantine period (when most Greek New Testament manuscripts were produced), see Nadezhda Kavrus-Hoffmann, "Producing New Testament Manuscripts in Byzantium: Scribes, Scriptoria, Patrons," in *The New Testament in Byzantium*, ed. D. Krueger and R. S. Nelson (Washington, DC: Dumbarton Oaks, 2016), 117–45.

2. This idea of process follows from the dictum of Parker: "Every written work is a process not an object," meaning that each copy is only one small witness to the totality of an entire literary work. David C. Parker, *An Introduction to the New Testament Manuscripts and Their Texts* (Cambridge: Cambridge University Press, 2008), 21.

when we look at its manuscripts, made from the second to the nineteenth centuries. When we turn our attention to the manuscripts, we start to break down the veneer of consistency that permeates modern English Bibles and the Greek critical editions that stand behind them, and we glimpse the many ways that readers from the ancient world onward have read, interpreted, and framed their sacred traditions. Manuscripts enable us to see the ways the texts, their frames, and the perspectives of readers change over time.

In the contemporary world, still dominated by the printed book, we tend to think of texts, especially sacred ones, as inert and easily duplicated. The history of the New Testament shows the exact opposite to be the case. The most sacred traditions are those most susceptible to change as new readers and communities work to recontextualize their scriptures for new times and questions. The enduring relevance of the New Testament is what has led to its many and varied forms and formats since its narratives were first written and its letters first dispatched in the first century CE.

My view of the New Testament as a body of literature defined by change stands in contrast to some popular views on the Bible that emphasize its invariability, internal consistency, and essentially static nature. These theological traditions that shape some understandings of the Bible have their own interesting histories and ongoing discourse. However, I think something else, something much richer is true: the variability of the New Testament that we see in its manuscripts is evidence that the God presented in the New Testament is complex, engaged with people, and profound. Variation doesn't undermine the sacredness of the work; it demonstrates its perceived importance and the imperative to pass it on, to make it relevant for new times and ideas. We ignore the things we don't care about, letting them lie in a stolid stance, gathering dust in a basement somewhere, while we engage and reshape the things that are important to us. Jennifer Wright Knust is right when she argues that "like human bodies and undertakings, texts, paratexts and works endure only insofar as they are cared for, repaired, reconstituted, and remade. Works pass away when they fail to become something else."[3]

3. Jennifer Wright Knust, "The New Testament Text, Paratexts, and Reception His-

The Bible as Change

From my view, the New Testament is not just an immaterial text floating in the penumbra to be reconstructed in one ideal, perfect way in the form of a printed book. We can try to make it this if we wish, but it's more significant when we let it be what it is: a diverse set of narratives and letters that have been remade each time they are copied and printed by people, people who have had to negotiate many conflicting technological, theological, and political realities and possibilities. Passing the New Testament on from one generation to another requires reworking as an essential ingredient, and these alterations are not always superficial. As David C. Parker notes, "The activities of scribes, typesetters, software developers, and editors do not just tinker with the accidentals and appearance of the New Testament. They have made the New Testament what it is . . . a collection of books which has come into being as a result of technological developments and the new ideas which both prompted and were inspired by them."[4] The New Testament is something that we make, something we imbue with significance, and something that is the product of the literary, theological, and technological context in which it was made.[5] It changes because it's important to us.

---

tory," in *The Oxford Handbook to the Textual Criticism of the Bible*, ed. T. Wasserman and S. Crawford (Oxford: Oxford University Press, forthcoming).

4. Parker, *Textual Scholarship*, 2–3.

5. Parker, *Textual Scholarship*, 12: "The New Testament is—and always has been—the result of a fusion of technology of whatever kind is in vogue."

Chapter 2

Materiality, Layout, and Paratext

Because of its importance to many communities over time, the New Testament has been subject to change in multiple ways. Textual critics—who have long been the primary arbiters of knowledge about the New Testament's manuscripts within biblical studies—tend to focus on changes to the text. They are concerned with variant readings, the activities of scribes that lead to textual change, and judging which form of a text might be earliest, among other things. There continues to be a lively discourse about textual change in the New Testament, its causes, and its significance for theology and history. But the New Testament changes in ways that extend beyond its text. These changes are not recorded in the apparatus of a critical edition; they are visible only when we look at the manuscripts themselves and consider their materiality, layout, and, most importantly for this book, paratextuality.

Materiality

The changes that I'm thinking about are easily observable, even if, like most people, you can't read Koine Greek, have never looked at a medieval manuscript, or have never thought about Bibles in an academic way. Anyone can peruse a book shop and see that some changes are *material* without even opening the book. What type of cover is there? Hardback? Paperback? Is it a handsome leatherbound tome or a paperback pocket edition? Does it use the tissue-thin paper or the thicker, sturdier stuff? Does it have a fancy in-built threaded bookmark? Are indents cut out of the fore-edge so you can flip right to 1 Corinthians if you wish? These *material* changes don't necessarily alter the text or the literary message of the New Testament. And while some differences are necessitated by developments in book technology and the desire of publishers to sell copies, the *materiality* of the books we read convey ideas about function, utility, and status of the text between the covers. Based on their work with manuscripts at Montecassino, Marilena Maniaci and Giulia Orofino put the same point this way: "In the Bible as a book, an impalpable and highly codified context can translate into a multitude of material forms which, over the centuries, can be seen to adapt to cultural and doctrinal needs."[1]

In other words, books change because we need them to, because our views on them and their significance change with time and other factors. For example, hardback covers with notches on the fore-edge place Bibles alongside reference books like dictionaries, while paperback versions of a standard size suggest comparisons to modern novels. The physical form of the book influences our initial approach to what we have before us.

The materials are important to consider because they contribute to the ways that books communicate. Brian Cummings argues that "a book is a physical object, yet it also signifies something abstract, the words and meanings collected within it. Thus, a book is both less and more than its contents alone. A book is a metonym for the words that we read or for the thoughts that we have as we read them."[2] As an object with specific

---

1. Marilena Maniaci and Giulia Orofino, "Making, Writing and Decorating the Bible: Montecassino, a Case Study," in *Scribes and the Presentation of Texts*, ed. B. A. Shailor and C. W. Dutschke (Turnhout: Brepols, 2021), 62. The material forms of books are subject to constant change in response to many factors. Format matters because, as David C. Parker notes, "Not only does the English-speaking world know the Bible by its format, it also formulates its view of the contents according to it." *The Living Text of the Gospels* (Cambridge: Cambridge University Press, 1997), 185. On ancient materiality in a broader sense, see Cornelia Ritter-Schmalz and Raphael Schwitter, eds., *Antike Texte und ihre Materialität: Alltägliche Präsenz, mediale Semantik, literarische Reflexion* (Berlin: de Gruyter, 2019).

2. Brian Cummings, "The Book as Symbol," in *The Book: A Global History*, ed. M. F. Suarez, SJ, and H. R. Woudhuysen (Oxford: Oxford University Press, 2013), 93. See also Laura Feldt and Christian Høgel, "Reframing Authority—the Role of Media and Materiality," in *Reframing Authority: The Role of Media and Materiality*, ed. L. Feldt and C. Høgel (Sheffield: Equinox, 2018), 1 (and the other studies in their volume), who

physical properties, books and manuscripts communicate through the combination of their texts and materiality, even beyond their textual content. This reality holds true whether we're talking about modern printed English Bibles or an ancient papyrus manuscript of Paul's letters in Greek. How a book is made says something about its text and what we should do with it. Because of this fact, we do the New Testament a disservice when we mine the manuscripts only for their texts, setting aside their other signifying features.

Laying Out the Text

The tradition of change to the New Testament extends beyond the materials used to make the book to the way the text is laid out for us to read. *Layout* matters.[3] Numerous choices face us when thinking about how to

---

note that when it comes to the book, "Forms of mediation and materiality play key roles in any constitution, contestation, or transformation of authority, and that new understanding of authority can be gained by focusing on how authority is created, contested, or transformed in different historical eras and cultures." James W. Watts makes the point more succinctly: "*Scriptures are icons.* They are not just texts to be interpreted and performed. They are material objects that convey religious significance by their production, display, and ritual manipulation." "Three Dimensions of Scriptures," in *Iconic Books and Texts*, ed. J. W. Watts (Sheffield: Equinox, 2013), 11. Kristina Myrvold and Dorina Miller Parmenter, "Religious Miniature Books: Introduction and Overview," in *Miniature Books: The Format and Function of Tiny Religious Texts*, ed. K. Myrvold and D. M. Parmenter (Sheffield: Equinox, 2019), 1–11 comment suggestively on the role of size in function and status of books and manuscripts, as does Eyal Poleg, *The Material History of the Bible: England 1200–1553* (London: British Academy, 2020), 3–13. See David Ganz and Barbara Schellewald, eds., *Clothing Sacred Scriptures: Book Art and Book Religion in Christian, Islamic, and Jewish Cultures* (Berlin: de Gruyter, 2019) for the aesthetic aspects of "clothing" the Bible.

3. I have argued elsewhere that layout plays a role in understanding that relationship between scripture, traditions, and revelation as it plays out within the New Testament's manuscripts, Garrick V. Allen, "Text and Tradition: David Brown and New Testament Textual Criticism," in *The Moving Text: Interdisciplinary Perspectives on David Brown and the Bible*, ed. G. V. Allen, C. R. Brewer, and D. F. Kinlaw III (London: SCM, 2018), esp. 9–11. On the significance of layout in the Dead Sea scrolls, see Lindsey A. Askin, "Scribal Production and Literacy at Qumran: Considerations of Page Layout and Style," in *Material Aspects of Reading in Ancient and Medieval Cultures: Materiality, Presence and Performance*, ed. A. Krauß, J. Leipziger, and F. Schücking-

make a book as complex as a Bible or any of its smaller units, and this is true whether you're a scribe, ruling parchment in tenth century Constantinople to make a gospel book for a local community, or a modern editor, working with a publisher to make copies that will appeal to some subset of readers. Knust rightly points out that "each medieval Greek text captures hundreds if not thousands of small, usually anonymous decisions made incrementally over time."[4] What type and size of script or font do we use? How many columns do we use? How should we mark section breaks—subtitles, indents, or some other way? Who decides where the section breaks go? What else do we include with the biblical text—chapter and verse numbers, page numbers, variant readings, cross-references, or some combination of these things? What colors do we use for the text? Are we making something austere for the serious reader using only black ink? Or do we make parts of the text red, green, yellow, or gold? These are questions that people who have passed on the New Testament have been asking themselves since scribes started to make copies of the earliest Christian texts. Answers to these questions shape the way that people perceive the text itself, directing our attention as readers to different parts of the tradition. Even if we choose not to change the text of the New Testament, its arrangement need not remain static. Issues of layout are complex when it comes to the Greek New Testament.[5]

Jungblut (Berlin: de Gruyter, 2020), 23–36, who notes that "the neat and uncluttered spacing of so many Qumran scrolls, again, seems to be based on the importance of the text" (32). On layout and its significance in other manuscript cultures and traditions, see, for example, Poleg, *Material History*, 13–18; Liv Ingeborg Lied, *Invisible Manuscripts: Textual Scholarship and the Survival of 2 Baruch* (Tübingen: Mohr Siebeck, 2021), 35–44; Michael Philip Penn, "Know Thy Enemy: The Materialization of Orthodoxy in Syriac Manuscripts," in *Snapshots of Evolving Traditions: Jewish and Christian Manuscript Culture, Textual Fluidity, and New Philology*, ed. L. I. Lied and H. Lundhaug (Berlin: de Gruyter, 2017), 221–41; and H. J. Martin and J. Vezin, eds., *Mise en page et mise en text du livre manuscrit* (Geneva: Cercle de la Librarie, 1990).

4. Jennifer Wright Knust, "The New Testament Text, Paratexts, and Reception History," in *The Oxford Handbook to the Textual Criticism of the Bible*, ed. T. Wasserman and S. Crawford (Oxford: Oxford University Press, forthcoming).

5. There are multiple different layout possibilities for the New Testament. When it comes to the catena manuscripts of the New Testament (copies of New Testament books that come with extracts from various ancient and medieval writers),

The Importance of Paratexts

More vital for our understanding of change and its significance to the New Testament, and the features that we will turn our attention to for this book, are the other things that appear between the two covers of a Bible beyond the biblical text itself. Things like prologues, tables of contents, lists of various kinds, extracts from scholars or religious leaders, many sorts of marginal notations, images, and other add-ons encourage readers to interpret the text in particular ways. These items, which the French literary critic Gérard Genette coined as *paratexts* (literally the things around the text; *para* = around), appear in some form in every kind of book from antiquity to today.[6]

---

see H. A. G. Houghton and D. C. Parker, "An Introduction to Greek New Testament Commentaries with a Preliminary Checklist of New Testament Catena Manuscripts," in *Commentaries, Catenae and Biblical Traditions,* ed. H. A. G. Houghton (Piscataway, NJ: Gorgias, 2016), 1–35; H. A. G. Houghton and D. C. Parker, eds., *Codex Zacynthius: Catena, Palimpsest, Lectionary* (Piscataway, NJ: Gorgias, 2020); William R. S. Lamb, *The* Catena in Marcum: *A Byzantine Anthology of Early Commentary on Mark* (Leiden: Brill, 2012); and Georgi R. Parpulov, *Catena Manuscripts of the Greek New Testament: A Catalogue* (Piscataway, NJ: Gorgias, 2021). In catena traditions, scribes had a choice as to how to locate the commentary in relation to the text of the New Testament itself. They could arrange the commentary around the upper, outer, and lower margins of the main text (see figure 2.2), or they could insert the commentary between the sections of main text that they comment upon, thus breaking up the linear narrative of the text itself. This choice impacts how people engage with the manuscript and conceive its text. The book of Revelation, for example, is often transmitted along with the sixth- or seventh-century CE commentary of Andrew of Caesarea, which either regularly interrupts the main text or is sometimes arranged around the main text in the margins. On the layout of Andrew's commentary, see Garrick V. Allen, *Manuscripts of the Book of Revelation: New Philology, Paratexts, Reception* (Oxford: Oxford University Press, 2020), 74–120.

6. Gérard Genette defines paratexts somewhat amorphously as the things that "surround [the text] and extend it, precisely in order to *present* it ... to *make present*, to ensure the text's presence in the world, its 'reception' and consumption in the form of ... a book.... The paratext is what enables a text to become a book and be offered as such to its reader.... The paratext is a *threshold* ... a *vestibule* that offers the world at large the possibility of either stepping inside or turning back.... [The paratext] is a zone not only of transition but also of *transaction*." *Paratexts: Thresholds of Interpretation*, trans. J. E. Lewin (Cambridge: Cambridge University Press, 1997), 1–2. In other

Materiality, Layout, and Paratext

Bibles are no different. Because of the importance of the New Testament for many communities, it has gathered a significant variety of paratexts, none of which were made by the authors of the New Testament themselves. Although not attached to the New Testament when its works were initially written, these items shape the ways that the text is read and persist across space and time as the Greek tradition was read and copied again and again. Paratexts are the products of tradition and readers, ranging from the sparse titles that head Paul's letters in the papyri manuscripts (figure 2.1), to complex marginal notations (catenae), lection data, and cross-references of a deluxe twelfth-century Byzantine gospel book (figure 2.2). These manuscripts, made about a millennium apart, are both equally genuine representations of the New Testament, even if they offer very different frames for reading the text and preserve different combinations of the New Testament's works. Scripture and tradition live side by side in a mutually beneficial relationship on the pages of the New Testament's manuscripts. Paratexts open a window

---

words, paratexts are the things around the text: "a title, a subtitle, intertitles; prefaces, postfaces, notices, forewords, etc.; marginal, infrapaginal, terminal notes; epigraphs; illustrations; blurbs, book covers, dust jackets, and many other kinds of secondary signals." *Paratexts*, 3. Not all of these items are relevant for discussing manuscripts of the New Testament—dust jackets, for example, are the products of modern print cultures, not ancient scribes—but it is still possible to identify and analyze the paratextual traditions specific to particular manuscript or book cultures, especially because paratextuality "is first and foremost a treasure trove of questions without answers." Gérard Genette, *Palimpsests: Literature in the Second Degree*, trans. C. Newman and G. Prince (Lincoln: University of Nebraska Press, 1997), 4. On paratexts in New Testament manuscripts, see Matthew R. Crawford, *The Eusebian Canon Tables: Ordering Textual Knowledge in Late Antiquity* (Oxford: Oxford University Press, 2019), 21–28; Patrick Andrist, "Toward a Definition of Paratexts and Paratextuality: The Case of Ancient Greek Manuscripts," in *Bible as Notepad: Tracing Annotations and Annotation Practices in Late Antique and Medieval Biblical Manuscripts*, ed. L. I. Lied and M. Maniaci (Berlin: de Gruyter, 2018), 130–49; and Allen, *Manuscripts*, 44–52. On the relevance of paratexts for other manuscript traditions, see Rosalind Brown-Grant et al., eds., *Inscribing Knowledge in the Medieval Book: The Power of Paratexts* (Berlin: de Gruyter, 2019); Liv Ingeborg Lied and Marilena Maniaci, eds., *Bible as Notepad: Tracing Annotations and Annotation Practices in Late Antique and Medieval Biblical Manuscripts* (Berlin: de Gruyter, 2018); and Laura Jansen, ed., *The Roman Paratext: Frame, Texts, Readers* (Cambridge: Cambridge University Press, 2014).

FRAMING THE NEW TESTAMENT

Figure 2.1. The end of Hebrews and start of 1 Corinthians with multiple paratexts: a page number in the top margin (71), a stichometric notation at the end of Hebrews (a count of lines in the work), *paragraphoi* (lines extending into the margins that divide the letters), and a title in 1 Corinthians (literally "to the Corinthians 1") *(P46, Dublin, Chester Beatty, CBL BP II, f.38).* © *The Trustees of the Chester Beatty Library, Dublin*

Materiality, Layout, and Paratext

Figure 2.2. Gospel of Mark, starting at 1:10, surrounded by many different paratexts, including catenae in the margins (extracts from ancient commentary traditions explaining the text), Eusebian notations in the left margin (part of a cross-reference system), and liturgical notations between the lines in the left and right margins (giving information on when to read these texts in the Orthodox liturgical year) *(GA 2604, Dublin, Chester Beatty, CBL W 139, 124r)*. © The Trustees of the Chester Beatty Library, Dublin

into the literary imagination of past readers and bookmakers, showing us how people worked to communicate the significance and relevance of the text to future readers and how the texts of sacred traditions were reimagined from one generation to the next.[7]

The paratextual possibilities available to those who make Bibles are vast, and we continue to make new ones every time we make a new translation or repackage one for a new audience. The creation of paratexts is a practice that goes back to the scribes who copied the earliest papyri, like the manuscript in figure 2.1, which is perhaps the earliest copy of Paul's letters bound in a single codex that we still have.[8] The making of paratexts to shape scriptural traditions has only accelerated. This reality makes paratextuality central to my argument that scripture is something constantly negotiated afresh as we read and pass on sacred traditions. And while the paratexts that we find in manuscripts differ in important ways from the paratexts we find in modern English printed Bibles, it's instructive to look at what happens when we read the same New Testament text with different paratexts pitched to very different target audiences. The variation of paratexts and annotation in modern Bibles is a microcosm, the result of a rich history of paratextual invention that we see in the manuscripts.

---

7. See, for example, Liv Ingeborg Lied, "Epistles from Jerusalem: The Paratexts of Syriac 2 Baruch and the Peshitta Jeremiah Corpus," *Religions* 13 (2022), https://doi.org/10.3390/rel13070759, and Eva Mroczek, *The Literary Imagination in Jewish Antiquity* (Oxford: Oxford University Press, 2016), for views on the relationship between text and paratext in early Jewish traditions.

8. This manuscript (P46, CBP Pap II) is part of the Chester Beatty Biblical Papyri located in Dublin. Images of the entire collection, or at least the parts of it that are held in Dublin, can be found here: https://viewer.cbl.ie/viewer/search/-/-/1/RANDOM/DC%3Abiblicalpapyricollection/ (accessed 2 May 2022). This manuscript has several paratexts, including titles, page numbers, stichometric notations (counts of lines in each letter), and corrections to the text made by multiple readers. These features show that Paul's letters had begun to emerge as a group of literary texts transmitted together and that multiple different people were interested in the specific wording of the text.

Chapter 3

Matthew in the Scofield Bible

To illustrate the consequences of different paratexts on the same story, let's start by reading Jesus's speech in Matthew 24, sometimes called the Olivet Discourse. In Matthew's version of the final trip to Jerusalem, Jesus is quite busy, leading up to and even beyond his crucifixion. (Most characters are not so active after their executions.) In addition to his lengthy speech about the end of the age in the Olivet Discourse, he curses a fig tree, disputes with his opponents, and tells some spicy parables. But the central part of what Jesus does in Jerusalem, and the part that is often most confusing to readers, is his speech concerning the signs of the end and the final judgment in chapter 24.[1]

In this private speech to his disciples, Jesus continues his denunciations of Jerusalem and its authorities, declaring that the temple will soon be destroyed and that this will be a sign of the end of the age. He encourages the disciples to endure in the face of increasing chaos, defined by war, false messiahs, familial strife, opaque rumors, and persecution. Those that stand firm will be saved. These vague descriptions become somewhat more specific when Jesus refers to something that Matthew thinks his audience will already know: the "desolating sacrilege standing in the holy place, as was spoken by the prophet Daniel—let the reader understand" (24:15).[2] When this sign occurs, those in Judea should flee

---

1. This text has parallels in Mark 13 and Luke 21. See Ian Boxall, *Matthew through the Centuries* (Oxford: Wiley Blackwell, 2019), 348–63, for a detailed overview of the chapters and its significance within Matthew.

2. English Bible translations in this book come from the NRSV, often with small adjustments based on my reading of the Greek text.

to the mountains. Woe to those who are pregnant and nursing mothers because suffering will abound until the sun is darkened and the stars fall from heaven. Then the Son of Man will appear in heaven, send his angels, and gather the faithful.

Unfortunately, the time of these troubles is unknown to all except God, for the Son of Man's coming is like the days of Noah, which probably is not a good thing for most people, considering how the flood story in Genesis 6–9 plays out. Be ready, Jesus says, because "you do not know on what day your Lord is coming" (24:42). If you do not keep watch, the master will return and cut his servants to pieces. There will be weeping and gnashing of teeth.

Jesus's pep talk to his disciples in Matthew 24 is, at first glance, confusingly negative, drawing on apocalyptic imagery with which most modern readers are not immediately familiar. So, what do we do with it? Do we read it like a partial road map to the end times? It is, after all, an apocalyptic text with angels, disappearing people, suffering, destruction, and cosmic disorder.[3] Surely, there must be a logic to this text as it appears in Matthew's narrative.[4]

Themes from this speech appear elsewhere in Matthew, and the discourse reinforces the significance of Jesus's actions and his death and resurrection in the story—they have cosmic significance, so much so that they initiate the end of the age and the eternal age of God's rule, like a small stone that eventually starts an avalanche. The crucifixion leads somewhere—in Matthew's view, to a new creation. Matthew gives us a glimpse of this reality when he says that at Jesus's death, tombs were

---

3. On apocalyptic traditions in Matthew, see Kristian Bendoratis, "Apocalypticism, Angels, and Matthew," in *The Jewish Apocalyptic Tradition and the Shaping of New Testament Thought*, ed. B. E. Reynolds and L. T. Stuckenbruck (Minneapolis: Fortress, 2017), 31–51, who argues that "Matthew is unique in its frequent display of apocalyptic elements" among the gospels (31). It is now widely recognized that apocalyptic thought shaped early Christian identity and literary output, including the content of the New Testament. See Benjamin E. Reynolds and Loren T. Stuckenbruck, eds., *The Jewish Apocalyptic Tradition and the Shaping of New Testament Thought* (Minneapolis: Fortress, 2017).

4. For one take on the logic of the passages, see Vicky Balbanksi, "Mission in Matthew against the Horizon of Matthew 24," *New Testament Studies* 54 (2008): 161–75, who connects Matthew 24 with the call to mission in 28:16–20.

Matthew in the Scofield Bible

opened and the dead walked around Jerusalem (27:52–53). But the details of the Olivet Discourse, like this tantalizing note about resurrected people wandering the streets, remain obscure; the narrative doesn't give us any explicit interpretation of Jesus's sayings here or any explanation of the significance of the dead being raised. What does it mean that "many will come in my name, saying, 'I am the Messiah'" (24:5)? What is a false prophet, and what does it mean that they will lead people astray (24:11)? What is the sacrilege of desolation (25:15)? How do I keep watch? And this text raises larger historical questions as well. The temple was destroyed by the Romans in 70 CE, and the eternal reign of God and final judgment have not yet materialized (as far as I can tell). Was Jesus overly optimistic about the timing of the end? Sure, Matthew makes it appear that he's not privy to the details of the timeline (24:36), but how should we read this text nearly two millennia later?

One way to answer some of these questions is to take a cue from the paratexts that accompany this discourse in various Bibles. When we read these texts in two very different modern versions—the Scofield Reference Bible and the Green Bible (discussed in the next chapter)—we come to very different conclusions about the significance of this passage and what we ought to do with it. These conclusions are shaped first and foremost by the paratexts in these versions.

First: the Scofield Reference Bible. The copy that I have is a reprint of the second edition of 1917 with large print, red letters for the words of Jesus, and fancy storage box (probably aimed at an older readership).[5] This edition has the text of the King James Version (KJV) of 1611, framed with prologues, in-text commentary, and indexes. Ironically, the paratexts to the edition espouse a theology unknown to the seventeenth century when the translation was initially made.[6] The paratexts of this version

---

5. Published by Oxford University Press.
6. See Todd R. Mangum and Mark S. Sweetnam, *The Scofield Bible: Its History and Impact on the Evangelical Church* (Milton Keynes: Paternoster, 2009), 1. There is no guarantee that paratexts for any literary tradition represent the text in ways intended by their authors or translators. On the KJV and its history, see Gordon Campbell, *Bible: The Story of the King James Versions 1611–2011* (Oxford: Oxford University Press, 2010), esp. 241–48 for analysis of the huge impact of the Scofield Reference Bible on American evangelical culture and thought.

were made by Cyrus Ingerson Scofield (1843–1921), a Confederate soldier, lawyer, evangelical preacher, and premillennial dispensationalist, who believed that he was living near the end of the age, just before the literal thousand-year reign of God.[7] Scofield's life is complex and obscured by dueling apologetics and polemics, but the paratexts he produced in partnership with eight consulting editors—yes, all of them white men—made his eponymous reference Bible a highly influential bestseller that remains in print. Even today, it is one of the most profitable books in the history of Oxford University Press.[8] It helped to shape the twentieth-century home Bible study movement in America, reinforced the eschatology of modern evangelicalism, and deeply influenced conservative politics in the United States.[9] It has many imitators. In essence, Scofield took his preferred version of the English Bible—the KJV—and attached a set of paratexts to it that reflected his own theology, which had a particularly acute focus on and detailed view of the end times.

The entire Bible is prefaced with a text written by Scofield, somewhat threateningly entitled "Introduction (To Be Read)." It describes the rationale for making the edition and offers a "panoramic view on the Bible," a grand narrative that readers are urged to adopt before they read from Genesis to Revelation. We learn that this Bible was made to enable readers to access "all the greater truths of divine revelation . . . so that the reader may for himself [sic] follow the gradual unfolding of these," culminating in "Jesus Christ and New Testament Scriptures." Scofield also provides commentary-filled footnotes within the biblical text to elucidate difficult passages, along with "alleged discrepancies or

---

7. See C. I. Scofield, *Rightly Dividing the Word of Truth, Being Ten Outline Studies of the More Important Divisions of Scripture* (1896) for a fuller treatment of his theology in his own words, and see Mangum and Sweetnam, *Scofield Bible*, 53–133, for the theological roots of Scofield's project and the theology represented by his Bible.

8. The Scofield Reference Bible was the first book published by Oxford University Press to reach a million units sold (Mangum and Sweetnam, *Scofield Bible*, 7). Arno C. Gaebelein (one of the original consulting editors of the edition, writing a real piece of hagiography and apologetics for the Scofield Bible) notes that by the mid-century, more than two million copies had been sold. *The History of the Scofield Reference Bible* (Our Hope Publications, 1943; repr., Spokane, WA: Living Word Edition, 1991), 11.

9. On the influence of the Scofield Bible, see Mangum and Sweetnam, *Scofield Bible*, 169–97.

contradictions," working to describe the unity and consistency of a literal interpretation of scripture on all points. He also includes other readerly helps, like simple definitions of complex theological terms "submitted to, and approved by, a very large number of eminent students and teachers of all the evangelical bodies." There are also modern equivalents for weights and measures, prefaces for each biblical book, a new paragraphing arrangement for the text, breaking it up into segments that align with Scofield's reading, and notes on the dispensations and literal interpretations of prophecy, among other things.[10] The short preface to the second edition also notes that Scofield added the dates of the biblical chronology of James Ussher (1581–1656), a Church of Ireland archbishop, polymath, and chronologist who placed the creation of the earth at 4004 BCE.[11] If you are at all familiar with modern evangelical theology, you can easily see how Scofield's paratextual interventions, even including the rearrangement of the biblical text itself into different sections, continue to shape literal readings of the Bible and other interpretive practices. Only by changing the arrangement of the text and its framework can Scofield maintain a literal reading of the unchanging text.

This point becomes even clearer when we look at his "panoramic view of the Bible." This short preface contains five propositions about

10. Scofield's textual rearrangement and division of the biblical text has many ancient precursors. See Peter M. Head, "Punctuation and Paragraphs in P66 (P.Bod.II): Insights into Scribal Behavior," in *Studies on the Intersection of Text, Paratext, and Reception*, ed. G. R. Lanier and J. N. Reid (Leiden: Brill, 2021), 3–29.

11. On Ussher, see Alan Ford, *James Ussher: Theology, History, and Politics in Early-Modern Ireland and England* (Oxford: Oxford University Press, 2007). And on Ussher's "biblical chronology" in the context of sixteenth- and seventeenth-century scholarship, see James Barr, "Why the World Was Created in 4004 B.C.: Archbishop Ussher and Biblical Chronology," *Bulletin of the John Rylands University Library of Manchester* 67 (1985): 575–608. Ussher's timeline has had significant impact on young earth creationist movements who read the Bible literally to argue that the world is only about six thousand years old. His work was cutting edge scholarship in its time, but the chronology and the young earth theories it supported have been undermined, even by evangelical scholars, since the theory of evolution came into popular consciousness. On the debate around Ussher's chronology, see Ronald L. Numbers, "'The Most Important Biblical Discovery of Our Time': William Hebry Green and the Demise of Ussher's Chronology," *Church History* 69 (2000): 257–76.

what the Bible is and argues that the parts of the Bible are inaccessible without some overarching view of the whole. For Scofield, "The Bible story and message is like a picture wrought out in mosaics: each book, chapter, verse, and even word forms a necessary part, and has its own appointed place." Therefore, the Bible is one book with a single, harmonious, progressively unfolding message that flows from Genesis to Revelation, but it is also a book of books, meaning that each book within the Bible is like a chapter in the entire story, entirely self-sufficient apart from the rest. The biblical books also fall into groups, which inform humanity's ongoing relationship with God in various ways and increase our knowledge of Jesus Christ, who is the "central theme" of the Bible. If you're turning to Matthew 24 with these (somewhat contradictory) ideas in mind, you are already motivated to see how Jesus's speech fits into a broader and progressive narrative that is ultimately leading to the end of the age. Decoding his vague description of the events smooths out some of the complexities of the text.

Scofield's assertions in these prefaces are reinforced by (surprise!) even more prefaces. The shaping of interpretation is heavy-handed in this edition, and the preface that precedes the Four Gospels is highly prescriptive. The fact that the gospels create a "personality" of Jesus but not a "biography" shows the religious importance of these stories, "that through these narratives we should come to see and know Him whom they reveal." Without a doubt, Scofield thinks the gospels are "divinely perfect as revelation," even if incomplete on the details of Jesus's early life. The "living Christ" is available to those who read these texts so long as the reader has an "ungrieved Spirit." The remainder of the preface to the gospels reinforces theological ideas about the relationship between Israel and the church, between Jews and gentiles, issues that are central to Scofield's view of the end and his dispensationalist theology.[12]

The final preface to contend with in our reading of the Olivet Discourse is the one to Matthew specifically. In it, Scofield argues that Matthew was written in 37 CE, a period well before the destruction of the second temple by the Romans in 70 CE, which means that anything Jesus says about the temple in Jerusalem must be read as genuine prophecy,

---

12. See Scofield, *Rightly Dividing the Word*.

Matthew in the Scofield Bible

not a retrospective shaping from the author of Matthew as most modern scholars see it.[13] The remainder of the text is a dense and elaborate discussion of covenantal theology from Matthew's perspective. Scofield explores Jesus's actions and their relationship to the Davidic (2 Samuel 7) and Abrahamic covenants (Genesis 15), a distinction that "determines the purpose and structure of Matthew. It is peculiarly the Gospel for Israel; and, as from the death of Christ, a Gospel for the whole world."

Even before getting to Matthew 24, the Scofield Bible has set the reader up to read Jesus's speech with certain ideas in mind through its paratexts. The prefaces, nested one within the other, tell the reader about the edition, the Bible as a self-actualized object, the Gospels as a fourfold collection, and Matthew specifically. They reinforce the ideology and perspective of their creator. Scofield's goal was to shape godly men (all pronouns in these texts are masculine) to read the Bible literally and to attend to themes relevant to a form of end-times thinking defined by detailed mapping of historical events on top of biblical prophecy.

But prefaces are not the only paratexts that shape our reading of the Olivet Discourse. The lower margin of most pages in the Scofield Bible are replete with lengthy explanations of the biblical text. Often viewed as the greatest of Scofield's paratextual innovations,[14] these notes hit

---

13. Scofield's dating of Matthew does cohere closely to the tradition that Matthew wrote the gospel eight years after Jesus's ascension, a note found in many subscriptions or end-titles to Matthew in the manuscripts. For example, many texts after Matthew read something like "End of the Gospel of Matthew. Written by him in the Hebrew language in Jerusalem eight years after Christ's ascension," a time that corresponds closely with Scofield's assertion. It's most likely that Scofield has followed Ussher's date here, especially since the preface concludes with a chronological notation from Ussher that Matthew covers a period of thirty-eight years. Modern scholars view Matthew as an expansion of Mark, written after the destruction of the temple in Jerusalem by the Romans in 70 CE (although opinions range from 40 to after 100 CE), based mainly on the discourse in Matthew 24. See W. D. Davies and D. C. Allison, *Matthew 1–7* (London: T&T Clark, 1988), 127–38.

14. Mangum and Sweetnam, *Scofield Bible*, 7, go so far as to say that the Scofield Bible was the first Bible to have commentary "included beneath the text of Scripture itself." This is a vast overstatement in light of the manuscripts that include both text and commentary or catena. The manuscripts of the New Testament anticipate Scofield's work in many ways by over a millennium, and often provide more enlightening

upon themes similar to those mentioned in the prefaces and sometimes take up more than half the page. Scofield composed three annotations for Matthew 24: a lengthy introductory note that incorporates the chapter into Scofield's overarching end-times scenario, a short discussion on the "abomination of desolation" (24:15), and an explanation of the word "generation" in 24:34. All the notes are organized around Scofield's eschatology, or view of the end times. The third note on the word "generation," commenting on Matt 24:34 ("Verily I say unto you, this generation shall not pass, till all these things be fulfilled" [KJV]), reads:

> Gr. *Genea*, the primary definition of which is, "race, kind, family, stock, breed." (So all lexicons.) That the word is used in this sense here is sure because none of "these things," i.e. the worldwide preaching of the kingdom, the great tribulation, the return of the Lord in visible glory, and the regathering of the elect, occurred at the destruction of Jerusalem by Titus, A.D. 70. The promise is, therefore, that the generation—nation, or family of Israel—will be preserved unto "these things"; a promise wonderfully fulfilled to this day.

Scofield made this note because a literal reading of the verse as it is rendered in the KJV might have signified that Jesus was wrong. He changes the meaning of the text without changing the words by appealing to alternative meanings in the underlying Greek text. In the discourse, Jesus discusses the signs of the end, suggesting that this time is rapidly approaching. Just as one knows that summer is near when a fig tree begins to bloom (24:32), so too will one know when the end is near; the end stands before our door even now (24:33). If we read verse 34 alone as it's translated, then Jesus expects the end to come before "this generation" has passed. Obviously, Scofield has a problem with this apparent contradiction—if these things happened within a generation of Jesus's speech, then what are we still doing here? Did we miss the end of the age? Certainly not! Instead, the underlying Greek word for "gen-

---

commentary. And paratextual innovation was central to the tradition of the English Bible-making from its earliest periods. See Debora Shuger, *Paratexts of the English Bible, 1525–1611* (Oxford: Oxford University Press, 2022).

eration" (γενεά) means something else. It must mean a metaphorical nation or family. A literal interpretation raises uncomfortable questions, so we should make use of its metaphorical meaning. Because none of the things predicted by Jesus occurred when the temple was destroyed by the Romans, then it must mean something else, something that is continually relevant for our present day. Jesus has not returned, so "generation" must mean something other than what it says; it must refer to the family of Israel, which Scofield connects to the church.[15] Paratext shapes the biblical text in its own image.[16] This example is typical of the rhetoric of the paratextual notes in the Scofield Reference Bible, which work, sometimes quite hard, to make the text say what it must mean according to Scofield's grand narrative.

As you may have guessed by now, I'm no big believer in Scofield's eschatology or the sometimes tortured ways he goes about making his paratexts do the interpretive work. But the point is that his paratextual interventions direct readers to the features of the biblical text that are central to his theology. The Scofield Bible, and every other version or edition is a product of the paratext. Scofield's work, whatever we think about it, is part of a longer tradition that has enabled Bibles to become what they are for us today. Since antiquity, scholars, scribes, and readers have been shaping how people read and interpret the New Testament. As we will see in the following chapters, there are dozens of different prefaces that frame the gospels in the manuscripts and a complex system of prefaces to the New Testament's letters. For example, the prologue to Acts that is part of the Euthalian apparatus (see chapter 8), describes the work of the editor who, like Scofield, divided the text into small units and wrote prefaces for each work. We also get in the prologue a summary of

---

15. Scofield is not the only one to adopt an approach along these lines for this text. See Philip La Grange Du Toit, "'This Generation' in Matthew 24:34 as a Timeless, Spiritual Generation akin to Genesis 3:15," *Verbum et ecclesia* 39 (2018): e1–e9.

16. Beyond the explicit comments, the Scofield Reference Bible has multiple other paratexts that aid in reading. For example, it creates numerous cross references to parallel texts in the gospels in the center column of the page, offers alternative readings to difficult words, and prints all of Jesus's first-person speech in red. Some of these are older conventions, but they are combined with Scofield's idiosyncratic notes to give a more interpreted Bible to his ideal readers.

the Acts narrative, which describes its author's background and the two main movements of the book: Jesus's ascension and the work of Paul.[17] Scofield shows us the power of prefaces to shape reading and perception, even if we don't accept his theological positioning.

The other paratextual "innovations" of the Scofield Reference Bible, like highlighted text, commentary extracts, and developed cross-reference systems, are features that go back to late antiquity and continue to develop well into the age of print.[18] In the Scofield Reference Bible, we see the continuation of a long tradition of change where paratexts imbue new meanings or add new contexts to an old text, which is itself not entirely static.[19] It's just that this version of the changing New Testament is commercially viable and organized to appeal to people who are interested in decoding the events preceding the end of the world like a set of directions. It's not my ideal way of reading biblical works, but the edition shows the power of paratexts to change reading habits, shape culture, and give new life to an old text.

---

17. See Vemund Blomkvist, *Euthalian Traditions: Text, Translation and Commentary* (Berlin: de Gruyter, 2012), 113–17.

18. Short bits of commentary around the text of the New Testament, for example, appear regularly in medieval copies of the New Testament, composed of extracts from other ancient Christian writers. Modern scholars call these comments located in the margins of New Testament manuscripts catenae.

19. Although it is not wildly unconstrained, the text of the Greek New Testament itself changes as well. And I'm not just talking about the many endings of Mark (e.g., Claire Clivaz, "Mk 16 im Codex Bobbiensis. Neue Materialien zur *conclusion brevior* des Markusevangeliums," *Zeitschrift für Neues Testament* 47 [2021]: 59–85; and Mina Monier, "Mark's Endings in Context: Paratexts and Codicological Remarks," *Religions* 13 [2022]: art. 548, https://doi.org/10.3390/rel13060548) or the complex tradition of the woman caught in adultery in John 7:53–8:11 (e.g., Jennifer Knust and Tommy Wasserman, *To Cast the First Stone: The Transmission of a Gospel Story* [Princeton: Princeton University Press, 2018]). The text changes in more small-scale ways as well in the manuscripts that reflect the interpretive choices of scribes and readers (e.g., David C. Parker, *The Living Text of the Gospels* [Cambridge: Cambridge University Press, 1997]; and Garrick V. Allen, "The Apocalypse in Codex Alexandrinus: Exegetical Reasoning and Singular Readings in New Testament Greek Manuscripts," *Journal of Biblical Literature* 135 [2016]: 859–80).

Chapter 4

Matthew in the Green Bible

Another example of paratextual innovation, and one that moves in quite a different direction, is the Green Bible, published by HarperCollins in 2008, with the subtitle "A Priceless Message That Doesn't Cost the Earth." The Green Bible is printed on paper from "environmentally and socially well managed forests" (which, exactly, I'm not sure), and instead of printing Jesus's words in red ink, it prints the text of over one thousand passages related to "creation care" in green. It's a clever play on older paratextual conventions and one that's designed to appeal to those who believe that people of faith ought to care for the world that God has made. Again, the emphasis of this edition is on the creation of new paratexts, reframing an existing English translation, the New Revised Standard Version (NRSV). The in-text notes are significantly scaled back in comparison to the Scofield edition. They are adopted directly from the translators of the NRSV, who used them to highlight variant readings in the underlying Greek tradition or to clarify potential alternative translations. Besides printing some passages in green, the Green Bible doesn't alter the NRSV in any way. Instead, it creates an even more developed set of prefaces from a series of Christian environmentalists, famous scholars, and influential religious leaders, like Archbishop Desmond Tutu and John Paul II, each of whom prime the reader to engage the Bible with an eye toward the goodness of creation and the responsibility to care for what God has made.

Covering 121 pages before you even run into "In the beginning" (Gen 1:1), the prefaces make the case for personal responsibility for the environment. Preface writers make multiple arguments: climate change is a threat to the most vulnerable, and we have a moral obligation to act

(Desmond Tutu); ignorance of the non-human world makes us preoccupied with our own importance (Dave Bookless); creation is a process, not a one-off event, and it speaks a language we can understand (Ellen Bernstein); humans have a special responsibility to care for creation with love (Barbara Brown Taylor); and eschatology, environmentalism, and the new creation are intimately related (N. T. Wright). In short, we have a moral imperative to care for the poor and seek justice by caring for what God has made.

This idea is further reinforced by nearly one hundred pages of green paratexts at the end of the edition, including the "Green Bible Trail Guide," an aid to Bible study attentive to green themes, a resource guide for making practical changes that benefit the environment, and lengthy indexes that encourage green reading practices and cross-reference. The text of the Bible hasn't changed, but the material placed on either end of it has. And these frames—these paratexts—change our focus when we come back to the Olivet Discourse.

The end-times focus of Matthew 24 is still prominent in the Green Bible. Jesus's disciples still ask him, "What will be the sign of your coming and of the end of the age?" (24:3). But the focus is not on deciphering a road map of defined events or on clarifying inconvenient details; instead, the perspectives of the prefaces, combined with the green text, emphasize the role of creation and its catastrophic unmaking in the apocalyptic imagination of the earliest Christian communities. Instead of fretting about the meaning of the word "generation" in a long footnote, the editors print three passages in green. In verses 7–8, for example, Jesus notes that "nation will rise against nation and kingdom against kingdom, and there will be famines and earthquakes in various places: all this is but the beginning of the birth pangs." Highlighting this portion of Jesus's speech draws attention to the shared fates of humanity and creation—just as people will devolve into strife, so too will the earth fall out of harmony with the created order, manifesting in famine and earthquakes. The end of the age is manifest in human conflict and in creation's undoing.

The idea that creation will begin to unravel before the end is reinforced in verses 29–30, also printed in green. Following days of suffering, Jesus says, "The sun will be darkened, and the moon will not give its light; the stars will fall from heaven, and the powers of heaven will be shaken.

Matthew in the Green Bible

Then the sign of the Son of Man will appear in heaven, and then all the tribes of the earth will mourn, and they will see 'the Son of Man coming on the clouds of heaven' with power and great glory." These passages are reworkings of prophetic texts from Jewish scripture (Isa 13:10; 34:4; Zech 12:10, 14; Dan 7:13) that speak about the coming of the Lord and the reversal of Israel's fortunes.[1] But in the Green Bible, we're not guided to make these intricate connections. Instead, the green text directs our attention to the cosmic dimension of the end of the age, helping us to see the interconnectedness of creation, the significance of Jesus's actions in Jerusalem that ultimately led to his execution, and the impending urgency of his return from the heavenly realm. Although it intervenes directly in the text in a more nuanced way, the Green Bible and its paratexts shape our experiences as readers and point us relentlessly to one specific topic.

The Green Bible's presentation of Matthew 24 is only part of a longer tradition of paratextual developments. For example, some manuscripts offer access to commentary on specific passages. Matthew 24 is quite literally framed by commentary in GA 2604 (Dublin, CBL W 139, diktyon 13571), a twelfth-century copy of the Gospels held at the Chester Beatty in Dublin (figure 4.1). The second half of verse 29 begins on the first line of the text, and right above the first letter is a small gold alpha. This little Greek letter draws our attention to the golden alpha in the upper margin, the text of which continues down the right margin and into the lower margin. Remarkably, this note is interested, like Scofield, in the eschatological events that precede the end.[2]

However, the commentary in GA 2604 is not the only paratext present. Gold ink is also used for the capital letters that protrude into the left margin and mark new sections in the text, drawing attention to aspects of the text like the red and green print in modern Bibles. We can also see part of a developed cross-referencing system, the Eusebian apparatus,

---

1. For a more technical interpretation of these traditions and their interrelationships, see Garrick V. Allen, *The Book of Revelation and Early Jewish Textual Culture* (Cambridge: Cambridge University Press, 2017), 112–22.

2. The text is close to the note recorded in John Anthony Cramer, *Catenae graecorum partum in Novum Testamentum*, vol. 1, Catenae in evangelia s. Matthaei et s. Marci ad fidem codd. Mss. (Hildesheim: Georg Olms, 1967), 200–202.

Figure 4.1. Matthew 24:29–32 with catena, text division, and one Eusebian cross-reference in the left margin *(GA 2604, Dublin, CBL W 139, 101r)*. © *The Trustees of the Chester Beatty Library, Dublin*

in the left margin next to the large kappa. The text reads 259₂, which means that this is the 259th section in Matthew's Gospel, and that this passage has parallels also in Mark and Luke. If we turn to the second

Matthew in the Green Bible

Figure 4.2. Canon Table 2 showing texts shared by Matthew, Mark and Luke *(GA 2604, Dublin CBL W 139, 6r)*. The parallel for the 259th section of Matthew can be found in the third to sixth columns in the first line of the third box down (σνθ for Matthew, ρμη for Mark, σμζ for Luke). © *The Trustees of the Chester Beatty Library, Dublin*

table at the start of the manuscript (figure 4.2), we can find the precise locations of this text's parallels in Mark and Luke.[3] There are many ways to frame the text of the New Testament, and our modern Bibles are often

3. For more on the Eusebian system, see chapter 7.

less interesting or ephemeral repackagings of older traditions that we find in the manuscripts.

The examples of the Scofield and Green Bibles show that one way to think of paratexts is as maps for reading.[4] Sometimes, they're directional maps, like a treasure map, designed to point you to one conclusion; sometimes, they simply represent a space, showing you the possibilities. The Scofield Reference Bible is more directional, while the Green Bible is more representational, but both guide readers through Matthew 24 while borrowing and reworking conventions found in abundance in the manuscripts of the New Testament. These modern editions use different English translations, yes, but the differences between them are not really in the text of the Bible they adopt, but in the paratexts they offer. In Scofield, we see a picture of the end of the age defined by the literal fulfillment of prophecies in a definite order. Any evidence to the contrary is explained in such a way that it falls into line with what we already know the Bible must say. The end goal is always in primary focus. The Green Bible adopts an alternative orientation, one that stresses care for creation as a way to care for the poor and vulnerable, as a way to worship God, and as a way to actively practice a faithful life in a time of crisis, although in a way that is relentlessly apolitical. It makes creation care an issue of personal responsibility, not a call to critique and work to change larger economic and political systems. We might be more drawn to one approach over the other, but both editions use the same strategy to make the case for their interpretations and emphases.

There are of course innumerable modern Bible editions on the market, each of which present different translations alongside innovative paratexts to different audiences, including *She Reads Truth* and the *(In)courage Bible*, as well as study Bibles of various kinds, such as children's Bibles, teen *Adventure Bible*, *American Patriot's Bible*, and *Orthodox Study Bible*, among many others. The list goes on. If there is a market, there's a Bible for it, especially in America. The point is that the Scofield and Green Bibles are two species in a very complex biblical

---

4. This metaphor is also used to describe the Eusebian apparatus in Jeremiah Coogan, "Mapping the Fourfold Gospel: Textual Geography in the Eusebian Apparatus," *Journal of Early Christian Studies* 25 (2017): 337–57.

ecosystem defined by evolution and change. And this tradition of change runs through the entire history of the New Testament, from its earliest manuscripts through to the different types of Bibles available in English translations today.

In recent years, scholars have made much of the changes to the biblical text and the importance of the ways that manuscripts were produced for interpreting the text. But what we have largely ignored is the paratexts and their effect on reception, reading, and interpretation. When we turn to the manuscripts and get behind our modern Bibles and critical editions, we find ourselves in a new world with a new set of possible maps. The New Testament's manuscripts and their variability show the importance that people from the past attributed to this collection. Manuscripts place our modern Bibles in the context of their own history. They put to rest the idea that there has ever been one Bible, one consistent set of works in a defined order with fixed texts that then can be interpreted in only one perfect way intended by their authors. The manuscripts invite us to think about scripture in new, open ways, to find and engage with the complexities and contradictions inherent to sacred traditions and, by extension, the faithful life. The line between text and paratext, between scripture and tradition, has never been as clear as it tends to be in our popular imaginations. There is no one right way to make or read a Bible (even though I can think of several ways that miss the mark).

The idea that scripture changes—that the texts, order of works, and paratexts of the New Testament in the manuscripts are never entirely stable—might be threatening to some people. Even in his introduction to the Green Bible, Dave Bookless expresses this concern:

> Part of me reacts badly to the idea of a "Green Bible." Niggling away in some small corner of my mind is a train of thought which goes like this: "The Bible is the Bible—if it's God's word then don't mess with it! Surely we should let the whole Bible speak to us without picking and choosing a few favorite bits and highlighting them in Green? Don't we run the risk of squeezing it into a mold of our own creating?"

The reality is, though, that as soon as parts of the New Testament began to be copied by the earliest Christian communities and circulated to new recipients, we began to shape the words into a "mold of our own creating." Bibles are not self-sufficient or obvious. Changes to the Bible are invitations to explore its depth and complexity anew and to encounter how previous generations of people understood their sacred traditions. Whenever we copy a text, frame it with paratexts, and select the materials on which we will write the words, we make the work anew. Bibles are the product of human choice. Sacred texts were never unassailable. Instead, they invite engagement, leading to change in the struggle to create significance from these works.[5] Paratexts give us new insights into our sacred texts, but they also tell us a lot about the people who made them.

---

5. Working with early print Bibles, William H. Sherman assumed that "the most active readers of the sixteenth and seventeenth centuries would have set down their pens and pressed their palms together in a posture of quiet (if not altogether passive) veneration. When I later returned to the Bibles to complete my survey, I learned how wrong I have been." Sherman's observations extend in many ways also to the Greek manuscripts, as we will see. *Used Books: Marking Readers in Renaissance England* (Philadelphia: University of Pennsylvania Press, 2010), 73.

TITLES

I want to start our exploration of paratexts by beginning where most books start: with titles. My earliest memory of a book is tied to my first time visiting a library. Sometime in the early 1990s at the Mill Creek branch of the Sno-Isle library system, I found a book with the tantalizing title *How Many Trucks Can a Tow Truck Tow?* It posed an alluring question that required a creative answer, delivered in satisfying alliteration. As my mom read it to me, I learned that the book was indeed about a tow truck and how many tow trucks it might be capable of towing. The title rhymed, just like the book. The essence of the story—its main question and style of delivery—was encapsulated in its title.

Now, *How Many Trucks Can a Tow Truck Tow?* is not a work of high literary art. Nevertheless, like nearly all ancient and modern literature, its title serves an important function in relation to the work. Not only does it work as a shorthand for everything inside the book, but it is also crafted for a particular audience (children under five, especially those who like trucks and big machines) and accurately previews the content and delivery of the prose. Like the title, the book is terse, alliterative, fast paced, imaginative. The title is the question that the book answers.

Professional titologists—literary scholars who focus on the effects and semiotics of titles, drawing originally on French discussions of textual pragmatics[1]—usually turn their attention to

---

1. See the early generative and highly technical discussion between Leo H. Hoek,

more culturally generative works of literature and visual arts, analyzing the titles of early modern French novels, paintings, or poetry. But regardless of their objects of study, titologists are generally convinced that titles are crucial aspects of whatever artwork they label and that they are evidence of reception that help us understand the ways these works were read and understood in various contexts. Titles are subject to change in terms of their wording, location, and relationship to the main text.[2] It is in these changes that titles hold up a mirror to the time and place of their making, giving us a glimpse into how readers conceived of a given literary work.[3] As Paola Buzi notes in an article on titles in Coptic manuscripts, these glimpses are never simple to interpret and rarely contribute to a grand narrative about the work.[4] But

---

La marque du titre: Dispositifs sémiotiques d'une pratique textuelle (Paris: Mouton, 1981); and Claude Duchet, "La Fille abandonée et la bête humaine, Eléments de titrologie Romanesque." *Littérature* 12 (1973): 49–73. The debate is summarized in Gérard Genette, *Paratexts: Thresholds of Interpretation*, trans. J. E. Lewin (Cambridge: Cambridge University Press, 1997), 55–56. This discussion, focusing primarily on early modern French novels, revolved around questions of label (what do we call the different aspects of titles?), the intertextuality of titles in multiple directions, and their literary functions.

2. See Genette, *Paratexts*, 64–75 on these variables, although they do not comport precisely with the situation in ancient and medieval manuscript traditions. On the suitability of Genette's categories for these traditions, see Garrick V. Allen, *Manuscripts of the Book of Revelation: New Philology, Paratexts, Reception* (Oxford: Oxford University Press, 2020), 46–48; Patrick Andrist, "Toward a Definition of Paratexts and Paratextuality: The Case of Ancient Greek Manuscripts," in *Bible as Notepad: Tracing Annotations and Annotation Practices in Late Antique and Medieval Biblical Manuscripts*, ed. L. I. Lied and M. Maniaci (Berlin: de Gruyter, 2018), 130–35; and Matthew R. Crawford, *The Eusebian Canon Tables: Ordering Textual Knowledge in Late Antiquity* (Oxford: Oxford University Press, 2019), 21–28.

3. Medieval and ancient works were often retitled as they began to be printed in the form of critical editions. See, for example, the works of Chaucer in Victoria Louise Gibbons, "The Manuscript Titles of *Truth*: Titology and the Medieval Gap," *Journal of the Early Book Society for the Study of Manuscripts and Printing History* 11 (2008): 197–206, who notes that titles were not essential to some works of lyric poetry in Middle English.

4. Paola Buzi, "New Testament Titles in the Coptic Manuscript Tradition: An Overview," *Religions* 13 (2022), https://doi.org/10.3390/rel13060476: "What is the func-

because we expect titles in conventional places in our printed books, they become ingrained parts of what we read; we rarely reflect on their significance in our rush to understand the main text. They are the gristle we cut around to get to the steak. But without the fatty parts, the meat lacks flavor.

Despite what I suspect is our general ambivalence toward titles, Giancarlo Maiorino, exploring titular traditions in early modern and post-modern literature, argues that "interpretation begins with the title, which is the seed that contains the tree. As the literary nutshell that offers an introductory overview of etymological roots, semantic complexity, and literary echoes, the title ought to loom as large in the reader's mind as it does on the book's spine."[5] In my experience, this is not usually how most people read literature, especially the titles of the New Testament that are (for the most part) very well known and often used as shorthand for ideas their works contain. Nonetheless, I think Maiorino is right that "the relationship between title and text covers complexities and contradictions that cannot be overlooked."[6] Titles are micro-texts unto themselves, formulations that signpost to things like plot, genre, style, and themes located in their works.[7] Titular forms

---

tion of a title? What is its temporal relationship with the text it is attributed to? How certain can we be about the contemporaneity of a title and the text with which it is associated? Can we use a title to univocally identify a text? Everybody who has dealt with titles of ancient works is aware that these questions are not easy to solve, and, more importantly, the answers change from literary tradition to literary tradition."

5. Giancarlo Maiorino, *First Pages: A Poetics of Titles* (University Park: Pennsylvania State University Press, 2008), 2. John Fischer puts it more directly: "The unique purpose of titling is hermeneutical: titles are names which function as guides to interpretation." "Entitling," *Critical Inquiry* 11 (1984): 287.

6. Maiorino, *First Pages*, 2.

7. For a short manifesto and clever treatise on how titles and subtitles ought to function in modern literature, see John Barth, *The Friday Book, or, Book-titles should be Straightforward and Subtitles Avoided: Essays and Other Nonfiction* (New York: Putnam, 1984), ix–xiv. Of course, titles can also be satirical, subverting expectation when you begin to read the main text, like Jonathan Swift's *A Modest Proposal For preventing the Children of Poor People From being a Burthen to Their Parents or Country, and For making them Beneficial to the Publick*, commonly known as *A Modest Proposal*.

constitute a type of paratext that "create[s] zones of transaction between readers and writers as well as zones of transition between literary traditions."[8] They add value to the main text, or at least they ought to.[9] As we know from the empirical sciences, titles have cognitive functions, altering the ways we interact with texts and artworks based on their concreteness and relationship to the item they label.[10] And, as Esther Brownsmith, Liv Ingeborg Lied, and Marianne Bjelland Kartzow demonstrate, sometimes a title is all that remains of an ancient work.[11]

Titles exist in some form for nearly every kind of literature, including sacred traditions, both ancient and modern. As such, they are a type of paratext common to literature more broadly but overlooked when it comes to the New Testament in particular. In many cases, titles are essential parts of the meaning-making process.

---

8. Maiorino, *First Pages*, 2.

9. See Graham Francis Badley, "Un-doing a Title," *Qualitative Inquiry* 20 (2014): 287.

10. E.g., Marie Lippmann et al., "The Concreteness of Titles Affects Metacognition and Study Motivation," *Instructional Science* 47 (2019): 257–77; Jennifer Wiley and Keith Rayner, "Effects of Titles on the Processing of Text and Lexically Ambiguous Words: Evidence from Eye Movements," *Memory & Cognition* 28 (2000): 1011–21; and H. Leder, C.-C. Carbon, and A.-L. Ripsas, "Entitling Art: Influences of the Title Information on Understanding and Appreciation of Paintings," *Acta Psychologica* 121 (2006): 176–98.

11. Esther Brownsmith, Liv Ingeborg Lied, and Marianne Bjelland Kartzow, "A Jubilee of Fifty Books Known Only by Title," *Journal for the Study of the Pseudepigrapha* 32 (2023): 376–98.

Chapter 5

THE TITLES OF THE NEW TESTAMENT

Like most other literature we read, the New Testament's titles are simultaneously overlooked and ubiquitous. They're everywhere, at different locations and in different forms, but we rarely stop to consider them or their significance, even though they are essential to the interpretive process.[1] If you pick up a Bible today, you're likely to find the title (or at least a version of it) on the spine, dust jacket, front cover, title page, and as a running title in the upper margin of every other page. You're also likely to find titles for each biblical book, subtitles or headings for various sections within each book (usually written by modern editors), and perhaps even titles at the end of the work or at the end of sections. Titles are mobile in relation to the texts they describe. Every time we read anything—Bibles, a novel, an academic tome, a collection of essays, an academic journal, a magazine, a newspaper, a website—we encounter titles, which have various relationships to the texts they label and which we often consume without much active thought. Like most paratexts, they are hidden in plain sight. This is especially true of the New Testament, where in many cases, readers have an overriding concern to interpret the main text without realizing that their engagements with that text are mediated by paratexts.

---

1. John Fischer, "Entitling," *Critical Inquiry* 11 (1984): 296: "Attending to titles, even subtitles, is in some instances absolutely essential to understanding, evaluating, and interpreting." Jerrold Levinson argues that "the title of an artwork is an invariably significant part of that work, which helps determine its character, and not just an incidental frill devoid of import, or a mere label whose only purpose is to distinguish it from its fellows.... Titles of artworks are often *integral parts* of them, constitutive of what such works are." "Titles," *Journal of Aesthetics and Art Criticism* 44 (1985): 29.

TITLES

Titles are an important species of paratext due to their omnipresence and flexibility. Gérard Genette, speaking about early modern French novels, notes that

> the title as we understand it is actually . . . an artificial object, an artifact of reception or commentary, that readers, the public, critics, booksellers, bibliographers . . . and titologists (which all of us are, at least sometimes) have arbitrarily separated out from the graphic and possible iconographic mass of a "title page" or cover.[2]

In other words, titles are set off from the main text in various ways and deeply connected to the texts they label, reflecting a work's reception. They are also some of the earliest instances of reception for a work, offering us a unique view into ancient interpretations within a specific context. The New Testament's titles are the spaces where interpretation and the forging of canons began to make their mark on the sacred text.[3] Today, their presentation in printed Bibles is the product of hundreds of choices made by anonymous people from antiquity onward. They are the result of mass print technologies, the desire to make books look attractive on the shelves, and the ways that people read. The location of the title vis-à-vis the main text, along with the intended audience and function, change as ancient literature is transmitted.[4]

From antiquity onward, bookmakers, interpreters, editors, and readers have had a hand in shaping the New Testament's titles. Titles are

---

2. Gérard Genette, *Paratexts: Thresholds of Interpretation*, trans. J. E. Lewin (Cambridge: Cambridge University Press, 1997), 54–55.

3. Fischer, "Entitling," 298: "Not all artworks need to be titled. But when an artwork is titled, for better or worse, a process of interpretation has inexorably begun."

4. Genette makes this point even for eighteenth-century French novels, which are creatures of early modern print cultures. *Paratexts*, 64–103. Manuscript cultures offer even more space for development since each copy needs to be made by hand in a bespoke way. On early titling traditions in other ancient traditions, see Menico Caroli, *Il titolo iniziale nel rotolo librario Greco-egizio* (Bari: Levante, 2007); Francesca Schironi, ΤΟ ΜΕΓΑ ΒΙΒΛΙΟΝ: *Book-Ends, End-Titles, and Coronides in Papyri with Hexamatric Poetry* (Durham: American Society of Papyrologists, 2010); and Jean Irigoin, "Titres, sous-titres et sommaires dans les œuvres des historiens grecs du Ier siècle avant J.-C. au Ve siècle après J.-C.," in *Titres et articulations du texte dans les œuvres antiques*, ed. J.-C. Fredouille et al. (Paris: Institut d'Études Augustiniennes, 1997), 127–34.

ripe for interpretive changes because they signal what we should expect when we come to the text without necessarily altering the text itself. We learn about the genre of the work, its topic, key idea, or main character. The information we gain from these deductions, often subconsciously, configures our reading strategies and shapes what we imagine we will find between the covers. For example, we learn about the genre of the New Testament works (*Letter* of Paul to the Romans), their purported authors (Gospel *according to Luke*), intended recipients (Letter *to the Philippians*), and many other things. The titles of the New Testament set our expectations by offering us information on the genre, content, supposed author, or the work's relationship to other parts of the corpus.

There are two important points about the New Testament's titles that I want to explore further. First, at their earliest stages, the works of the New Testament were essentially untitled texts in search of a label. Titles were invented by subsequent readers to organize emerging Christian scripture into collections and to distinguish similar works, be they letters or narratives, from one another. None of the titles we commonly use in reference to these works were written by their authors.[5] Paul didn't affix *Romans* at the top of the letter when he posted it off from Corinth in the capable hands of Phoebe the deacon; Mark never flipped back to the start of his gospel and wrote *Gospel according to Mark* above "The

---

5. This is true for much ancient and medieval literature. See, for example, Victoria Louise Gibbons, "The Manuscript Titles of *Truth*: Titology and the Medieval Gap," *Journal of the Early Book Society for the Study of Manuscripts and Printing History* 11 (2008): 197–206. Another problematic concept is that of the "author," not only because many New Testament works are functionally anonymous (the Gospels, Acts, 1 John, Hebrews) but because the production of ancient literature was always a collaborative process that involved composition, revision, copying, and later editorial processes to put works into conversation with one another. Paul's voice may be the dominant one in the letters attributed to him, but he often wrote with named coworkers, and the people who carried the letters for him also appear as characters in the text and as figures of note in the title. The subscription to Romans, for example, often notes that it was carried by "Phoebe the deacon," who likely played a role in communicating the letter and its contents to the recipients. Although the titles present authorship in a straightforward way, the reality is much more complex. On the role of letter carriers in antiquity, see Peter M. Head, "Named Letter-Carriers among the Oxyrhynchus Papyri," *Journal for the Study of the New Testament* 31 (2009): 279–99.

beginning of the gospel of Jesus Christ, Son of God."[6] The production and early transmission of these works are more complex than this reconstruction, but the point remains: the titles for biblical works were made by anonymous readers, scholars, and compilers *after* they were initially written and transmitted. How the New Testament went from a series of individually circulating texts to a corpus of sacred literature is, in part, a story of titles, labels, and organization.

The date at which titles were attached to these works, especially the gospels, has been a significant point of discussion in the broader conversation on the origins of the Four Gospels collection. Martin Hengel, for example, argued that the formulaic title for the four gospels, *Gospel according to Matthew* (εὐαγγέλιον κατὰ ματθαῖον) for example, was an early development that enabled the four works to witness a single gospel message and to distinguish between each story when read in early Christian communities.[7] Similarly, Silke Petersen makes the case that the emergence of titles was the result of an organic process necessitated by the ways that early Christian communities read the gospels in combination with one another.[8] The consistency of the way the now-canonical gospel titles were formed asserts that they are a group of texts that belong together, are literarily related in some way, and that they tell a similar story.[9]

---

6. Bruce M. Metzger, *The Canon of the New Testament: Its Origin, Development, and Significance* (Oxford: Clarendon, 1987), 302: "Originally none of the documents now included in the New Testament had the titles to which we have become accustomed in the headings of the different books in traditional English versions."

7. Martin Hengel, *Die Evangelienüberschriften* (Heidelberg: Universitätsverlag, 1984), 47–51. On this topic, see Matthew D. C. Larsen, "Correcting the Gospel: Putting the Titles of the Gospels into Historical Perspective," in *Rethinking "Authority" in Late Antiquity: Authorship, Law, and Transmission in Jewish and Christian Tradition*, ed. A. J. Berkovitz and M. Letteney (New York: Routledge, 2018), 78–103.

8. Silke Petersen, "Die Evangelienüberschriften und die Entstehung des neutestamentlichen Kanons," *Zeitschrift für die neutestamentliche Wissenschaft und die Kunde der älteren Kirche* 97 (2006): 250–74.

9. On the earliest witnesses to the titles of the New Testament, see Garrick V. Allen, "Titles in the New Testament Papyri," *New Testament Studies* 68 (2022): 156–71; and Simon J. Gathercole, "The Titles of the Gospels in the Earliest New Testament Manuscripts," *Zeitschrift für die neutestamentliche Wissenschaft und die Kunde der älteren Kirche* 104 (2013): 33–76.

The Titles of the New Testament

The titles create attributions of authorship for works that are functionally anonymous in an effort to put these texts in conversation with one another, to bind them into a corpus.[10] The titles are something that early readers made as they grappled with how to put these works into dialogue and began to conceive early canonical collections of works that once circulated independently. From one perspective, the New Testament exists only because its titular traditions enable readers to distinguish between similar works and offer ways to subdivide the collection according to genre (Gospels, Catholic Epistles/Praxapostolos) or author (Paul). The very phrase *New Testament* is itself a title that describes later editorial work on the part of ancient readers. The New Testament is, ironically, a later editorial contrivance, a literary entity that none of the authors of any of its works could have foreseen.

The second point I want to make is that the New Testament's titles have continually changed from antiquity through to our modern Bibles. They were not fixed in antiquity and then remained untouched; they have been a consistent space of interpretive engagement within a set of traditional boundaries. Unlike modern titles of popular books which tend to contract over time in popular imagination,[11] the titles of the New Testament expand as they're preserved in the many thousands of Greek manuscripts copied from the second to the nineteenth centuries, offering more specific information about the work by placing it within

---

10. In "Correcting the Gospel," Larsen argues that the names attached to the gospels were not meant to ascribe authorship to these works in their ancient context, but to signal a persona responsible for editing an essentially unauthored, fungible, and growing tradition. Regardless of the veracity of this intriguing hypothesis, the names attached to the gospels have usually been understood as the authors of these works.

11. Genette, *Paratexts*, 70 notes that titles tend to decrease in size as people engage with them. A good example is Daniel Defoe's 1719 novel we know as *Robinson Crusoe*, originally published as *The Life and Strange Surprizing Adventures of Robinson Crusoe, of York, Mariner: Who lived Eight and Twenty Years, all alone in an un-inhabited Island on the Coast of America, near the Mouth of the Great River of Oroonoque; Having been cast on Shore by Shipwreck, wherein all the Men perished but himself. With An Account how he was at last strangely deliver'd by Pyrates. Written by Himself.* Note that this title contains a proper title (up to the colon), a summary of the entire plot in great detail, and a note on the fictive author (Defoe presents his work as the transcription of the fictional Crusoe).

the larger context of the collection. These changes are not uncontrolled. They fluctuate within a set of confines, not unlike what we find if we open different modern Bibles. Consider the inscription for 1 Timothy in various modern English Bibles:

- *1 Timothy* (ESV)
- *The First Book of Timothy* (Orthodox Study Bible)
- *The First Letter of Paul to Timothy* (NRSV)
- *The First Epistle of Paul the Apostle to Timothy* (Scofield)

These titles are not entirely dissimilar. None of them refers to the letter as the *Third Epistle of Donny*, *2 Francesco*, or *Fifty Shades of Paul*. But which one is the "real" title? The name Timothy is always present, and each title signals that there is probably a subsequent letter to attend to, creating a link with whatever text is entitled something like 2 Timothy. But they each call the text a different thing. Is it a book, a letter, or an epistle? How does the designation change how we approach the text? The Scofield Bible and the NRSV also mention Paul, with Scofield mentioning his apostolic status. Does this designation change our valuation of the text's message or its authority? These changes in modern Bibles reflect the patterns we see in ancient and medieval variations of the titles in the manuscripts. Small deviations can have big effects on the way we, as readers, approach these texts. Giving authors names and designations attempts to pre-instill the authority of the work's message. Calling 1 Timothy a book instead of a letter plays down its occasional nature: 1 Timothy, along with other New Testament letters, addresses specific issues at specific times, and we are not always privy to the underlying issues being addressed.[12] Calling it a book signifies its ongoing relevance and accessibility—it becomes something made for our consumption, something that is complete within itself.

When we make, print, and read the New Testament today, regardless of language or version, we partake in a long history of paratextual change. The variation present in titles for works of the New Testament across a broad span of history—even now with modern printed English

---

12. See, for example, the famous article by John Barclay, "Mirror-Reading a Polemical Letter: Galatians as a Test Case," *Journal for the Study of the New Testament* 10 (1987): 73–93.

Bibles—demonstrates that readers and editors play a key role in the ongoing use and reshaping of Bibles. Paratexts are the main vector for this change, and the titles are an overlooked but ubiquitous example of this type of dynamic.

When scholars have analyzed the New Testament's titles, they've focused almost entirely on the gospels.[13] Traditionally, the more effusive of the New Testament's titles have been viewed as "misinformation," since their assertions about authorship and provenance do not cohere with what modern scholars think about the origins of these works and the people who wrote them.[14] The shortest forms of the title are the ones that usually appear in our critical editions and, therefore, in our modern Bibles. In other words, most scholars have thought that titles are useful for understanding the earliest scholarship on the gospels, but that subsequent longer forms of the titles are of little relevance since they have no claim to being the earliest designation. Due to the laser-like focus on New Testament scholarship on the first and second centuries, lots of useful information on the titles from later periods has been overlooked.

Thanks in part to a research project I am currently leading in Glasgow called *Titles of the New Testament: A New Approach to Manuscripts and the History of Interpretation* (2020–2025), we now have significant and innovative information on the texts, aesthetics, and locations of thousands of titles in our Greek manuscripts.[15] This new information, in combination with what we know about the titles from recent critical editions, gives us a novel vantage point on the dynamics of change in the titles and what they reveal about the New Testament's essential substance. With this new information in mind, we can zoom in on the titles of the book of Revelation and the Catholic Epistles.

---

13. Or, if you're me, the book of Revelation, Garrick V. Allen, "Paratexts and the Reception History of the Apocalypse," *Journal of Theological Studies* 70 (2019): 600–632.

14. See Bruce M. Metzger, *Manuscripts of the Greek Bible: An Introduction to Palaeography* (Oxford: Oxford University Press, 1981), 40.

15. See Garrick V. Allen and Kelsie G. Rodenbiker, "Titles of the New Testament (TiNT): A New Approach to Manuscripts and the History of Interpretation," *Early Christianity* 11 (2020): 265–80.

Chapter 6

Titles in Revelation and the Catholic Epistles

The book of Revelation is a good example of the ways that titles change, especially because it's an outlier in its transmission among the other New Testament works in the Greek tradition. The earliest title for Revelation in its Greek manuscripts is, simply, "Apocalypse of John."[1] This title comes in part from the first words of the text—"Revelation (or Apocalypse) of Jesus Christ" (ἀποκάλυψις Ἰησοῦ Χριστοῦ)—but the responsibility for the work in almost every version of the title is transferred from Jesus to John. As the English word "reveal" suggests, the term "revelation" (or "apocalypse") refers to an unveiling or a manifestation; John becomes the conduit for the unfurling of this vision. In total, there are fifty-two different titles preserved for Revelation in its Greek manuscripts, giving us lots of additional information on John, Patmos, and the meaning of the work.[2] For example, three manuscripts from the fifteenth and sixteenth centuries (GA 2055, 2064, and 2067) call Revelation the "Apocalypse of St. John the Apostle, Evangelist, and Theologian, which is an explanation of the mysteries of God."[3] Another title in a manuscript cop-

---

1. Even though these early manuscripts (and a few others) share this title, they do not agree on the spelling of John (ιωανου or ιωαννου) or Revelation (αποκαλυψις or αποκαλυψεις). On Revelation and its titles, see Garrick V. Allen, *Manuscripts of the Book of Revelation: New Philology, Paratexts, Reception* (Oxford: Oxford University Press, 2020), 44–73; Garrick V. Allen, "Paratexts and the Reception History of the Apocalypse," *Journal of Theological Studies* 70 (2019): 600–32.
2. You can see each title and its English translation in Allen, *Manuscripts*, 68–73.
3. ἀποκάλυψις τοῦ ἁγίου ἀποστόλου καὶ εὐαγγελιστοῦ ἰωου τοῦ θεολόγου δήλωσις

ied in the year 1847, probably from a printed copy of the New Testament, provides a litany of adjectives for John and his identity, tying Revelation very closely to the beloved disciple in John's Gospel:

> *The Apocalypse of the Honored Evangelist, the one upon the breast, Dear, Virgin, Beloved by Christ, John the Theologian, Son of Salome and Zebedee and adopted son of the Mother of God, Mary, and a Son of Thunder*[4]

There has never been one single title for the book of Revelation, and this is true in degrees also for the rest of the New Testament. The varied titles we encounter in the manuscripts preserve not only an apparently straightforward authorial attribution, but significant traditions tied to apostolic figures such as "John the Theologian."

The reality of Revelation's changing titles is further complicated when we consider that the New Testament's manuscripts have four different kinds of titles: inscriptions (titles at the beginning of a work), subscriptions (titles at the end of a work), *kephalaia* (titles for subsections within a work), and, in some manuscripts, running titles, often appearing in the upper margins. The fifty-two titles I've counted in Revelation's Greek manuscripts account only for its inscriptions and subscriptions. These do not include the titles of the seventy-two chapters for Revela-

---

αὐτη τῶν θυ μαρτυρίων (transcription from GA 2064). The additional information on what an apocalypse is comes from Andrew of Caesarea's commentary. For an English translation, see Eugenia Scarvelis Constantinou, *Andrew of Caesarea: Commentary on the Apocalypse* (Washington, DC: Catholic University of America Press, 2011).

4. GA 1775 (Mt. Athos, Panteleimonos, 110; diktyon 22248). See also Bruce M. Metzger, *The Canon of the New Testament: Its Origin, Development, and Significance* (Oxford: Clarendon, 1987), 301–4. This title is located directly below an icon and precedes another commentary title connected to Andrew of Caesarea. This manuscript creates a commentary to Revelation drawn from the Andrew, Oecumenius, and Arethas traditions, while also abbreviating its main text. Nonetheless, it shares many readings with the Erasmus edition, suggesting that the scribe had access to a printed text at some point in the production process. See Darius Müller, "Abschriften des Erasmischen Textes im Handschriftenmaterial der Johannesapokalypse," in *Studien zum Text der Apokalypse*, ed. M. Sigismund, M. Karrer, and U. Schmid (Berlin: de Gruyter, 2015), 228–31.

tion composed by Andrew of Caesarea in the late sixth or early seventh century that are often present in many manuscripts (even when the commentary is not), or the few that preserve running titles of one kind of another.[5] Titology is relevant for thinking about ancient literature because the New Testament's titles are complex and subject to change as literature is passed from one generation to another. The titles of the book of Revelation are persistent spaces for framing reading experiences. As such, they offer oft-overlooked evidence for the reception of Revelation and for traditions of manuscript production in various contexts. What we call a thing reflects and alters how we conceive of and use it.

The Catholic Epistles, Titles, and Canon

Change is also found in the collection of letters known as the Catholic (or General) Epistles: James, 1–2 Peter, 1–3 John, and Jude. Going back at least to Eusebius, scholars have raised questions about this collection: can all the letters be attributed to the apostles whose names are attached to them? Who put this collection of letters together? What is the logic of their arrangement and message? What role did they play in the larger canonical process? Already in the fourth century, Eusebius knew that there were "seven letters called Catholic" (*Hist. eccl.* 2.28.24–25), but he acknowledged that there was debate around their authenticity. These questions persist in modern discourse on these works.[6] The titles of these letters offer a viewpoint into the strategies that scribes and read-

---

5. For an English translation of Andrew of Caesarea's seventy-two subtitles (and his commentary), see Constantinou, *Andrew of Caesarea*, 45–50. For the Greek text of Andrew's commentary and accompanying paratexts, see Josef Schmid, *Studien zur Geschichte des griechischen Apokalypse-Textes*, part 1, Der Apokalypse-Kommentar des Andreas von Kaisareia (Munich: Karl Zink, 1956).

6. See, for example, Matthias Klinghardt, "Wie und warum ist der Jakobusbrief ins Neue Testament gekommen? Der Jakobusbrief als kanonisches Pseudepigraph," *Zeitschrift für Neues Testament* 25 (2022): 85–95, who argues that James was composed especially to be part of the emerging New Testament canon and that it was never transmitted apart from this collection. I disagree that we can reconstruct a specific "canonical edition," but the order and arrangement of the Catholic Epistles as we now have it was an intentional choice at some point in the transmission. The conventional ordering is also subverted in some copies that place Jude after James,

ers employed to make the Catholic Epistles a corpus. The titles are key innovations that created and perpetuated this collection.

Let's start with James, the first of the Catholic Epistles in most manuscripts. According to the most substantial modern edition of the Catholic Epistles, there are thirty-five different titles in Greek for James, the simplest being *Epistle* (or *Letter*) *of James* (Ἰακώβου ἐπιστολή or ἐπιστολή Ἰακώβου).[7] Most English Bibles have some version of this title. From it, we learn the identity of the author (the genitive is a standard way to denote authorship) and the type of thing we are about to read—a letter. None of this is groundbreaking; it's easily deduced from the epistolary form of the first few verses (Jas 1:1–2).

However, the titles for James are not static. Many include elements that make assertions about canon and the collection of the seven Catholic Epistles more generally. The titles and other paratexts that become attached to the Catholic Epistles work diligently to assert that these letters do indeed belong together and that they are connected to the earliest phases of Christian history.[8] For example, most formulations include the adjective "catholic" or "general" (καθολική) for James and the other letters to assert that these works do indeed form a literary collection and that their intended audiences are more general than the specific situations that stand behind Paul's letters. The titles in GA 312 (London, British Library, Add. 5115–5116, diktyon 38771), an eleventh-century copy of Paul,

---

probably because they are both presented as the biological brothers of Jesus (e.g., GA 61 and 326).

7. See Barbara Aland et al., eds., *Novum Testamentum Graecum Editio Critica Maior*, IV/1, 2nd ed. (Stuttgart: Deutsche Bibelgesellschaft, 2013), 1.

8. For recent discussions of the canonicity of the Catholic Epistles, the process of their collection and composition, and the consequences for reading these letters, see Darian R. Lockett, *Letters from the Pillar Apostles* (Eugene, OR: Pickwick, 2017); David R. Nienhuis, *Not by Paul Alone: The Formation of the Catholic Epistle Collection and the Christian Canon* (Waco, TX: Baylor University Press, 2007); and Robert W. Wall, "A Unifying Theology of the Catholic Epistles: A Canonical Approach," in *The Catholic Epistles and Apostolic Tradition*, ed. K. W. Niebuhr and R. W. Wall (Waco, TX: Baylor University Press, 2009), 13–40. These discussions revolve around questions of pseudonymity, composition, and the theological inevitability of the canonical processes, but they overlook the evidence of reception preserved in manuscripts that preserve these works.

Acts, and the Catholic Epistles, each include this word: "Catholic Epistle of James" (Ἰακώβου καθολικὴ ἐπιστολή), "First Catholic Epistle of Peter" (ἐπιστολὴ καθολικὴ πέτρου. πρώτη), and so on. This shared feature, incorporated by those who copied these works, connects the seven Catholic Epistles as a subcorpus of the New Testament, a group of letters distinct from Paul's collection.

The concern to demarcate the Catholic Epistles as a collection is even clearer in other examples. In GA 056 (Paris, BnF, Coislin gr. 26, diktyon 49168), a tenth-century copy of Paul, Acts, and the Catholic Epistles with commentary, James is clearly denoted as the start of this broader collection (56v):[9]

> Beginning of the Seven Catholic Epistles:
> Epistle of James
>
> ἀρχὴ τῶν ζ καθολικῶν ἐπιστολῶν:
> ἐπιστολὴ Ἰακώβου

Titles create distinctions between letters, but they are also used to distinguish between the various groups of works that make up the New Testament, which was a concern for readers from antiquity onward.[10] Many Greek manuscripts distinguish between the New Testament's constituent subcorpora: the Gospels, Paul's letters, the Praxapostolos (Acts and the Catholic Epistles), and Revelation. The Catholic Epistles are usually presented as a unit, even in Codex Alexandrinus, a fifth-century complete Bible codex which includes a subscription at the end of Jude that reads "Acts of the Holy Apostles and the Catholics."[11] This subscrip-

---

9. Images are available at the holding institution's website: https://gallica.bnf.fr/ark:/12148/btv1b110001885/f1.image [accessed 16 August 2023].

10. This is true for some copies of Paul's letters, e.g., GA 2197, where we read "End of the 14 Letters [of Paul]" (τέλος τῶν ιδ̄ ἐπιστολῶν) after Hebrews and before James (356v), and for the Gospels, e.g. GA 961, where we read "End of the four Gospels" (τέλος τῶν τεσσάρων εὐα[γγελίων]) following the subscription to John (244r).

11. An interesting counterexample is GA 368 (Florence, Biblioteca Riccardiana, 84, diktyon 17083), a fifteenth-century manuscript that compiles all the Johannine literature in the New Testament, preserving John, Revelation, and 1–3 John in this order.

Titles in Revelation and the Catholic Epistles

tion connects the Catholic Epistles through their defining shared feature and connects them to Acts, creating a nascent Praxapostolos collection. This reality is clear, too, at the ending of the Catholic Epistles in some manuscripts. At the end of Jude in GA 307 (Paris, BnF, Coislin gr. 25, diktyon 491670), a copy of Acts and Catholic Epistles produced in the tenth century, we don't find a subscription to this short letter as we do for the other works in this manuscript.[12] Instead, we find an enlarged and ornamental title for the Catholic Epistles (figure 6.1):

With God, end of the Catholic Epistles

σὺν θ̄ω̄ τέλος τῶν καθολικῶν επιστολῶν

The desire to demarcate the Catholic Epistles as a subcorpus is a pervasive concern in the titles of the individual letters and in the titles at the start and end of the collection. These manuscripts want readers to consider the Catholic Epistles as an independent collection within the broader umbrella of the New Testament. Their inherent connectedness and defined order, reinforced by the titles and other paratexts, is one thing that enables them to exist within the canonical tradition.[13]

The titles also reinforce the place of the Catholic Epistles in the canon by explicitly connecting their authors to the first Christian generation, tapping into an existing network of traditions about the presumed authors of these letters.[14] In parallel with the expanding stories and apocry-

---

12. For example, James concludes with the subscription "Epistle of James" (ἰακώβου ἐπιστολή, 206v).

13. Some titles also order the letters. For example, in GA 467, 621, and 1243, James is entitled "First Catholic Epistle of James" (ἰακώβου ἐπιστολὴ καθολικὴ ᾱ). See also Lockett, *Letters*, 105–15.

14. Some titles make identification of the authors of 1–2 Peter and 1–3 John with the apostles Peter and John obvious, even though 1 John isn't a letter and the author of 2–3 John refers to himself as "the Elder." The inscription to 1 John in GA 2674, for example, refers to John the Theologian, an appellation often found in Revelation's titles and sometimes also in subscription to John's Gospel (e.g., GA 412 and 577). This descriptor ties together the Johannine literature in the New Testament more broadly. In some cases, the inscriptions to 1 Peter refer to the author as an apostle, further connecting these letters to the Peter we see in the gospels (e.g., GA 049, 1127, 1735,

Figure 6.1. Subscription to the Catholic Epistles *(GA 307, Paris, BnF, Coislin grec 25, 254v)*. Bibliothèque nationale de France

phal narratives attached to apostolic figures in late antiquity,[15] the titles reinforce the apostolicity of these letters by explicitly connecting them to specific figures. Some titles, for example, assert that the author of James is James, the "brother of God" (ἀδελφοθέοιο or ἀδελφοθέου), a leader of the early church in Jerusalem (e.g., Matt 13:55; Mark 6:3; Acts 12:17; Gal 2:9; Eusebius, *Hist. eccl.* 2.23.1).[16] The inscription to James in GA 1501 (Mt. Athos, Great Lavra Monastery, A 79, diktyon 27007, thirteenth century) reads "Catholic Epistle of James the Apostle and Brother of God"

---

and 1838). On the construction of Peter's identity in light of paratexts, see Kelsie G. Rodenbiker, "The Second Peter: Pseudepigraphy as Exemplarity in the Second Canonical Petrine Epistle," *Novum Testamentum* 65 (2023): 109–31, esp. 126–29.

15. On the functions of apocryphal stories of the apostolic past, see Tobias Nicklas, "Retelling Origins: Stories of the Apostolic Past in Late Antiquity," in *The Apostles Peter, Paul, John, Thomas and Philip with Their Companions in Late Antiquity*, ed. T. Nicklas, J. E. Spittler, and J. N. Bremmer (Leuven: Peeters, 2021), 1–20, who argues that apocryphal stories create "landscapes of memory" and connections to physical objects. Titles function in similar ways by physically bracketing material manuscript copies of scriptural texts. They are the traditional memories that shape reading and interpretation.

16. See Luke Timothy Johnson, *Brother of Jesus and Friend of God: Studies in the Letter of James* (Grand Rapids: Eerdmans, 2004), 4–9, for a portrait of James as an early church leader in Jerusalem.

(Ἰακώβου ἀποστόλου τοῦ ἀδελφοθέου, ἐπιστολὴ καθολική). By identifying the author as a particular James, one with a leadership role in the early church and a biological connection to Jesus, the title adds gravitas to the message of the letter, filling out the picture of its author and the larger context in which it was written.[17] The same holds true for Jude, who is also identified as a "brother of God" or "brother of James" in some titles.[18] The title connects the content of the letter to a larger landscape of historical memory, creating a new and specific context for understanding the work's message.

With the moniker "brother of God," James takes on the mantle of a kind of early ecclesial communication to a broad audience, following the declaration in 1:1 that the letter is for the "the twelve tribes in the diaspora." Some titles specify the addressees further, suggesting that the letter was intended for different kinds of Jewish communities. The inscription in GA 1739 (Mt. Athos, Great Lavra Monastery, B 64, diktyon 27116, tenth century) calls James "Catholic Epistle of James: Letter of James the Brother of God to the Hebrews" (Ἰακώβου ἐπιστολὴ καθολική. γράμμα πρὸς ἑβραίους Ἰακώβου ἀδελφοθέοιο). GA 94 (Paris, BnF, Coislin gr. 202bis, diktyon 49342, thirteenth century) is even more specific: "Catholic Letter of James to the Believing Jews in the Diaspora" (καθολικὴ ἐπιστολὴ Ἰακώβου πρὸς τοὺς ἐν τῇ διασπορᾷ πιστεύσαντας ἰουδαίους). This title envisions the addressees as Jews who follow Christ, as opposed to dispersed Jewish communities more generally.[19]

Conclusion

The patterns that we see in the changes to the titles of the Catholic Epistles are commensurate with the titles for the New Testament's other

---

17. For traditions on James's identity, see Dale C. Allison Jr., *James* (London: Bloomsbury, 2013), 3–32. Another title also locates James as written from Jerusalem, offering further ecclesial authority to the work's message: "Catholic Epistle of James, written from Jerusalem" (καθολικὴ ἐπιστολὴ Ἰακώβου γραφεῖσα ἀπὸ ιελημ) (GA 330).

18. For example, in the subscription to Jude in GA 88, "Catholic Epistle of Jude the Brother of James" (ἰούδα ἀποστόλου ἀδελφοῦ Ἰακώβου ἐπιστολὴ καθολική).

19. There is debate about the intended addressees, but Johnson argues that the twelve tribes "most naturally suggests Jewish Christian readers." *Brother of Jesus*, 7.

works. As the most widely transmitted collection of texts that have come to us from the ancient world, the New Testament's Greek manuscripts preserve a surprising variety in their paratextuality, including in the various forms of their titles. This brief sampling of titles associated with Revelation and the Catholic Epistles shows that later scribes and readers used titles as a space to frame reading experiences and to extend traditions related to venerable figures and the literature associated with them. Our interpretation of these texts is impacted by our view of the author's persona and identity, the scope of their intended addressees, their connection of the text to other parts of the New Testament, and the place and time of their initial production.

The material context in which we encounter works like the Catholic Epistles, be it a modern English Bible, a critical edition of the Greek text, or an ancient manuscript, is both a product of the cultures in which we read and a catalyst for directing interpretations. The titles we find in Bibles that we pick up in the pews or in our grandma's basement are only one of many options for naming these works. This reality has consequences for what we think the New Testament is. Because it doesn't exist in any one ideal form, format, or language, the New Testament is something that is never fully apprehended in any one manuscript or printed book. It is something more complex—a collection of thousands of manuscripts, printed books, and now digital texts, in hundreds of languages, formats, and materials. It is an omnibus of all its possible iterations. Each copy is something tangible, but that physicality only gives us access to one example of the whole, even if the entire New Testament text is contained in that copy we hold in our hands. When we hold a modern Bible, we touch the curated product of centuries of interpretation and scholarship, an entryway to the vast and messy tradition of scriptural engagement. The titles begin to show us this complexity and reveal the ways that sacred traditions have been mediated by generations of anonymous readers, scribes, and scholars.[20] We become part of

---

20. In other words, the manuscripts and their paratexts help us to "read the scribe" and "read the reader," in the words of Erik Kwakkel, "Decoding the Material Book: Cultural Residue in Medieval Manuscripts," in *The Medieval Manuscript Book: Cultural Approaches*, ed. M. Johnston and M. van Dussen (Cambridge: Cambridge University Press, 2015), 60–76.

a much more expansive story that connects us to the "authors" of these works, but only mediated through the centuries of grappling, change, and thought that have gone before.

Paratexts, including titles, played a major role in shaping the New Testament as we now have it, influenced by interpretive traditions, the various commentary traditions, and the social function of the manuscripts. Revelation's titles, for example, connect the Apocalypse with the author of John's Gospel and even at times the Johannine letters. Despite early uncertainty about the authenticity and apostolic authorship of some of the Catholic Epistles, the titles work to create a defined set of seven letters in a (mostly) consistent order. They reflect the interpretive choices that led to the incorporation of the Catholic Epistles into most (but not all) forms of the New Testament canon and enabled the continuing existence of this tradition. The malleability of the titles is an essential ingredient that authorizes ongoing engagement with sacred traditions. Change is a potentially revelatory aspect of tradition, revealing new insights about scripture and its contexts. The variation we see in the titles played a significant role in the production of a canon that many consider unchanging, but canon is something that must be continually negotiated by readers and communities of faith.

CROSS-REFERENCES

When I was about ten, my mom signed me up for Vacation Bible School at a Baptist church in Everett, Washington. She was a single parent and needed a week of free childcare in the summer. One of our neighbors attended the church, which added a layer of comfort. Entering this unfamiliar context was, thankfully, more fun than confusing. The music was overly cheerful, and they kept trying to get us to do an altar call (whatever that was), but there was also time for play and pizza. The balance between sitting still listening to long-winded talks about Jesus and free time was, for the most part, bearable.

One of the games we played still sticks with me, mostly because of its unjust bias toward the church kids. We were each given a Bible, and the woman leading the group read off a random verse with no context. "As he came out of the temple, one of his disciples said to him, 'Look, Teacher, what large stones and what large buildings!'" "Jesus wept." And so on. The first person to find the passage and place their finger on the words won. Naturally, I failed to find a single text, although I remember being amazed that the church kids could flip from book to book in this huge volume and find specific words and phrases. How did they know this odd conversation about the size of a temple was in Mark 13? How did they know that the phrase "Jesus wept" only appeared in John? I was in over my head.

I learned an obvious lesson that day: the Bible is a big, complex book. Even if we just take the New Testament, it's a multifaceted collection comprised of twenty-seven works of different lengths in different genres. Although we often think of the New Testament as a single collection bound between two covers that runs from Matthew to Revelation in a fixed, inevitable order, the manuscripts present many different possible combinations and arrangements. Out of the nearly 5,700 known Greek manuscripts that preserve parts of the New Testament, only fifty-two were designed to preserve all twenty-seven New Testament works when they were first produced as far as we can tell. Of these fifty-two manuscripts, only four preserve the order of works we're used to seeing in our modern English Bibles, and these are quite late, made from the fourteenth to sixteenth centuries.[1] It was not until Paris in the thirteenth century that full Bibles in Latin became widespread, and as Chiara Ruzzier has recently shown, this was a remarkable development that required significant technological innovation.[2]

The New Testament as we often experience it today, a thing bound as a single book in a well-defined, consistent order, is a relatively recent phenomenon, more the product of print culture than an unchanging historical inevitability. The standardization of the

---

1. See Ulrich Schmid, "Die Apokalypse, überliefert mit anderen neutestamentlichen Schriften—eapr-Handschriften," in *Studien zum Text der Apokalypse*, ed. M. Sigismund, M. Karrer, and U. Schmid (Berlin: de Gruyter, 2015), 421–41. The four that preserve the modern English order are GA 296 (sixteenth century), 367 (fourteenth century), 886 (fifteenth century), and 1626 (fifteenth century). This reality is why the Tyndale House Greek New Testament (Crossway, 2017) and the Robinson/Pierpont Byzantine Textform edition (Chilton, 2005) place the Catholic Epistles between Acts and Paul's letters, following a common pattern found in the manuscripts. Of course, over 2,500 of the manuscripts in the *Liste* are lectionaries (excerpted and re-arranged texts to correspond to the Orthodox liturgical calendar), but it is striking how few Greek manuscripts preserve the order of works that modern readers of English Bibles are familiar with. David C. Parker formulates the problem this way: "While early Christianity may have come to make lists of authoritative books, there were no authoritative copies of them." *The Living Text of the Gospels* (Cambridge: Cambridge University Press, 1997), 188.

2. Chiara Ruzzier, *Entre Université et ordre mendiants: La production des bibles portatives latines au XIIIe siècle* (Berlin: de Gruyter, 2022).

New Testament as a printed object made it possible for the church kids at VBS, familiar with the basic order and content of mass-produced Bibles, to wipe the floor with me in the find-the-verse game. They were able to navigate its pages with a certain level of expertise. There was a way to locate whatever it was you were looking for, aided by their familiarity with the conventions of printed Bibles: chapter and verse numbers, book divisions and fixed sequences, and subtitles. The paratexts did some heavy lifting for them.

The questions that I want to explore in the following chapters are how, before the advent of print, did readers find their way through the New Testament, and what do these pathways show about how people read these texts? If the number of works, their order, and paratextuality differ sometimes drastically from copy to copy, how could readers navigate the New Testament? How do the possibilities of reading embedded in these tools relate to how we approach these texts today? The ability to know what works are arrayed within a codex, their order, their internal literary structures, and their relationship to other texts they sit next to is basic to reading and interpretation.

Modern Bibles have multiple structures to help navigate these complexities. Even in a time when the twenty-seven works of the New Testament are fixed in a typical order, we still need help to find our way, and the tools offered to us by publishers are determined by the intended audience of a given edition. Some of these navigation aids take the form of material changes to the book. A good example is the thumb index, a series of notches made in the fore-edge of the book, a tool for locating the start of a work or textual subdivision. The presence of a thumb index communicates that this book is a compilation, a collection, but don't be afraid, you can still make your way. Another way to save your place and to navigate the New Testament is the ribbon or attached bookmark. These have become conventional aspects of what makes a "fine Bible" (at least according to Cambridge University Press).[3]

---

3. "Recognizing a Fine Bible," Cambridge University Press, accessed August 9, 2023,

In addition to these physical alterations to the book, most modern Bibles include paratexts that aid in wayfinding: tables of contents, running titles, chapter and verse numbers, indexes, page numbers, subheadings with parallel passages, and more. These navigational paratexts—items that aid users in locating themselves within a codex or within a longer literary work—are so commonplace that we often overlook their utility, viewing them as the incidental extras that must come along with the literature we read. This book that you're now reading has these features too, including chapters, titles, table of contents, page numbers, and indexes. Some of these things are conventions of modern publishing generally, not specific to Bibles. And even some of the more conventional paratexts that we now associate with Bibles, like consistent chapter and verse divisions, weren't invented until the sixteenth century when they first appeared in Stephanus's 1551 printed Bible.[4] Looking at the paratexts shows that our modern Bibles are indeed just that: very modern.

Some of the paratexts that we find in Bibles today have ancient and medieval forerunners. When we pick up a Bible, we look through the shadows of previous navigation systems, contrived in late antiquity for the New Testament, that enabled readers to do

---

https://www.cambridge.org/bibles/about/recognizing-fine-bible. On bookmarks and manuscripts, see Georgios Boudalis, "Straps, Tabs and Strings: Book-Marks in the Codices of the St Catherine's Monastery in Sinai," *Journal of Paper Conservation* 20 (2019): 81–105.

4. Modern chapter and verse divisions were first introduced into the Greek New Testament in the 1551 edition printed in Geneva by Robert Estienne, also known as Stephanus (although previous attempts had been made in Latin by Sanctes Pagninus in 1528 and by Stephen Langton, who introduced chapter divisions, in the thirteenth century). See William Weavers, "The Verse Divisions of the New Testament and the Literary Culture of the Reformation," *Reformation* 16 (2011): 161–77; Ezra Abbot, *The Authorship of the Fourth Gospel and Other Critical Essays* (Boston: Ellis, 1888), 464–67; Isaac H. Hall, "Note on Early Verse-Divisions of the New Testament," *Journal of Biblical Literature* 10 (1891): 65–69; and Bruce M. Metzger, *The Text of the New Testament: Its Transmission, Corruption, and Restoration*, 2nd ed. (Oxford: Oxford University Press, 1968), 103–4. On Langton's intervention, see Christopher de Hamel, *The Book: A History of the Bible* (London: Phaidon, 2001), 124. On the finding devices of early print books, some of which overlap with manuscripts of the New Testament, see Ann M. Blair, *Too Much to Know: Managing Scholarly Information before the Modern Age* (New Haven: Yale University Press, 2010), 132–60.

new things with their sacred traditions. Most of these systems for cross-reference and navigation developed out of the pioneering context of the library of Caesarea Maritima in Palestine in the third and fourth centuries CE, spearheaded by the prolific work of Origen, Eusebius, and their collaborators.[5] This highly generative context became a space for experimenting with the utility of the codex, similar to the type of book familiar today where gatherings of pages are bound between two covers. The development of the codex, emerging views on the canon of sacred scripture, and an intellectual setting of innovation coalesced to create new paratexts that impacted what people did with the New Testament for well over a millennium. Caesarea is the main headwater of the New Testament's navigational paratexts.

Origen, Eusebius, and many other anonymous people created the paratextual machinery by which people navigated Bibles, and traces of these systems are found in nearly every manuscript copy of the Greek New Testament in existence. The history of this context has been explored in many places and from many angles in recent years.[6] What I want to do, building on this work, is to explore how the scholarship undertaken in Caesarea fundamentally shaped the ways that people moved within and around the New Testament by taking a close look at two systems connected to this context, beginning with Eusebius's paratexts to the gospels.

---

5. For an overview on the relationship between book history and scholarship in this context, see Anthony Grafton and Megan Williams, *Christianity and the Transformation of the Book: Origen, Eusebius, and the Library of Caesarea* (London: Belknap, 2006). See also Gregory Peter Fewster, "Finding Your Place: Developing Cross-Reference Systems in Late Antique Biblical Codices," in *The Future of New Testament Textual Scholarship: From H. C. Hoskier to the Editio Critica Maior and Beyond*, ed. G. V. Allen (Tübingen: Mohr Siebeck, 2019), 155–79.

6. On the library of Caesarea see, e.g., Andrew Carriker, *The Library of Eusebius of Caesarea* (Leiden: Brill, 2003); Marko Frenschkowski, "Studien zur Geschichte der Bibliothek von Cäsarea," in *New Testament Manuscripts: Their Texts and Their World*, ed. T. J. Kraus and T. Nicklas (Leiden: Brill, 2006), 53–104; Paul Hartog, "Pamphilus the Librarian and the Institutional Legacy of Origen's Library in Caesarea," *Theological Librarianship* 14 (2021): 22–34.

Chapter 7

Eusebius and His Paratextual System

Eusebius of Caesarea (c. 260–330 CE) was a prolific author, commentator, historian, and bishop. His vast body of work, especially his ten-book *Ecclesiastical History*, has deeply influenced reconstructions of the earliest layers of Christian history and preserves many fragments of now lost works.[1] Perhaps his greatest achievement, however, is not a historical narrative or commentary, but a paratextual system for the Gospels: the canon tables.[2] In the past ten years or so, there has been a resurgence of scholarly interest in the canon tables and the system crafted by Eusebius to assist readers of the Gospels.[3] Martin Wallraff, the first person to produce a critical edition of the system, refers to it as "the king of New Testament paratexts" because of its utility and widespread

---

1. On Eusebius's corpus, see Jeremiah Coogan, *Eusebius the Evangelist: Rewriting the Fourfold Gospel in Late Antiquity* (Oxford: Oxford University Press, 2022), 97–100. Eusebius also used lists and columns in other works, including his *Chronicon*, Psalms list, and *Onomasticon*. See Martin Wallraff, *Die Kanontafeln des Euseb von Kaisareia: Untersuchung und kritische Edition* (Berlin: de Gruyter, 2021), 17–20; and Wallraff, "The Canon Tables on the Psalms: An Unknown Work of Eusebius of Caesarea," *Dumbarton Oaks Papers* 67 (2013): 1–14.

2. The English word "canon" comes from the Greek κανών, meaning "list," "table," "rod," or "standard." We're not talking about "canons of scripture" or authoritative lists, but about tables of parallels that can be read both horizontally and vertically.

3. For recent large-scale studies, see Matthew R. Crawford, *The Eusebian Canon Tables: Ordering Textual Knowledge in Late Antiquity* (Oxford: Oxford University Press, 2019); Alessandro Bausi, Bruno Reudenbach, and Hanna Wimmer, eds., *Canones: The Art of Harmony* (Berlin: de Gruyter, 2020); and Coogan, *Eusebius the Evangelist*. On the role of the book in early Christianity, which regularly touches on Origen and Eusebius, see Harry Y. Gamble, *Books and Readers in the Early Church: A History of Early Christian Texts* (New Haven: Yale University Press, 1995); and Martin Wallraff, *Kodex und Kanon: Das Buch im frühen Christentum* (Berlin: de Gruyter, 2013).

transmission.[4] Nearly every manuscript copy of the gospels in Greek and other languages preserves some portion of this system devised by Eusebius in the early fourth century. It includes three elements, which appear in the manuscripts in various combinations: textual divisions and marginal annotations, tables of textual parallels, and a preface known as the *Letter to Carpianus*.[5] Together, these elements create what Wallraff calls a "complex comprehensive artwork," a set of structures that comprises a symbiotic relationship with the gospel texts that it represents and organizes.[6] The Eusebian system is a major paratextual achievement that has underwritten large swathes of scholarship on the gospels since.

The system capitalizes on the idea that the Four Gospels can be bound together in one book. Modern Bible readers take this reality for granted, but important changes in third- and fourth-century book technology allowed these works to be bound between the same covers, enabling readers to compare parallel passages and traverse the long narratives of Jesus's life and activity found in Matthew, Mark, Luke, and John in new ways.[7] In some sense, the Eusebian system acted as an interactive map, as Jeremiah Coogan calls it, making it possible for people to find

4. Wallraff, *Kanontafeln*, 3: "Die Kanontafeln sind der König der neutestamentlichen Paratexte."

5. The Eusebian material is still found in some editions of the New Testament, including the Nestle-Aland[28] hand edition. The canon tables were first added to the 7th edition; see E. Nestle, "Die Eusebianische Evangeliensynopse," *Neue kirchliche Zeitschrift* 19 (1908): 50–51, 93–114, and 219–232. For an overview of the system, see Garrick V. Allen and Anthony P. Royle, "Paratexts Seeking Understanding: Manuscripts and Aesthetic Cognitivism," *Religions* 11 (2020), https://doi.org/10.3390/rel11100523; and Jeremiah Coogan, "Mapping the Fourfold Gospel: Textual Geography in the Eusebian Apparatus," *Journal of Early Christian Studies* 25 (2017): 343–44. On the date of the system see Wallraff, *Kanontafeln*, 9–12.

6. Wallraff, *Kanontafeln*, 3: "komplexen Gesamtkunstwerk."

7. The codex and its form are central to the work of Eusebius and others in his context. Matthew R. Crawford argues that the canon tables and other of his works are "part of Eusebius' larger programme of experimenting with the codex form to find innovative ways to present complex data." "Ammonius of Alexandria, Eusebius of Caesarea and the Origins of Gospels Scholarship," *New Testament Studies* 61 (2015): 16–17. On book production in late antiquity, see Georgios Boudalis, *The Codex and Crafts in Late Antiquity* (New York: Bard Graduate Center, 2018); and Leila Avrin,

Eusebius and His Paratextual System

Figure 7.1. Canon Table 1: passages shared by all four gospels *(GA 2604, Dublin, CBL W 139, 5r)*. © *The Trustees of the Chester Beatty Library, Dublin*

their own pathways through the gospels based on the questions they brought to the text and the structure of Eusebius's juxtapositions.[8]

Scribes, Script and Books: The Book Arts from Antiquity to the Renaissance (London: British Library, 1991), 159–75, and 205–29.

8. See Coogan, "Mapping," 337–57, who argues that the Eusebian system creates a canonical space that underwrites further intellectual engagement with these works.

65

The first feature of the Eusebian system is a set of chapter divisions called *kephalaia* (κεφαλαία). These divisions break down the narrative of each gospel into discrete, numbered textual units of varying length, 1,162 in total. Matthew usually has 355 chapters, Mark has 233, Luke has 342, and John has 232.[9] Instead of subdividing each gospel into chapters and verses like modern Bibles, Eusebius broke up each narrative into a single, linear set of units. In a time before the modern chapter and verse systems, this numeration allowed readers to identify texts in a highly specific way.[10] Instead of telling your friend to go read the Sermon on the Mount in Matthew 5–7 (as we now know it), you would tell them to read Matthew 24–62. Or if you needed to stop reading Mark because your kids were fighting in the other room again, you could remember that you stopped at chapter 155 (what we know as Mark 13:35–37) and pick up there after bedtime.

The numbering of texts was Eusebius's first step to facilitating cross-references between the gospels. He then plotted these chapter numbers, representing the texts they label, on a set of ten tables, the second major part of the system (figure 7.1).

A distinctive feature of the tables is their often highly elaborate artistic presentation, but their main literary function is to facilitate comparison across the gospels.[11] Each table presents texts (represented by

---

9. The total number of divisions differs from manuscript to manuscript. On Eusebius's numerations, see Wallraff, *Kanontafeln*, 20–27; on variants, see pp. 47–63.

10. There is another ancient chapter system for the gospels, often called the *kephalaia* system, which breaks up the gospels into much larger units. In this system Matthew has sixty-eight chapters, Mark has forty-eight, Luke has eighty-three, and John has eighteen. These *kephalaia* are titled, giving readers a summary of the content. For example, chapter 5 in Matthew is titled "Regarding the Beatitudes," covering the entirety of the Sermon on the Mount (Matt 5:1–7:29). The Eusebian chapters, however, break up the Sermon into thirty-eight different sections. Usually, these two ancient systems coexist in the manuscripts. See Garrick V. Allen, "The Possibilities of a Gospel Codex: GA 2604 (Dublin, CBL W 139), Digital Editing, and Reading in a Manuscript Culture," *Journal of Biblical Literature* 140 (2021): 409–34.

11. On the art-historical value of the canon table tradition, often highly illuminated with colorful architectural features and animals, see the classic study by Carl Nordenfalk, *Die spätantiken Kanontafeln*, 2 vols. (Göteborg: Isacsons, 1938). See also Ewa Balicka-Witakowska, "Carl Nordenfalk," in *Canones: The Art of Harmony*, ed. A. Bausi, B. Reudenbach, and H. Wimmer (Berlin: de Gruyter, 2020), 1–16, who contextualizes Nordenfalk's work. Speaking on the significance of the decoration in Armenian manuscripts, Crawford notes that the ornamentation bears symbolic

their *kephalaia* numbers) that the gospels share in various combinations, beginning with the first table, which shows passages shared by all four gospels and continuing to Table 10, with its four lists of texts unique to each gospel (see Table 7.1).

TABLE 7.1. *Parallels presented in each canon table*

I	Matthew // Mark // Luke //John
II	Matthew // Mark // Luke
III	Matthew // Luke // John
IV	Matthew // Mark // John
V	Matthew // Luke
VI	Matthew // Mark
VII	Matthew // John
VIII	Mark // Luke
IX	Luke // John
X	Four lists where each gospel has a unique passage

By placing the numbers on one of the ten tables, readers can immediately see which other gospels have parallels to the selected passage. For example, from the first line in figure 7.1 (which reads Matthew 166, Mark 82, Luke 94, John 17) readers know that these chapters in each gospel are related in some way. Or, if you noticed that a passage was placed on Table 6, then you would immediately know that it was a passage shared only by Matthew and Mark but absent in Luke and John, at least according to Eusebius. If you want to explore the parallels to Matthew 166 further, you could then flip to each numbered section in the other gospels and compare their texts or extract them in parallel columns as shown in table 7.2:

---

significance and that the decorative program was "intended as a defined progression through an imagined architectural space leading to some sort of culmination." *Eusebian Canon Tables*, 248. On the reception of the tables in other languages, see Crawford, *Eusebian Canon Tables*, 125–284; Judith S. McKenzie and Francis Watson, *The Garima Gospels: Early Illuminated Gospel Books from Ethiopia* (Oxford: Manar al-Athar, 2016), 83–117; Wallraff, *Kanontafeln*, 27–30; and Rolf Strøm-Olsen, "The Propylaic Function of the Eusebian Canon Tables in Late Antiquity," *Journal of Early Christian Studies* 26 (2018): 403–31.

CROSS-REFERENCES

TABLE 7.2. *Comparison between four passages in Canon Table 1*

Matt 166 (16:13–20)	Now when Jesus came into the district of Caesarea Philippi, he asked his disciples, "Who do people say that the Son of Man is?" And they said, "Some say John the Baptist, but others Elijah, and still others Jeremiah or one of the prophets." He said to them, "But who do you say that I am?" Simon Peter answered, "You are the Messiah, the Son of the living God." And Jesus answered him, "Blessed are you, Simon son of Jonah! For flesh and blood has not revealed this to you but my Father in heaven. And I tell you, you are Peter, and on this rock I will build my church, and the gates of Hades will not prevail against it. I will give you the keys of the kingdom of heaven, and whatever you bind on earth will be bound in heaven, and whatever you loose on earth will be loosed in heaven." Then he sternly ordered the disciples not to tell anyone that he was the Messiah.
Mark 82 (8:27–30)	Jesus went on with his disciples to the villages of Caesarea Philippi, and on the way he asked his disciples, "Who do people say that I am?" And they answered him, "John the Baptist; and others, Elijah; and still others, one of the prophets." He asked them, "But who do you say that I am?" Peter answered him, "You are the Messiah." And he sternly ordered them not to tell anyone about him.
Luke 94 (9:18–20)	Once when Jesus was praying alone, with only the disciples near him, he asked them, "Who do the crowds say that I am?" They answered, "John the Baptist; but others, Elijah; and still others, that one of the ancient prophets has arisen." Then he said to them, "But who do you say that I am?" Peter answered, "The Messiah of God."
John 17 (1:41–42)	He first found his brother Simon and said to him, "We have found the Messiah" (which is translated Anointed). He brought Simon to Jesus, who looked at him and said, "You are Simon son of John. You are to be called Cephas" (which is translated Peter).

The passages that Eusebius sets in parallel in this example are not identical in their wording or length. Matthew's version is much longer, including a loquacious blessing from Jesus in response to Peter's messianic declaration. Luke's passage doesn't mention Caesarea Philippi and it lacks the warning in Matthew and Mark that the disciples remain silent. John's passage is significantly different, taking place when Jesus is calling his disciples. Instead of Peter speaking to Jesus, Andrew tells his brother, Peter, that Jesus is the messiah. Peter doesn't say anything but receives a new name from Jesus. Some versions of the table also include chapter 74 in John (6:68–69) as a parallel, where in response to many followers leaving Jesus, Peter proclaims, "Lord, to whom can we go? You have the words of eternal life. We have come to believe and know that you are the Holy One of God." Even if we take the two Johannine passages as a pair, the parallels differ in multiple ways from the content and narrative context of the parallels in the Synoptic Gospels. They both deal with Peter and Jesus's messianic identity, but their narrative setting does not align with the context of the interaction in the Synoptics.

By plotting chapters across each gospel and organizing these chapter numbers on a set of tables, Eusebius creates a tool for interpretation that both reflects his understanding of the gospels' interrelationships and that produces new possibilities for readers. Instead of reading each gospel from front to back in a linear way, readers can flip between works in an almost hypertextual way, moving between stories as they please and investigating the minute differences between the narratives of Jesus's life.

The tables are visual representations of intricate textual relationships as Eusebius saw them, giving a highly condensed overview of this tradition, necessitated by the fact that, although they have many similarities, the gospels differ from one another in important ways. The tables put texts into conversation with one another by placing them into parallel columns without breaking up the narrative of the gospels themselves, as multiple early scholars prior to Eusebius had done to facilitate textual comparison. Readers can decide to engage the gospels in a straightforward way from the start of Matthew to the end of John (or whatever order they happen to take in their manuscript), but the tables offer the possibility to read the gospels in a nonlinear way, jumping back and forth between related passages.

CROSS-REFERENCES

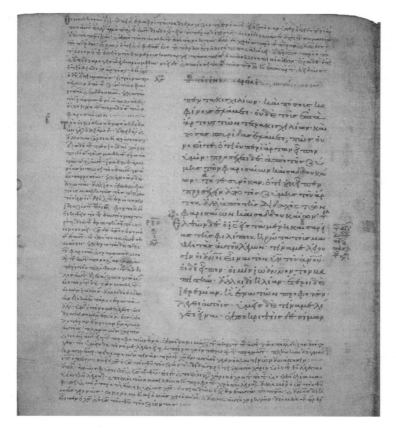

Figure 7.2. Matthew 166₁ in the left margin between main text and outer margin commentary *(GA 2604, Dublin, CBL W 139, 75v)*. © *The Trustees of the Chester Beatty Library, Dublin*

This kind of hypertextual reading is facilitated also by the fact that the number of the chapter and the number of the table to which the section belongs are often found in the margins of gospel manuscripts. For example, this passage in Matthew in GA 2604 (Dublin, CBL W 139, diktyon 13571), a twelfth-century gospel codex, has the numbers 166₁ ($\overline{\rho\xi\varsigma}/\overline{\alpha}$), showing readers the chapter number and, directly beneath it,

70

the number of the table to which it belongs (figure 7.2). The change in section is also signaled by the large gold epsilon from the main text that protrudes into the left margin. Other paratexts exist on this page as well, like chapter 33 in an alternative *kephalaia* system (with its title in the upper margin, "Regarding the questioning in Caesarea") and the notation in the right margin that says this passage is read on the Sunday feast day of the Holy Apostles Peter and Paul.[12] The point is that someone reading Matthew from front to back would not only recognize this as the 166th section, but also know immediately that this passage had parallels in all the other gospels because it was located on the first canon table.

The final ingredient in the Eusebian system is a prefatory letter addressed to a certain Carpianus which explains how the system functions.[13] Affixed as a preface to the gospels in some manuscripts, including in GA 2604 in a cruciform design, the *Letter to Carpianus* describes Eusebius's debt to his teacher Ammonius of Alexandria, lays out the way that each table portrays the parallel passages, and designates how the chapter numbers and table number should be copied out in the margins of the manuscripts. The *Letter* begins by noting that Ammonius "left behind for us the *Diatessaron-Gospel*, in which he placed alongside the [Gospel] according to Matthew the concordant sections from the other evangelists."[14] There is debate, but Eusebius likely describes a gospel

---

12. On the Byzantine liturgical system and the Eusebian apparatus, see Stefan Royé, "The Cohesion between the Ammonian-Eusebian Apparatus and the Byzantine Liturgical Pericope System in Tetraevangelion Codices," in *Catalogue of Byzantine Manuscripts in the Liturgical Context*, ed. K. Spronk, G. Rouwhorst, and S. Royé (Turnhout: Brepols, 2013), 55–116. On the alternative *kephalaia* or chapter-title system often found in gospel manuscripts, see W. Andrew Smith, *A Study of the Gospels in Codex Alexandrinus* (Leiden: Brill, 2014), 156–79; and Charles E. Hill, *The First Chapters: Dividing the Text of Scripture in Codex Vaticanus and Its Predecessors* (Oxford: Oxford University Press, 2022), 55–57. Some gospel manuscripts also preserve a table that creates parallels within this longer *kephalaia* tradition. For example, in GA 1443 (Mt. Athos, Great Lavra Monastery, A 6, diktyon 26934, copied in 1047, 90v), *kephalaion* 33 in Matthew is paralleled with Mark *kephalaion* 24 and Luke *kephalaion* 29.

13. On the letter to Carpianus, see Crawford, *Eusebian Canon Tables*, 295–96; Wallraff, *Kanontafeln*, 175–76; Coogan, *Eusebius the Evangelist*, 14–21, 100–102.

14. Translation from Crawford, *Eusebian Canon Tables*, 295–96.

harmony that has the entire text of Matthew in the left column with the parallels from other gospels rearranged and set alongside Matthew. Ammonius's *Diatessaron-Gospel*, which is no longer extant, facilitated comparison but at the expense of the narrative integrity of Mark, Luke, and John. This *Diatessaron-Gospel* was likely similar in format to Origen's *Hexapla*, which arranged the various versions of Jewish scripture in Hebrew and Greek in parallel columns to facilitate textual comparison.[15] Perhaps using Ammonius's division of Mark, Luke, and John to correspond to sections in Matthew as the raw material for his tables, Eusebius created a system that facilitated comparison, but without rearranging Mark, Luke, and John according to Matthew's narrative.[16]

Eusebius goes on to make just this point in this prefatory letter: "In order to preserve the body and sequence of the other [gospels] throughout and yet still be able to know the particular passages in each evangelist where they were moved by love for the truth to speak about the same things, I took my starting points from the labor of the aforementioned man [Ammonius], and, with the application of a different method, I have designed ten canons for you."[17] The narrative integrity of each gospel is preserved, while their similarities and differences are visualized as tables so that readers can compare parallel texts. The *Letter* concludes with a description of the context of each of the tables and the intended functioning of the system, designed to enable cross-referencing, where "you will find them [the gospels] saying similar things." The Eusebian

---

15. Although the *Hexapla* did not rearrange the sequence of texts in subsequent columns. On the *Hexapla*, see Natalio Fernández Marcos, *The Septuagint in Context: Introduction to the Greek Version of the Bible*, trans. W. G. E. Watson (Atlanta: SBL Press, 2000), 204–22; Peter J. Gentry, "The Septuagint and Origen's Hexapla," in *The T&T Clark Handbook of Septuagint Research*, ed. W. A. Ross and W. E. Glenny (London: T&T Clark, 2021), 191–206; and Anthony Grafton and Megan Williams, *Christianity and the Transformation of the Book: Origen, Eusebius, and the Library of Caesarea* (London: Belknap, 2006), 86–132.

16. Due to this debt to Ammonius, the chapters of the Eusebian system are sometimes called Ammonian sections, although this is a misnomer. See Crawford, "Ammonius of Alexandria," 1–29. On the somewhat enigmatic Ammonius and his intellectual work on the columnar *Diatessaron-Gospel* (and the work of Tatian before him), see Crawford, *Eusebian Canon Tables*, 56–84; Coogan, "Mapping," 346–52.

17. Translation from Crawford, *Eusebian Canon Tables*, 295.

system is intended to place side by side gospel texts that share commonalities of some kind.[18] It accomplishes this goal by creating literary and theological connections between texts, but the system's very existence highlights the invariable discontinuities and differences between the gospel narratives.[19] This tension makes the system a powerful tool for interpretation, for forging new reading pathways, and for thinking about the varying messages and specificities of each gospel.

The Eusebian system enjoyed a long and fruitful afterlife because it was fairly simple to use and addressed a fundamental problem: there are four versions of Jesus's life in the New Testament set right alongside one another.[20] The decision to juxtapose these narratives begs for a way to navigate these texts, to read them closely in relation to one another, to interrogate their every detail, and to understand how each story is a witness to the gospel writ large. The Eusebian system simultaneously creates and undermines the idea of a single gospel narrative.[21] It doesn't hide the messy truth that the gospels differ from one another; it gives readers ways to navigate their intersection and differences, to develop new ideas about their relationships; it offers a way through the fog of multiplicity, crafting a network that simultaneously acknowledges the differences between the gospels and the inextricable links between them.

This overview only begins to scratch the surface of the system's many interpretive possibilities, and it leaves out entirely the important discourse on the reception of this system in visual art and other media, an emerging area of study that Beatrice Kitzinger has recently explored.[22]

18. On the exclusivity of the system to the Four Gospels, see Coogan, *Eusebius the Evangelist*, 86.

19. As Coogan notes in his larger argument, the system is not concerned to explain away historical fissures in the narratives: "Eusebius' extensive juxtapositions render Gospel discrepancies *more* visible to the reader, not less." *Eusebius the Evangelist*, 116.

20. It also "has room for multiple intellectual projects." Coogan, *Eusebius the Evangelist*, 117. The system's ease of use is repeatedly asserted by Wallraff, who, for example, argues that "one can say that the system of Eusebius is marked simultaneously by minimal invasiveness and high efficiency and intellectual clarity." *Kanontafeln*, 13.

21. Coogan notes that "Eusebius's apparatus creates a canonical space and insinuates new routes through the canonical gospels for readers to follow." "Mapping," 354. See also Wallraff, *Kanontafeln*, 31–39.

22. Beatrice Kitzinger, "Eusebian Reading and Early Medieval Gospel Illumina-

However, the main point I want to make is that from a very early stage, Christian scholars exerted intellectual energy to create complex paratextual systems that allowed readers to navigate the gospels in equally complex ways. The gospels demand paratexts in light of their literary relationships and the import of their content. The Eusebian system is one way that you can find your way through part of the New Testament in a time before our modern chapter and verses. In many ways it is superior to the tools we use to navigate the gospels today.[23]

In contrast to reading a manuscript with the Eusebian system, it is difficult for the readers of most modern Bibles to quickly access parallel passages in the gospels. Some versions, like the Orthodox Study Bible, give parallels under its section subheadings that the modern editors have added to the text, but these are generally less capacious than the Eusebian system.[24] Even with this information in some versions, though, the gospels in modern Bibles are primarily designed to be read front to back, like a novel. In comparison to the manuscripts, there are fewer opportunities for cross-reference or awareness of differences in parallel passages without recourse to specialist tools like synopses, which place texts side by side in parallel columns in a way similar to Ammonius's *Diatessaron-Gospel*.[25] Of course, ancient and medieval people also read the gospels from front to back. Eusebius made sure this was still possible when he

---

tion," in *Canones: The Art of Harmony*, ed. A. Baussi, B. Reudenbach, and H. Wimmer (Berlin: de Gruyter, 2020), 133–71. For other explorations of the system's interpretive possibilities, see Francis Watson, *The Fourfold Gospel: A Theological Reading of the New Testament Portraits of Jesus* (Grand Rapids: Baker, 2016), 125–65; Matthew R. Crawford, "Do the Eusebian Canon Tables Represent the Closure or the Opening of the Biblical Text? Considering the Case of Codex Fuldensis," in *Canones: The Art of Harmony*, ed. A. Baussi, B. Reudenbach, and H. Wimmer (Berlin: de Gruyter, 2020), 17–27; and Crawford, *Eusebian Canon Tables*, 96–121.

23. A point made also by Watson, *Fourfold Gospel*, 105.

24. For example, at Matt 16:13, the Orthodox Study Bible offers the sub-heading "Jesus Is the Christ, the Son of God," inaugurating a section that runs to 16:20, longer than the Eusebian *kephalaion* that runs only to verse 16. Under this sub-heading, two parallels are offered: Mark 8:27–30 and Luke 9:18–21. The editors leave off the reference to John 1:41–42 entirely, creating their own set of cross-references that differ from the Eusebian system. Modern Bible editors continue the work of Eusebius when they identify parallels and divide the text by adding new subheadings.

25. The synopsis on my shelf is Kurt Aland, ed., *Synopsis of the Four Gospels* (United Bible Societies, 1972).

designed his system. But the paratextuality of most manuscripts allowed them to do different things that our modern Bibles don't readily facilitate—to quickly locate parallels, to compare similar texts, and to locate liturgical readings with ease. Our habits of reading have changed when it comes to the gospels, and this reality is revealed in the way we configure the paratexts in the Bibles we now read. The paratexts that accompany our Bibles influence how we read and, subsequently, how we interpret and understand the significance of our scriptural traditions. Some paratexts are better than others, and this applies to the ancient world as much as it does the modern. But once we've learned to see the paratext as a feature that alters our engagement with the text, we can begin to evaluate its particular function.

Chapter 8

Exploring the Euthalian Tradition

Closely connected to the Eusebian system and the intellectual context of the library of Caesarea, the Euthalian apparatus is a more complicated (and in many ways less elegant) set of paratexts.[1] The tradition is comprised of multiple paratexts with various interconnections, created after Eusebius's work and likely connected to the same intellectual center that fostered the canon tables: the library of Caesarea.[2] Unlike the Eusebian system, the Euthalian material is usually anonymous, although sometimes it is attributed to a mysterious Euthalius, an otherwise unknown person.[3] Instead of engaging the gospels, these paratexts are attached

---

1. The Euthalian prologue to Paul's letters quotes Eusebius's *Chronicon* and *Church History*. On the connection of the Euthalian tradition with Eusebius, see Garrick V. Allen, "Are There Ancient Editions of Paul's Letters? The Euthalian Apparatus as a Storehouse of Tradition," *Studia Theologica* 77 (2023): 1–31: "The Euthalian apparatus is a product enabled by the previous scholarship of Origen and Eusebius and it works to make us see it in that context" (23).

2. The date at which the different features of the Euthalian system were composed remains obscure, with proposals dating from the fourth to seventh centuries. This disagreement is one reason that so little attention has been given to the system and its features—it essentially has no native context. The Euthalian tradition does antedate the Eusebian material, and a colophon preserved in its earliest manuscripts (GA 015) and a few other copies note that "the book was compared with a copy in the library of Caesarea, written in the hand of the holy Pamphilus [Eusebius's teacher]," although this is at least a copy of a copy. Translation from Vemund Blomkvist, *Euthalian Traditions: Text, Translation and Commentary* (Berlin: de Gruyter, 2012), 16 (with minor alterations).

3. Scholars have proffered many arguments as to the identity of Euthalius and

Exploring the Euthalian Tradition

to Acts, the Catholic Epistles, and Paul's letters.[4] Parts of the Euthalian apparatus exist in nearly every Greek manuscript that contains these works.[5] This tradition is truly pervasive, mediating most readings of Acts and the New Testament's letters in Greek for over a millennium.[6] In a time before modern chapters and verses, one thing the Euthalian apparatus did was create ways for readers to find their place within the individual works it augmented and to begin to see thematic, conceptual, or theological connections between specific texts in the larger corpus.

---

his occupation, including Evagrius of Pontus, Evagrius of Antioch, and Euzoius of Caesarea. For an overview of scholarship, see Blomkvist, *Euthalian Traditions*, 8–33; Louis Charles Willard, *A Critical Study of the Euthalian Apparatus* (Berlin: de Gruyter, 2009), 111–27. The discussion of the provenance and authorship of the apparatus is highly speculative. See Günther Zuntz, "Euthalius = Euzoius?," *Vigilae Christianae* 7 (1953): 16–22, as a good example of erudite speculation.

4. The book of Revelation also has a commentary and text division system created by Andrew of Caesarea (with the help of his interpretive nemesis Oecumenius) in the late sixth or early seventh century. On Andrew and his system, see Garrick V. Allen, *Manuscripts of the Book of Revelation: New Philology, Paratexts, Reception* (Oxford: Oxford University Press, 2020), 74–120; Eugenia Scarvelis Constantinou, *Guiding to a Blessed End: Andrew of Caesarea and His Commentary in the Ancient Church* (Washington, DC: Catholic University of America Press, 2013); and Juan Hernández Jr., "Andrew of Caesarea and His Reading of Revelation: Catechesis and Paranesis," in *Die Johannesapokalypse: Kontexte—Konzepte—Rezeption*, ed. J. Frey, J. A. Kelhoffer, and F. Tóth (Tübingen: Mohr Siebeck, 2012), 755–74.

5. Nils Alstrup Dahl argues that the prefaces for each letter called the *hypotheses* or *argumenta* occur in 99 percent of manuscripts of Catholic Epistles, 90 percent of Paul's letters, and 80 percent of Acts (although Dahl does not consider these prefaces original to the Euthalian tradition). "The 'Euthalian Apparatus' and Affiliated 'Argumenta,'" in *Studies in Ephesians*, ed. D. Hellholm, V. Blomkvist, and T. Fornberg (Tübingen: Mohr Siebeck, 2000), 253. We are currently in the process of producing a catalogue of Euthalian features in all Greek manuscripts and only a small handful of the manuscripts we've examined thus far lack part of the system, and these are usually commentary manuscripts or quite fragmentary.

6. The system exists in other languages as well, like Armenian, Syriac, Gothic, Slavonic, and Georgian. It is almost entirely absent in the Latin tradition, however, which is another reason that modern scholars have overlooked it. See Willard, *Critical Study*, 95–108; and Neville Birdsall, *Collected Papers in Greek and Georgian Textual Criticism* (Piscataway, NJ: Gorgias, 2013), 215–42.

Among the many different lists, prologues, prefaces, and biographical texts that make up the possible constellations of the system (some of which I explore further in chapter 10 and at the beginning of the section "Traces of Use"), one feature enables cross-reference and wayfinding, albeit in a less sophisticated way than Eusebius: the chapter or *kephalaia* lists and their titles.[7] Beyond the short prefatory texts for each work called *hypotheses*, which were likely not part of the system in its earliest iterations, the chapter lists are the most pervasive aspect of the Euthalian tradition.[8] They are present even in GA 015 (Paris, BnF, suppl. gr. 1074), the earliest witness to the Euthalian system produced in the sixth century.[9]

Like the list for 1 Timothy in GA 015, every one of the New Testament's letters and Acts are divided into various numerated sections and subsections in some cases, each of which has a title. The tables usually occur before each work, as they do in Codex H (although only fragmentarily preserved in this instance). The first page of 1 Timothy's chapter list in GA 015 (6v) preserves the first four of the work's eighteen chapters:[10]

---

7. For a summary of the items that comprise the Euthalian apparatus, see Blomkvist, *Euthalian Traditions*, 8–10; Garrick V. Allen, "Early Textual Scholarship on Acts: Observations from the Euthalian Quotation Lists," *Religions* 13 (2022), https://doi.org/10.3390/rel13050435. A longer summary of each item can be found in Willard, *Critical Study*.

8. Dahl, "Euthalian Apparatus," 253–60.

9. On Codex H, see Henri Omont, *Notices sur un très ancient manuscript grec en oncialtes des Épîtres de saint Paul* (Paris: Imprimerie nationale, 1889). The manuscript is currently divided between holding institutions in Paris, Turin, Mt. Athos, Kyiv, Moscow, and St. Petersburg. Elina Dobrynina argues that Codex H should be dated to the eighth or ninth century since the accentuation was original to the first stage of production and not only input when the manuscript was re-inked. "On the Dating of Codex H (Epistles of the Apostle Paul)," in *Le livre manuscrit grec: Écritures, matériaux, histoire*, ed. M. Cronier and B. Mondrain (Paris: Centre d'Histoire et Civilisation de Byzance, 2020), 137–49. I am not yet convinced by her argument, but, regardless of date, Codex H is a key witness to the Euthalian tradition.

10. English translations from Blomkvist, *Euthalian Traditions*, 55, with minor alterations. The text and English translation of the lists can be found in Blomkvist, *Euthalian Traditions*, 45–73. For images see https://gallica.bnf.fr/ark:/12148/bt v1b8577515k.r=.langFR (accessed 16 August 2023).

α	Περὶ τῆς εἰς ἀγάπην θ̄ῡ ὁδηγίας τὴν ἀπροσδεῆ. νομικῆς ἀνάγκης	1	Regarding guidance to love God, which does not need the restraint of the law (1:3)
β	περὶ τῆς ἑαυτοῦ ἐκλογῆς εἰς εὐαγγελιστὴν. ἐκ διώκτου. κατὰ χάριν θ̄ῡ	2	Regarding his election as an evangelist from being a persecutor, according to the grace of God (1:12)
γ	παραγγελία περὶ πίστης καὶ εὐσυνειδήτου διακονίας ἧς ἄνευ κίνδυνος	3	Instruction regarding faithful service with a good conscience, without which there is danger (2:1)
δ	περὶ εὐχῆς, ὅτι ὑπὲρ πάντων ὅτι πανταχοῦ ἀκάκως ἀτράχως [σεμνῶς]	4	Regarding prayer, that it should be for all, everywhere, without evil, quiet and solemn (2:11)

The chapters are shorter than our modern divisions, but they are usually longer than the sections into which Eusebius divided the gospels (see table 8.1). Nonetheless, the division of each work into numerated sections, each with its own title, begins to make it possible to locate specific passages in each work, enabling readers to compare the subject matter of the table with the text itself.[11] The tables create a summary of the narrative, topics, and arguments of the works to which they are attached. These lists were made based on a close reading of the text (at least as the composer of the list understood them), focusing on ethical, moral, literary, and theological topics.[12]

11. Another part of the Euthalian apparatus (which is rather rare in the manuscripts), the lection list, divides each letter into three units of varying length: readings (ἀναγνώσεις), chapters (κεφάλαια), and lines (στίχοι). The list also notes how many quotations are in each reading. For example, the lection list for 1 John reads "Letter of 1 John, 1st reading: 3 chapters (1, 2, 3), 1 quotation (1), 150 lines. 2nd reading: 4 chapters (4, 5, 6, 7), 140 lines."

12. The tables may also be compared to a kind of ancient data management, enabling readers to quickly access specific bits of information pertinent to their reading

CROSS-REFERENCES

TABLE 8.1. *Number of chapters in the Euthalian tradition*

Work	Number of chapters
Acts	40 (+ 47 subtitles)
James	6 (+ 9 subtitles)
1 Peter	8 (+5 subtitles)
2 Peter	4 (+1 subtitle)
1 John	7 (+8 subtitles)
2 John	2 (+1 subtitle)
3 John	3 (+1 subtitle)
Jude	4 (+1 subtitle)
Romans	19 (+6 subtitles)
1 Corinthians	9 (+16 subtitles)
2 Corinthians	10 (+5 subtitles)
Galatians	12
Ephesians	10
Philippians	7
Colossians	10
1 Thessalonians	7
2 Thessalonians	6
Hebrews	22 (+8 subtitles)
1 Timothy	18
2 Timothy	9
Titus	6
Philemon	2

By placing these chapters on a list before each letter, readers can glean the basic structure, narrative, and content of each work by reading the titles in sequence. The titles for each chapter often function as pithy doctrinal statements, at least in the longer letters.[13] For example,

---

activities. See Ann M. Blair, *Too Much to Know: Managing Scholarly Information before the Modern Age* (New Haven: Yale University Press, 2010), 14–22.

13. In the shorter letters, like 2 John which has only three chapters, the titles mostly relate to the literary structure of the letter. Chapter 1 starts "after the prooemium," and chapter 3 simply reports the author's hope to visit (the prooemium and declaration of a visit are formal elements of ancient letters). Chapter 2, however, does

James's first chapter is entitled "Regarding steadfastness and firm faith. To the rich [in particular]: regarding humility." In this case, we get no information on the author, addressees, or the larger structure of the letter, only its initial concerns, with a special note directed to the wealthy. The remaining chapter titles continue in a similar fashion: "Regarding mildness, chastity, and good behavior, giving us a share in the blessing. And regarding wise and suitable speech" (chapter 2); "Regarding impartial love toward everyone according to the law" (chapter 3); "That not by faith alone, but by works (not one separately, but both together), is one justified" (chapter 4). Chapter 5 again makes a general statement, the specific topics of which appear as subtitles. "The reckless and unruly tongue destroys its master; it must be controlled for praise and glory to God," we are told. The subtitles give examples, following the structure of the letter's argument. Controlling one's tongue means peaceful behavior toward one another (3:13), seeking after divine wisdom (3:17), avoiding the strife that comes from love of pleasure (4:1), and repentance, forgoing the judgment of one's neighbor (4:8).

The chapter lists relay the topic of a given text while also drilling down into its specific ethical imperatives. They reflect a close reading of the text, a reality that allows them to act as a kind of summary comprised of terse declarative statements. A similar argument has been made by David Hellholm and Vemund Blomkvist, who suggest that the Euthalian system is a form of education literature, reflecting ancient *paraenesis* or instruction that uses the New Testament text as its foundation.[14] Regardless of how we designate the genre of these paratexts, whoever composed them paid close attention to the biblical texts and their admonitions.

Beyond working as summaries of the biblical works, the information in the tables regularly appears in the margins of the works themselves, physically dividing the text and offering overviews of the content em-

---

sum up one reading of the purpose of the letter: "One should not let heretics live in the house or greet them, because of [their] sin."

14. David Hellholm and Vemund Blomkvist, "Paraenesis as an Ancient Genre-Designation: The Case of the 'Euthalian Apparatus' and the 'Affiliated Argumenta,'" in *Early Christian Paraenesis in Context*, ed. J. Starr and T. Engberg-Pedersen (Berlin: de Gruyter, 2004), 467–519.

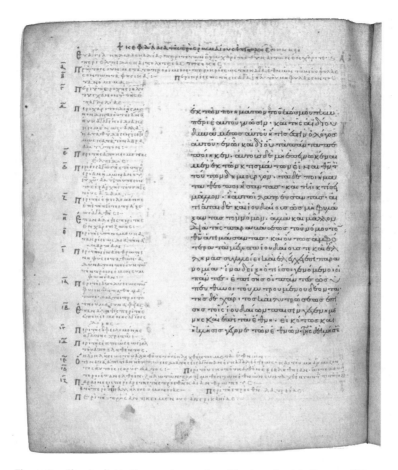

Figure 8.1. Chapter list to Romans in margins of the *hypothesis* to Romans *(GA 250, Paris, BnF, Coislin grec 224, 159v). Bibliothèque nationale de France*

bedded in the text as one reads the letters.[15] The chapter numbers and their titles even appear in the margins of manuscripts with no corre-

---

15. On the interpretive dimension of textual divisions, see Marjo Korpel, "Unit Delimitation as a Guide to Interpretation: A *Status Quaestionis*," in *Les delimitations éditoriales des Écritures—Editorial Delimitations of the Scriptures*, ed. G. Bady and M. Korpel (Leuven: Peeters, 2020), 3–33.

Exploring the Euthalian Tradition

sponding tables in many instances.[16] The Euthalian chapter divisions become the main way that readers divided most of the New Testament for over a millennium. In cases where both the table and marginal annotations exist, readers can cross-reference the information in the tables with the marginal notations. Not only is it possible to then approximate where you are in the letter, but you can easily locate specific information by coordinating the chapter number and title in the list with the same information in the margins.

For example, if you were interested in learning about the topic of grace in Paul's letters, you could scan the table at the head of each work for this topic. Let's say you happen to be reading GA 250 (Paris, BnF, Coislin grec 224, diktyon 49365), an eleventh-century copy of Acts, the Catholic Epistles, Paul, and Revelation. Flipping to the section on Paul, you turn past the abbreviated Euthalian prologue to this corpus (151r) and the text on Paul's travels (151r) to the chapter list, which begins in the margins on 159v (figure 8.1).

Reading down the list, you come to chapter 4 (Δ): "Regarding grace, the only way that people are justified since they are not judged according to their kind, but equally according to the gift of God, following the example of Abraham." This title is substantial, giving the topic (grace), the argument that Paul makes about it (that people are equally judged according to God's gift), and the evidence he adduces (the example of Abraham). You'll certainly want to locate this text and digest the argument in greater detail and nuance. But how do you locate it within the larger narrative of Romans?

In this case, you find the start of Romans with its nice ornamental headpiece and start flipping pages, looking for any indication that you've located chapter 4. A few pages later, on 167r, you see something: a small delta (Δ, 4) in the left margin and a few lines of text, identical to the title in the list, located between the main text and the marginal commentary in the lower margin (figure 8.2).

You begin to read from the words "what then" (τί οὖν), today the start of Rom 3:9, working your way carefully through Paul's dense discourse

---

16. For example, see GA 627, 633, 644, 676, 796, and 832. Many manuscripts also have chapter lists but no corresponding markings in the text itself (e.g., GA 101, 909, 918, 921, and 1067).

Figure 8.2. Chapter 4 in Romans according to the Euthalian system with marginal commentary *(GA 250, Paris, BnF, Coislin grec 224, 167r)*. *Bibliothèque nationale de France*

on justification, law, faith, and grace. Eventually, the discussion turns to Abraham as an example of the point Paul is trying to make (Rom 4:1–25), just as the title of the chapter notes. Eventually, you encounter a small epislon (ε̄, 5) in the upper margin a few pages down (170v) next to the title for chapter 5 ("Regarding the awaiting hope"), signaling the end of this chapter that deals with grace. This is a long section (comprising Rom 3:9–

Exploring the Euthalian Tradition

4:25 in the modern chapter and verse system), but it delineates a textual unit with a consistent theme: Paul's exposition on justification and an example, drawn from Jewish scripture, that supports his argument. The title boils down the main topic of the chapter to impartial grace, even though the word "grace" only appears once in the passage (Rom 3:24, "they are now made righteous by his grace as a gift"). The chapter list enables you to locate a specific passage by cross-referencing the list with the marginal notations in the manuscript. The title also allows you to find a passage that discusses the topic you're interested in.

In addition to finding your way to a specific passage that addresses a particular topic, the chapter lists help you cobble together a synopsis of similar passages that deal with questions of grace or Abraham. As you read through the lists at the start of each work, you are able to compile the following places to check further to compare against Paul's highly intricate argumentation in Romans (table 8.2).

TABLE 8.2. *Synopsis of chapter titles whose topics relate to Romans kephalaion 4*

Chapter	Title
Romans summary	Gospel teaching regarding those with and those without the grace of Christ, regarding hope and spiritual citizenship
Romans 7 (6:1–23)	Repetition regarding the life in grace
2 Corinthians 10 (10:1–18)	The story of his [Paul's] own toils, his aim, and the grace in him, so that the Corinthians may not join the imposters
Galatians 5 (3:7–9)	That also Abraham was justified by faith, as an example for us
Galatians 9 (4:21–5:1)	That there is no need to be enslaved under the law, if we follow the example of the free wife of Abraham and their legitimate son
Ephesians 3 (2:1–22)	Regarding gentiles and Jews becoming God's through Christ, for the sake of hope according to grace

CROSS-REFERENCES

Chapter	Title
Ephesians 6 (4:1–16)	Exhortation about unifying love, even if the gifts of grace are distributed to common benefit
1 Timothy 2 (1:12–17)	Regarding his election as an evangelist from being a persecutor according to God's grace
Titus 4 (2:9–15)	On slaves, how they can serve in a way worthy of the grace of Christ
Hebrews 6 (4:11–5:10)	The horror of judgment by the word that [cuts] through everything, and the goodness of the priestly grace of him who suffered like us in a human way
Hebrews 9_1 (7:6–10)	That he [Melchizedek] was more honored than Abraham
1 John 2_1 (2:12–17)	Exhortation about the grace of each according to his age, and regarding the putting off of the loving of the world
Acts 2_1 (1:23–26)	Regarding the substitution by Matthias, chosen through prayer by God's grace
Acts 4_1 (4:5–14)	Investigation of the high priests as they were concerned about the event, their decision about the miracle, and Peter's confession of the power and grace of Christ

In addition to the summary title for the whole of Romans (which often appears next to the main title, but is not numerated), there are thirteen other possible texts to look up that touch on the question of grace and/or the significance of Abraham, mostly in Paul, but also in the Catholic Epistles and Acts. Even without reading these texts, the titles suggest good places to start, especially Galatians and Ephesians where Paul also discusses grace in the context of justification and the consequences for Jews and gentiles. You might also be interested to explore how God's grace enacts change in those who experience it, either in Paul's election as discussed in 1 Timothy or in the selection of Matthias as an apostle in Acts. Or perhaps you'd like to explore Peter's view on the "power and grace of Christ" as Luke expounds in his speech in Acts.

Exploring the Euthalian Tradition

The chapter titles provide options for reading across the New Testament, especially in manuscripts that have the chapter lists of the gospels and Revelation as well as the Euthalian lists.[17] From these lists, readers can craft their own topical nonlinear reading pathways, even if the lists were not necessarily designed to be used in this way. These readings then raise new questions determined by the structure of the lists, their titles, and other paratexts in each manuscript.[18] There is no table of corresponding parallels like we find in the Eusebian canon tables, nor is there a set of doctrinal positions coordinated to particular texts as we see in the Latin tables of Priscillian of Avila,[19] but the Euthalian chapter lists implicitly offer readers the raw material to craft their own ways through the tradition. Euthalius (or whoever was responsible for these paratexts) drew upon the list as a way to organize knowledge, summarize the complicated messages of one side of ancient converstations, and give readers ways to find themselves within the broader corpus of the New Testament.

There are important differences between the Eusebian system and Euthalian chapter lists when it comes to navigation. Eusebius's system is designed to impact readings of four narrative works with similar subject

---

17. On Revelation's list of seventy-two chapters, attached to the Andrew of Caesarea commentary, see Eugenia Scarvelis Constantinou, *Andrew of Caesarea: Commentary on the Apocalypse* (Washington, DC: Catholic University of America Press, 2011), 45–50. On the chapter lists of the gospels, see Hermann von Soden, *Die Schriften des Neuen Testaments in ihrer ältesten erreichbaren Textgestalt hergestellt auf Grund ihrer Textgeschichte*, 1/1 (Göttingen: Vandenhoeck & Ruprecht, 1911), 402–11. See also, more generally, Sabine Mainberger, "Musing about a Table of Contents: Some Theoretical Questions Concerning Lists and Catalogues," in *Lists and Catalogues in Ancient Literature and Beyond: Toward Poetics of Enumeration*, ed. R. Laemmle, C. S. Laemmle, and K. Wesselmann (Berlin: de Gruyter, 2021), 19–34; and Joseph A. Howley, "Tables of Contents," in *Book Parts*, ed. D. Duncan and A. Smyth (Oxford: Oxford University Press, 2019), 65–79.

18. See also Blomkvist, *Euthalian Traditions*, 121–25.

19. See T. J. Lang and Matthew R. Crawford, "The Origins of Pauline Theology: Paratexts and Priscillian of Avila's *Canons on the Letters of the Apostle Paul*," *New Testament Studies* 63 (2017): 125–45; and T. J. Lang, "Arts of Memory, Ancient Manuscript Technologies, and the Aims of Theology," *Religions* 13 (2022), https://doi.org/10.3390/rel13050426.

matter; Euthalius's lists are for letters with more disparate content. Eusebius connects a preface, marginal notations, and tables in a tight set of interrelations; the Euthalian material is more flexible in its connections to other paratexts.

Despite these differences, however, both traditions are associated with the scholarly context of Caesarea, where the tools to navigate the Greek New Testament were forged in the fires of creative scholarship and technological change. More importantly, both systems allow readers to wayfind through the New Testament, to locate themselves within the broader scriptural tradition and to do things with these texts, and to manage interpretive information about them. The modern chapter and verse system we now take for granted is a latecomer to this game, the product of print and global economies. Our modern paratexts help us to do some of the same things: to recall a short phrase with specificity by simply quoting a set of numbers, for example (more people know that John 3:16 is somehow relevant than know what the text says). But the main difference between most modern navigational paratexts and those crafted within the cultural ambit of the library of Caesarea is that these ancient paratexts encourage readers to jump around. While the Eusebian and Euthalian system makes it possible for people to continue to read in a linear way, their substance encourages people to flip back and forth, to raise new theological questions, and to perhaps find some answers (at least as far as the New Testament cares about what they are asking). The type of generative, dynamic reading stimulated by these paratexts, a reading that allows you to move with little effort from one passage to another across a codex, is hard to do in a modern Bible without a high level of expertise. Today printed Bibles are designed to encourage people to read front to back, to enable a strategy of reading that emphasizes the work as the distinctive product of an author. But, as these ancient traditions show, this is not the only (or even the most interesting) way to read the New Testament. Paratexts reflect and shape the ways we read our sacred traditions.

Pervasive in the manuscripts for over a millenium, the Eusebian system and Euthalian tradition played outsized roles in how people read the Gospels, Paul, Acts, and the Catholic Epistles from late antiquity onward. These complex paratextual machines allowed people to identify particular texts, remember where they left off, and, most importantly, created opportunities to read across works, to compare them. With the Eusebian system we can compare parallel gospel passages in a nearly never-ending network, so long as we have the agility and endurance to keep flipping back and forth in a codex. The Euthalian system creates comparisons not through textual parallels but by thematic relationships based on the perceived topic of the various chapters its compiler crafted. These traditions show that paratexts are choices. They simultaneously open the New Testament up to new kinds of reading and foreclose the scope of its engagement, creating canonical spaces where creative readers can organize knowledge and represent the texture of the tradition. Paratexts make canons, give us ideas of what to do with them, and help us to make our way through them. Without paratexts there is no Bible.[20]

---

20. Paratexts have a habit of becoming shorthand for ad hoc collections of works that eventually come to be viewed as a corpus. See, for example, David Lincicum, "The Paratextual Invention of the Term 'Apostolic Fathers,'" *Journal of Theological Studies* 66 (2015): 139–48.

PREFACES

Writers like to have some control over what it is that people think about their work. One useful way to do this is through the preface, something that I, too, have opted to do in this book as a way to try to pre-explain what I've done, clarify technical issues, give context, and thank those who had a hand in shaping this book.[1] Even some of the New Testament authors begin their works with short texts that describe what it is that they have done or tell us their overarching concern. Luke tells his addressee, Theophilus, that he has written an "orderly account" based on eyewitness testimony so that "you might know the certainty of the things about which you were instructed" (Luke 1:1–4). John describes the preexistence and signifance of the Word, the light that shines in the darkness, thereby giving a poetic, cosmic summary of the narrative he then goes on to expound (John 1:1–18).[2]

Prefaces are what Dennis Duncan and Adam Smyth call "paradoxical forms" because they are usually written after the main

---

1. A good example of the power and ubiquity of the preface is the ingenious book by Glaswegian author and artist, Alasdair Gray, *The Book of Prefaces* (London: Bloomsbury, 2000).

2. On these texts, their functions, and relationships to other ancient literatures, see Loveday Alexander, *The Preface to Luke's Gospel: Literary Convention and Social Context in Luke 1:1–4 and Acts 1:1* (Cambridge: Cambridge University Press, 1993), who connects Luke's prefaces to historical, scientific, and early Jewish material; and Craig A. Evans, *Word and Glory: On the Exegetical and Theological Background of John's Prologue* (Sheffield: Sheffield Academic Press, 1993).

text is complete while appearing first.[3] Prefaces and other introductory discourses occupy "a sort of indeterminate space, supplementary to the text it introduces, but also crucial in setting certain interpretive wheels in motion; a self-effacing text that is also a document of control."[4] As such, prefaces are paratexts *par excellence*, taking up the liminal spaces between reader and text and between the work and the covers of the codex.

In addition to the occasional authorial preface, the works of the New Testament collected dozens of different prefatory texts from late antiquity onward that were written and propagated well after the New Testament had become a collection.[5] Preface making by later scholars, extractors, and commentators was one main way to shape the experience that readers had with these works, to key their attention to particular aspects, or to place its production in a definite context. Like other kinds of paratexts, prefaces are ubiquitous but overlooked in their diversity and effects. Preface writing is an ancient practice that extends well beyond Bibles, but the New Testament in particular has attracted a significant variety of prefatory traditions, some of which are new compositions and some of which are extracts from existing treatises. The Scofield Bible is a very recent example of a preface-happy edition, having prefaces at the level of the entire Bible, the New Testament, each

---

3. Dennis Duncan and Adam Smyth, "Introductions," in *Book Parts*, ed. D. Duncan and A. Smyth (Oxford: Oxford University Press, 2019), 3.

4. Duncan and Smyth, "Introductions," 3. Not all prefaces are as self-effacing as Duncan and Smyth suggest.

5. On various prefacing traditions for the gospels, for example, see Peter Darby, "The Codex Amiatinus *Maiestas Domini* and the Gospel Prefaces of Jerome," *Speculum* 92 (2017): 343–71; Donatien de Bruyne, *Prefaces to the Latin Bible* (Turnhout: Brepols, 2015), 153–208; H. A. G. Houghton, *The Latin New Testament: A Guide to Its Early History, Texts, and Manuscripts* (Oxford: Oxford University Press, 2016), 197–99; Robert S. Nelson, *The Iconography of Preface and Miniature in the Byzantine Gospel Book* (New York: New York University Press, 1980), 93–107; George Galavaris, *The Illustrations of the Prefaces in Byzantine Gospels* (Vienna: Verlag der Österreichischen Akademie der Wissenschaften, 1979), 25–28; and Hermann von Soden, *Die Schriften des Neuen Testaments in ihrer ältesten erreichbaren Textgestalt hergestellt auf Grund ihrer Textgeschichte*, 1/1 (Göttingen: Vandenhoeck & Ruprecht, 1911), 301–27.

subcorpus, and each work. When we look at ancient and medieval forms of the preface, we're looking back to the early stage of a phenomenon that is very much alive.

What I want to do here is give a brief overview of the New Testament's prefatory traditions. By preface, I mean any accompanying text that summarizes, contextualizes, explains, or otherwise engages one of the New Testament's works, written by someone other than the purported author.[6] This definition encompasses multiple nearly-synonymous English terms that describe front matter of some kind: preface, prologue, introduction, foreword, and others. There is little reason to distinguish between these technical terms, even though the Greek prefaces we will speak about do use various words to describe themselves, although there is little formal difference between the texts they describe. In the manuscripts, prefatory traditions are referred to as "prologue" (πρόλογος), "preliminary statement" or "proposal" (ὑπόθεσις), "introduction" or "prelude" (προοίμιον), "reminder" or "notes" (ὑπόμνημα), "summary" (ἀνακεφαλαίωσις), "notice" or "proclamation" (πρόγραμμα), a "preliminary notice" (προγραφή), or "list" or "notice" (ἔκθεσις), among others. Most of these words have broad semantic ranges—ἔκθεσις, for example, is used by Herodotus to describe the process of exposing a newborn child (*Hist.* 1.116)—and some of them refer to specific literary forms. The words ἔκθεσις and ἀνακεφαλαίωσις often entitle prefatory lists, although these lists too have their own short prefatory prose texts in some cases. These differences aside, there are no clear formal

---

6. Nowadays, of course, most authors write their own prefaces, but not all prefatory texts, like the foreword, are composed by the author. This definition also encompasses back matter like epilogues. Epilogues are less common than prefatory material in the Greek New Testament, but they do exist, especially in commentary and catena traditions. Andrew of Caesarea's commentary on the book of Revelation, for example, includes an epilogue in seven manuscripts composed by a later tradent of Andrew's commentary. See Garrick V. Allen, *Manuscripts of the Book of Revelation: New Philology, Paratexts, Reception* (Oxford: Oxford University Press, 2020), 106–7; and Josef Schmid, *Studien zur Geschichte des griechischen Apokalypse-Textes*, part 1, *Der Apokalypse-Kommentar des Andreas von Kaisareia* (Munich: Karl Zink, 1956), 267.

elements, besides perhaps length, that distinguish a πρόλογος from a ὑπόμνημα or a ὑπόθεσις from a πρόγραμμα, at least when it comes to the New Testament.

The point is not precisely what we call these introductory discourses but what they do to the readers who engage them by ambling through the authoritative frameworks that they provide. Like many of the features we've explored thus far, this process requires imagination and an accounting of how these features manifest in the manuscripts. Before moving on to look at the diverse prefatory aspects of the Euthalian apparatus in the following chapters, I want to highlight three basic features of New Testament introductory discourses by looking at a selection of prefaces to the gospels found, once again, in GA 2604: attribution, content, and the ways these paratexts are distinguished from the texts they're meant to inform.

As I've written elsewhere, GA 2604 is a heavily paratexted gospel book.[7] In addition to Matthew, Mark, Luke, and John, it contains multiple prefatory texts related to the gospels, including the *Letter to Carpianus* and the canon tables (which we discussed in chapter 7), chapter lists, and the *synaxarion* and *menologion* lists of liturgical readings. These items are prefatory, drawing our attention to marginal notations in the text related to the Eusebian tradition, the old chapter divisions and their titles, and the liturgical units marked with ἀρχή ("beginning") and τέλος ("end") notations. They point us to particular textual divisions and cross-references.

Even beyond this material, the codex preserves more direct prefatory texts, like "preliminary statements" (ὑποθέσεις) and "notes" (ὑπομνήματα) for each gospel. The ὑπόμνημα text for Matthew, for example, is entitled "Note on the Blessed Matthew the Evangelist" (ὑπόμνημα εἰς τ[ὸν] μακάριον ματθαῖον τὸν

---

7. See Garrick V. Allen, "The Possibilities of a Gospel Codex: GA 2604 (Dublin, CBL W 139), Digital Editing, and Reading in a Manuscript Culture," *Journal of Biblical Literature* 140 (2021): 409–34 for more technical details on the enumerative bibliography of the manuscript.

εὐαγγελιστήν), and gives personal information about the gospel's notional author.[8] We are told, among other things, that Matthew was from Galilee, a Hebrew by race and from the tribe of Benjamin, just like Paul, the sons of thunder, John the Theologian, and James, the first bishop of Jerusalem; that he was a tax collector, who did his work "with much greed" (πολλὰ τῆι πλεονεξίαι) but who was called out from his work, quoting Matthew's call in Matt 9:9; that he wrote his gospel eight years after Christ's ascension in the Hebrew language; and that he died in Syria on the tenth of November. Running about three pages, this biographical "note" fills out our picture of the work's author. The gospel itself has an anonymous narrator, and we glean no personal information from the text, so the preface fills the gap, giving us Matthew's background, his actions in the gospels (with an emphasis on his call to discipleship), his subsequent authoring of the gospel in Jerusalem, and his eventual death in Syria. The note creates an authorial narrative and offers further context for understanding the gospel and why it was written.

The "preliminary statement" (ὑπόθεσις) to Matthew (11v–12r) focuses on the content of the gospel instead of the construction of an authorial persona. We are told that Matthew begins his story with the birth of Jesus according to the flesh from the seed of David, referring to the genealogy (Matt 1:1–17), followed by his birth according to the Spirit, referring to the nativity story (Matt 1:18–2:23). The text then narrates the major movements of the story, from Jesus's baptism by John through to the resurrection.

These two types of prefaces, versions of which are found in many Greek manuscripts, prime the reader to observe particular elements of the gospels. Both prefaces are anonymous, passing themselves off as the authoritative arbiters of tradition, and they highlight different aspects of the gospel and its notional author. The "note" (ὑπόμνημα) preface creates an author figure, even though the gospel itself does not have an explicit authorial

---

8. The manuscript is online at the Chester Beatty's online viewer, starting here on 24r–25v, or a similar text can be found in von Soden, *Die Schriften*, 1/1, 305.

persona. At the same time it gives contextual information about Matthew's production, all of which modern scholars consider to be wrong: I don't know of anyone who still thinks that Matthew was written in the early 40s, in Jerusalem, in Hebrew. Yet, this tradition persists in the Greek manuscripts, appearing often as subscriptions or endtitles.

The "preliminary statement" (ὑπόθεσις) is a terse summary of Matthew's content, focusing on the beginning and end of the work. It evidences careful reading, noting the dual stories of Jesus's genesis in Matthew 1–3, one based on his lineage to Abraham (according to Joseph's line) and another based on his birth through Mary. The "preliminary statement" keys us to turn our attention to the narrative movements and events of Matthew, not necessarily toward the ethics of Jesus's teaching or some other possible focus. These features are anonymous, offer different content, and are located directly before each work they are intended to preface.

Two other prefatory works in GA 2604 are located before the start of Matthew, but they are oriented to the Four Gospels as a collection. Immediately after the "note" (ὑπόμνημα) preface (25v), we run into a text entitled "Preliminary Notice on the Holy Gospels from St. Maximos" (ἐκ τοῦ ἁγίου μαξίμου εἰς τὴν προγραφὴν τῶν ἁγίων εὐαγγελίων). As the title signals, this preface is extracted from a work by Maximus the Confessor, an important sixth- to seventh-century thinker. It is drawn from his *Ambigua* or *Book of Difficulties*, which deal with complex passages in Gregory of Nazianzus, a fourth-century writer.[9] The preface is created from *Ambiguum* 21.4–12, a passage that suggests the gospels are a pathway to higher spiritual thinking that can ultimately be accessed at the future consummation of the world. The gospels, we are told, constitute basic instruction that points us to realities beyond themselves. There are four versions of the story because the earth is made of up of four elements and defined by the four virtues.

---

9. For text and translation of the *Ambigua*, see Nicholas Constas, *On Difficulties in the Church Fathers: The Ambigua*, 2 vols. (London: Harvard University Press, 2014).

In this scheme, Matthew corresponds to earth and justice, Mark to water and temperance, Luke to air and courage, and John to ether and understanding, each marked by its distinctive features and emphases. The virtues articulated in each gospel teach the soul, which will ultimately return to God in the resurrection.

Unlike the "preliminary statement" and "note" for each gospel, this preface does not tell us anything about the purported authors of these texts and only briefly mentions the narrative features that define each account. Instead, the text argues that the fourfold structure of the canonical gospels reflects the structure of the created world and of the ethical realities of human behavior. This reality, then, has existential consequences for individuals since the gospels are only trailmarkers to the larger realities of existence in Christ, which we can only fully access at the end of the age. This extract from Maximus's work implicitly shows readers that they must look beyond the gospels and that they must prepare for the end. It highlights the eschatological nature of the narratives, which imply that Jesus's death and resurrection presage what will happen to the souls who believe at the end. This extracted preface places the distinctiveness of each gospel within a larger theological discourse.

There are other prefatory traditions in GA 2604, too, which appear in other manuscripts that preserve the gospels, including an extract entitled "Note on the Dormition of the Mother of God" (ὑπόμνημα εἰς τὸν κοίμησιν τῆς θ[εοτό]κου), which draws attention to Marian traditions in the texts and provides further context for her story beyond the narratives, and lists of definitions for Hebrew words in each gospel, entitled "Lexical Commentary on Hebrew Words in the Gospel according to Matthew" (ἑρμενεία λέξεων ἑβραϊκῶν. τὰ ἐν τῷ κατὰ ματθ[αῖον] εὐαγγελίῳ ἐμφερομένων), which directs readerly attention to the Semitic loan words in these texts, especially names, toponyms, and Jesus's non-Greek speech.[10] These prefaces point readers to certain aspects of the narratives,

---

10. On the Dormition text tradition see Stephen Shoemaker, *Ancient Traditions of the Virgin Mary's Dormition and Assumption* (Oxford: Oxford University Press, 2002).

be it an especially important character (Mary, the mother of Jesus) or a reality of the setting and characters of the texts (Hebrew loan words presented in Greek). Together, the prefatory texture of a manuscript like GA 2604 points readers in various directions, nudging them to pay attention to these features alongside consideration for the authorial personae of each text, important aspects of its narrative, and the existential realities to which these texts point. Prefaces set the agenda for any reading event, at least insofar as readers pay attention to them. The diversity of the New Testament's preface tradition—the combination of anonymity and named authors, the content these texts present, and their various locations in the manuscript in relation to the main text—is further evidence of lively paratextual tradition.

What I think is most interesting about the preface, as an ambient genre that lived off the New Testament in a kind of symbiosis, is just how optional these features are. Many ancient prose works, like Luke and John, preserve their own internal introductory discourses, and, while useful, no work requires a preface. The fact that so much intellectual energy and manual labor went into composing and then transmitting these features suggests that they became central aspects of what constituted the New Testament. In GA 2604, a total of thirty-five folia or seventy pages are devoted to prefatory material of one kind or another. Although optional, prefaces played an important role in shaping reading experiences and the interpretive attention of individual readers.

Prefaces of various kinds are good examples of the ways scripture and tradition interact. Traditional prefaces become an ingrained physical presence in most copies of the Greek New Testament, breaking down the firm boundary in our minds between text and paratext, or at least obscuring the distinction. Prefaces are revelatory insofar as they bring our attention to the imagined modes of production or literary features that affect our understanding of the scriptural work. Both scripture and tradition work hand in hand to renew engagment with the New Testament and to maintain its relevance for new times and questions, directing our gaze to different aspects of a work. Paratexts, like prefaces, are avenues through which the New Testament changes, not only in the configuration of texts that frame it in any given manuscript, but in the attention we give to certain features that the prefaces foreground. Attention is a key interpretive resource, and one that changes through time as new readers bring different questions and concerns to the text, as fashions change, and as theological debates evolve. Prefaces direct our limited attention and resources. In the next two chapters, I explore how the prefatory material in the Euthalian tradition directs our attention toward the book of Acts.

Chapter 9

Prologues and Division in Acts

Even more paratextually oppressive and complex than the gospels in GA 2604 is the Euthalian preface tradition. As I noted in chapter 8, parts of the Euthalian tradition are preserved in most manuscripts of Acts, the Catholic Epistles, and Paul's letters. Usually, this consists of the *hypothesis* and the chapter lists for each work. But in a handful of manuscripts, the Euthalian tradition is much more fulsome, encompassing a variety of prefaces that influence the things that readers do with these works in more complex ways.[1] Like the gospel prefaces, these items direct our attention to different features of the narrative, priming readers to key in on specific aspects of these multifaceted works. In this chapter, we'll take a closer look at the prefatory tradition for the book of Acts as represented in the *Euthaliana*. Other prefaces exist for Acts, often tied to the commentary traditions that accompany this work in some manuscripts, but the predominant prefacing tradition for Acts is tied to the Euthalian apparatus.[2]

---

1. Zacagni's 1698 edition of the Euthalian apparatus is a maximal representation of the features he had at hand in the Vatican library. *Collectanea monumentorum veterum ecclesiae graecae, ac latine quae hactenus in Vaticana Bibliotheca delituerunt* (Rome: Typis Sacra, 1698). Because this is the last edition produced of the Euthalian tradition and the primary way that scholars have accessed it, it has given the mistaken impression that the apparatus has a defined set of features in a fixed order, when in fact these items are migratory. They appear in various configurations in the manuscripts.

2. See for example the preface entitled "Introduction to the commentary on the Acts" (προοίμιον τῆς ἑρμηνείας τῶν πράξεων) in GA 056 (Paris, BnF, Coislin grec 26, diktyon 49168), 2r, which is often attached to Acts's commentary tradition. See Georgi R.

PREFACES

Figure 9.1. Title to the prologue to Acts *(GA 1162, Patmos, St. John the Theologian Monastery, 15, 1r)*

In addition to the chapter lists discussed in chapter 8, the Euthalian tradition includes multiple items that preface the New Testament works it engages. Acts alone is preceded, in various combinations, by a prologue (πρόλογος), a lection list ("summary of readings," ἀνακεφαλαίωσις τῶν ἀναγνώσεων), two types of quotation lists ("summary of divine witnesses," ἀνακεφαλαίωσις θείων μαρτυριῶν) that have their own introductory texts ("notice," πρόγραμμα), a "preliminary note" or *hypothesis* (ὑπόθεσις), and biographical texts that summarize Paul's travels (ἀποδημίαι παύλου), his martyrdom (μαρτύριον παύλου), or his final trip to Rome (πλοῦς παύλου).[3]

Parpulov, *Catena Manuscripts of the Greek New Testament: A Catalogue* (Piscataway, NJ: Gorgias, 2021), 161.

3. For a full overview of Euthalian features, see Vemund Blomkvist, *Euthalian Tra-*

Prologues and Division in Acts

It would be a tall order to explore how each of these items functions as a preface and how they're interrelated with one another in this context. So, instead of systematically examining each feature, I explore the effects of these traditions by focusing on one specific manuscript, in this case, GA 1162 (Patmos, St. John the Theologian Monastery, 15, diktyon 54259), an eleventh century copy of Acts, the Catholic Epistles, and Paul's letters with commentary extracts in the margins (catena). By working closely with one manuscript, it's possible to get an idea of how the larger tradition functions and begin to imagine how our reading of Acts would have been shaped if we had read it in this witness.

GA 1162 opens with the Euthalian prologue to Acts, entitled "Prologue of the Acts" (πρόλογος τῶν πράξεων), set with an ornamental headpiece frame (figure 9.1). The text of the prologue is similar to the text presented by Zacagni, in his 1698 edition, and by Blomkvist, running from 1r to the end of the first column of text on 2v.[4] It begins with a statement on the value of scriptural reading. Those "who yearn for immortality ... meditate day and night in their own souls on the words about the divine Word."[5] Living by the divine word enables readers to "turn their eyes upward to immortality itself," suggesting that, like the preface from Maximus the Confessor in the previous chapter, scripture signifies beyond itself by pointing to the future age. This sentiment underlines the preface writer's motivation for this task: helping others is (apparently) one way for him to avoid the mortal curse of envy. The author sees his

---

ditions: *Text, Translation and Commentary* (Berlin: de Gruyter, 2012), 8–9; Nils Alstrup Dahl, "The 'Euthalian Apparatus' and Affiliated 'Argumenta,'" in *Studies in Ephesians*, ed. D. Hellholm, V. Blomkvist, and T. Fornberg (Tübingen: Mohr Siebeck, 2000), 231–75; Louis Charles Willard, *A Critical Study of the Euthalian Apparatus* (Berlin: de Gruyter, 2009); and Günther Zuntz, *The Ancestry of the Harklean New Testament* (London: British Academy, 1945), 78–84. In some examples, the Euthalian prologue to Paul's letters prefaces Acts (e.g., GA 912, 1270, 1297, 1405, 1594, 1598, 1733, and 2963).

4. Zacagni, *Collectanea monumentorum veterum ecclesiae graecae*, 403–10; Blomkvist, *Euthalian Traditions*, 113–17.

5. Translations of the prologue from Blomkvist, *Euthalian Traditions*, 113–17, with some minor adjustments.

work of producing the prologue as a way to enable readers to achieve immortality. This is a high view of the power of the preface.

Next, the prologue describes how the author manipulated the biblical text, with much characteristic self-deprecation. He notes that he "read and wrote the apostolic book in verses," sending it on to one of "our fathers in Christ." Here we gain a glimpse of the prologist's scholarly approach. He carefully read the book and rewrote it by creating a new layout for the text. The word he uses to describe his writing activity (γράψας) refers both to his work of copying the text and to his editorial activity of arranging the text into units based on his own reading. He copied out the text of Acts but arranged it according to his own scheme of textual division.

Referring to his word as "mediocre" and to himself as "someone with no knowledge" (a commonplace way for authors to demonstrate humility), he passes on his reworked copy of Acts to his patron, following previous work on Paul's letters and the Catholic letters, begging forgiveness for any obvious shortcomings.[6] He goes on to praise his patron, a certain Brother Athanasius, who begets wisdom through his meditations on the scriptures, quoting the Shema and words of David in the Psalter as a way to drive home the point that reading scripture is a pathway to knowledge of God. We must never abandon the scriptures, he tells us. If we abandon scripture, punishment follows; if we give heed, scripture repays us with charity and delight. The prologue pleads for us to read since "the task of reading is instructive for us, as it every day, in small steps, trains and lifts up the soul to contemplate knowledge of beautiful things." It is priming us to read Acts as a form of spiritual sustenance which perfects our knowledge of God and prepares us for the age to come.

In the remainder of the text, the author of the prologue gets to the point. Expanding on the fact that he has divided the text into verses,

---

6. In the prologue to the Pauline corpus, which is much more substantial than that Acts prologue, the same author uses the metaphor of the completion of his work as a ship coming into harbor, a ship guided by the great hands of his patron, like Moses. The ship metaphor is another way to be unobtrusive and to claim completeness and closure for the editorial effort, which made their work part of a larger system of textuality. See Justin Willson, "The Terminus in Late Byzantine Literature and Aesthetics," *Word & Image* 38 (2022): 435–47.

he says that he was asked by his patron to read Acts and the Catholic Epistles with the correct pronunciation (κατὰ προσῳδίαν), to make some summaries (ἀνακεφαλαιώσασθαι), and to divide the text into small units. "And this I have done with zeal, without hesitation," he says. "Having organized the texts into verses (στιχηδόν) according to my own design, aiming at clear reading, I sent them to you."

The prologue concludes with a brief summary of the Acts narrative. We learn that Luke was a doctor from Antioch who, after becoming a disciple of Paul, wrote two books (Luke and Acts). Acts, then, is about the ascension, the coming of the Spirit, and the actions and miracles of the disciples. Paul's divine call, his apostleship and message, and the many dangers he faced are also central to the work.

The Euthalian prologue to Acts offers insight into the context of its own production (and the production of some other Euthalian features), into the motivations of the person who crafted these texts and the very basic plot features of Acts. This work is editorial in nature, changing the presentation of the text to cohere with the author's perceptions of its structure and significance. Most manuscripts that preserve Euthalian material, like GA 1162, don't have any special textual arrangement that might represent this work. GA 015 or Codex H, the earliest witness to the Euthalian tradition, may be a rare representative of this work since its text is divided into sense units demarcated by the indents of subsequent lines that belong to the same unit. It also preserves breathing marks and accents that assist in clear pronunciation. One of GA 015's editors, Henri Omont, calls this arrangement of text the "Euthalian method," but it is not entirely clear if the description in the prologue matches with what we see in GA 015.[7] Even if the textual arrangement described by the prologue's author is not present in GA 1162, this prefatory text attempts to set the parameters for the ways that readers engage Acts.

The prologue, however, is not the only preface that is concerned with the division of the text. The next item we encounter in GA 1162, in the second column of 2v, is the lection list. It's entitled "Summary of the Readings and which Chapters, Divine Witnesses, and Lines each con-

---

7. Henri Omont, *Notices sur un très ancient manuscrit grec en oncialtes des Épîtres de saint Paul* (Paris: Imprimerie nationale, 1889), 7: "la méthode euthalienne."

PREFACES

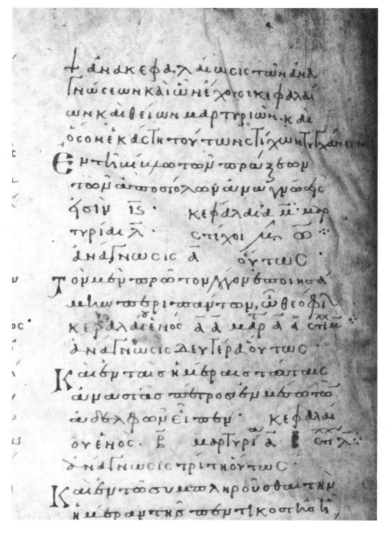

Figure 9.2. Start of the lection list *(GA 1162, Patmos, St. John the Theologian Monastery, 15, 2v)*

tain" (ἀνακεφαλαίωσις τῶν ἀναγνώσεων καὶ ὧν ἔχουσι κεφαλαίων καὶ θείων μαρτυριῶν. καὶ ὅσον ἑκάστη τούτων στίχων τυγχάνει, figure 9.2).

Prologues and Division in Acts

The lection list breaks up the text of Acts into three units of varying length: "readings" (ἀναγνώσεις), "chapters" (κεφάλαια), and "lines" (στίχοι). Additionally, it also counts the number of quotations in the work (μαρτυρίαι) and where they are located amidst the "readings." The list begins with an overview, starting on line 5 of figure 9.2: "In the book of the Acts of the Apostles there are 16 readings, 40 chapters, 30 quotations, and 2,800 lines." The list continues by giving information on each of the sixteen readings, including the start of the text (*incipit*) and the number of chapters, quotations, and lines for each section. For example, the entry for the first reading, which follows immediately from the overview, reads "Thus in the first reading: 'In the first book, Theophilus I wrote regarding everything' | 1 chapter 1 1, quotations 1 1, lines 40."

From this information, it's clear that the first reading, not surprisingly, begins at the outset of Acts since the incipit is the first nine words of Acts 1:1. We see that the first reading is coterminous with the first chapter since there is only a single chapter in this reading. It is the first chapter in this reading and the first in the work overall (hence the 1 1). The first reading and chapter comprise forty lines according to this scheme and there is one quotation in this section (the first in the section and the first in the work overall) referring to Acts 1:5, a passage about John the Baptist that the quotation lists (see below) see as a reference to Matt 3:11. The lection list gives no further information on the quotation, its precise location within the reading, or its source or significance, but it does map the intertextuality of the work within its various divisions. If we read on to the entry for reading 2, we can also define the boundaries of reading 1. The incipit to the reading 2 matches the text that we now know as Acts 1:15: "And in those days Peter stood up in the midst of the brothers and spoke." Reading 1, then, covers Acts 1:1–14, everything up to the immediate aftermath of Jesus's ascension.

TABLE 9.1. *Division of Acts according to the lection list in GA 1162*

Text	Reading	Chapters	Quotations	Lines
1:1–14	1	1 (1)	1	40
1:15–26	2	1 (2)	1 (2)	30
2:1–47	3	1 (3)	4 (3–6)	109
3:1–4:31	4	1 (4)	3 (7–9)	136

Text	Reading	Chapters	Quotations	Lines
4:32–5:42	5	2 (5–6)		100
6:1–8:1	6	2 (7–8)	9 (10–18)	220
8:2–40	7	4 (9–12)	1 (19)	120
9:1–31	8	1 (13)		95
9:32–11:26	9	3 (14–16)		250
11:27–14:28	10	6 (17–22)	6 (20–25)	300
15:1–16:40	11	2 (23–24)	1 (26)	200
17:1–18:28	12	3 (25–27)	1 (27)	180
19:1–21:14	13	3 (28–30)	1 (28)	240
21:15–25:26	14	5 (31–35)	1 (29)	293
25:27–26:32	15	2 (36–37)		268
27:1–28:31	16	3 (38–40)	1 (30)	119

In essence the lection list is a numerical representation of the narrative and structure of Acts, one that directs the readers' attention toward certain aspects of its literary texture. For example, the list highlights particular passages, especially the readings that are not subdivided into multiple chapters. Readings 1–4 and 8 stand out because they only preserve one chapter each and are among the shorter readings in terms of lines. These passages—including the ascension, the activity of the early followers of Jesus in Jerusalem, and Paul's prophetic call—stand apart from the longer sections later in the work that narrate Paul's travels. The way that Acts is divided acknowledges these passages as points of special interest that are not subdividable in their content.

The lists also prime readers to be alert for quotations as the only feature of the list that is not concerned with textual division. When the information in the lection list is laid out in a table (like table 9.1), we can see where the quotations are clustered. Noting that there is only one quotation in reading 14 (quotation 29), a lengthy section that encompasses what we now know as Acts 21:15–25:26, is of limited value. When we arrive at reading 14 or chapters 31–35, we know that we can expect to encounter very few quotations, but we don't learn anything about the quotation that does occur in this passage, including its location in that section, the text it references, or its narrative significance.[8] But if we

---

8. Quotation 29 in the lists is identified as a reference to Exod 22:28 in Acts 23:5.

were interested in inquiring further into Luke's quotation practices in Acts, we could shift focus to readings 3, 4, 6, and 10, where most of the work's quotations occur, tied to the activity and speeches of Peter and John in Acts 2–4, to Stephen's speech in Acts 7, and to Paul's speech to the Antioch synagogue in Acts 13.

Already the prefatory traditions attached to Acts in GA 1162 are thick with interpretive potential. The prologue and the lection list represent two very different approaches to the text. The former encourages a reading that is spiritually formative, pointing beyond the text to divine realities. The latter represents the narrative and some of its features in numerical form, encouraging types of reading that make use of the ways the text has been divided. Notably, these different approaches to Acts are mutually illuminating: the prologist's description of his activity, especially as it relates to textual division, clarifies why the lection list exists in the first place (it is the result of the editor's own "reading" and "writing" of the book of Acts). Similarly, the lection list informs our understanding of the prologue: its numerical representation of textual divisions and their content is one possible avenue for gaining access to the sustaining spiritual realities Acts offers. According to the prologist, proper division and pronunciation are key for attaining the message of the narrative. Altering the arrangement and divisions of a text shapes the way we understand its message. This is one concrete way that Bibles have continued to change, even when their wording remains more or less consistent.

Chapter 10

Making Lists Out of Acts

The lection list is not the only enumerative representation of the Acts narrative. The Euthalian tradition excels at the crafting of lists from the raw materials of scriptural texts. Once produced, these lists then influence the ways readers attend to the text, as we can see if we continue to read Acts in GA 1162.

The Short Quotation List

The prefaces to Acts in GA 1162 do not stop with the lection list. In fact, they build on the lection list's interest in quotations in the form of short and long quotation lists that appear immediately thereafter (3v–4r). The quotation lists and chapter lists are closely connected to the content and textual rhetoric of the lection list and they represent the earliest explicit engagement with the use of Jewish scripture in the New Testament.[1]

---

1. I have written about these lists in GA 1162 at length elsewhere: see Garrick V. Allen, "Early Textual Scholarship on Acts: Observations from the Euthalian Quotation Lists," *Religions* 13 (2022), https://doi.org/10.3390/rel13050435, as a supplement to this discussion.

Making Lists Out of Acts

TABLE 10.1. *Short quotation list in GA 1162*

Text	Translation
ἀνακεφαλαίωσις θείων μαρτυριῶν ὧν ἔχει ἡ βίβλος τῶν πράξεων τῶν ἀποστόλων. ἔχει δὲ μαρτυρίας. λα	Summary of the divine testimonies which the book of the Acts of the Apostles have; and there are 31 testimonies.
γενέσεως γ. η ι ια	Genesis III: 8, 10, 11
ἔξοδους. ζ ιβ ιγ ιδ ιε κθ	Exodus VI: 7, 12, 13, 14, 15, 29
δευτερονομίου α. ιε	Deuteronomy I: 15
βασιλειῶν πρώτης α. κ	1 Kingdoms I: 20
ψαλτηρίου ζ. β δ ε ς θ ιζ κβ	Psalter VII: 2, 4, 5, 6, 9, 17, 22
ἀμῶς προφήτ(ου) β. ις κς	Amos the Prophet II: 16, 26
ἰωὴλ προφήτου α. γ	Joel the Prophet I: 3
ἀγγαίου προφήτ(ου) α. ιη	Haggai the Prophet I: 18
ἠσαιόυ προφήτ(ου) δ. ιθ κγ κε λ	Isaiah the Prophet IV: 19, 23, 25, 30
ματθ(αιου) εὐαγγελίστ(ου) β. α κα	Matthew the Evangelist II: 1, 21
διατάξεων α. κη	(Apostolic) Constitutions I: 28
ἀράτου ἀστρονόμου α. κζ	Aratus the Astronomer I: 27
ἀμβακοὺμ προφήτ(ου) α. κδ	Habakkuk the Prophet I: 24
ὁμοῦ μαρτυρίαι λα. στίχοι ρκ	Together 31 witnesses, 120 lines

The short quotation list in GA 1162 (figure and table 10.1) is constructed around the order of the works as they are arranged in the Greek Old Testament, followed by quotations to other early Christian works (in this case, Matthew and the Apostolic Constitutions) and other ancient works (Aratus the Astronomer).[2] Each work that Acts references is followed by at least two numbers; the first is the total number of times that the work is referenced in Acts, and any other numbers that follow it identfiy the order of quotation when Acts is read from front to back. For example, the Psalter is quoted seven times and these quotations are the second, fourth, fifth, sixth, ninth, seventeenth, and twenty-second

---

2. Habakkuk is located last here probably because it was missed as the quotations to the prophets were written out and added at the end of the list to remedy the mistake.

PREFACES

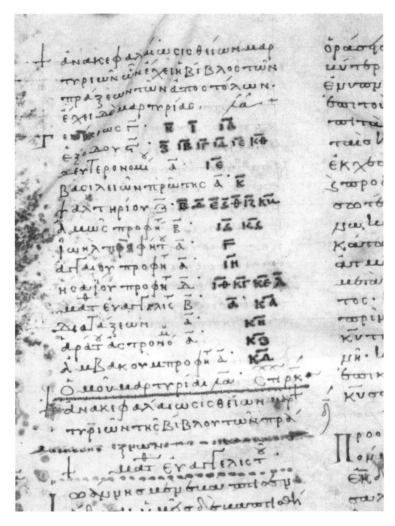

Figure 10.1. Short quotation list *(GA 1162, Patmos, St. John the Theologian Monastery, 15, 3v)*

quotations in Acts. The introduction and conclusion to the list note that Acts has thirty-one quotations, which differs from the lection list's thirty.

Making Lists Out of Acts

However, quotation fifteen, one of a string of quotations from Stephen's speech (Acts 7:40), is attributed to both Deuteronomy and Exodus.[3] So even though the list only goes up to thirty, it calls back to thirty-one sources in total.

Building from the lection list, the short quotation list further emphasizes the centrality of the quotations. The effort to create this list and other infrastructure around quotations suggests that the person who produced it saw these features as key to understanding the message of the work. To this end the short list shows the extent of Acts's intertextual network, which primarily consists of the Torah and Prophets, with special attention to Exodus, the Psalms, and Isaiah. It also suggests that Luke was already aware of the Gospel of Matthew and other early Christian texts, like the Apostolic Constitutions, even if most scholars today think that the Constitutions were produced after Acts. The list even takes Acts seriously enough to acknowledge that it references Aratus in a short snippet from Acts 17:28 where Paul speaks to the Athenians by referencing something "your own poets have said."[4]

Like the lection list, the short quotation list presents an aspect of the Acts narrative in numerical form. Without the lection list, however, the short list is only so useful. From it, we can see the serial order of the quotations: Acts quotes Matthew first, then the Psalms, then Joel, and so on. But we don't know where these quotations exist in Acts or what portion of Joel is quoted in the work. Only by returning to the lection list can we gain an idea of where these quotation occur in Acts, and even then it's only an approximation since we can only locate them within

---

3. The quotation lists for Acts differ in small-scale ways due to the ways they represent the quotation in Stephen's speech, where multiple utterances from Exodus, Deuteronomy, and Leviticus occur, although the quotation in Acts 7:37 (which closely corresponds to Deut 18:15–16, 19 and Lev 23:29) is not preserved in this version of the list. For more on the confusion here, which is also likely tied to the textual pluriformity of the Pentateuch in antiquity, see Allen, "Early Textual Scholarship"; Louis Charles Willard, *A Critical Study of the Euthalian Apparatus* (Berlin: de Gruyter, 2009), 37; and Nils Alstrup Dahl, "The 'Euthalian Apparatus' and Affiliated 'Argumenta,'" in *Studies in Ephesians*, ed. D. Hellholm, V. Blomkvist, and T. Fornberg (Tübingen: Mohr Siebeck, 2000), 249.

4. See Mark J. Edwards, "Quoting Aratus: Acts 17,28," *Zeitschrift für die neutestamentliche Wissenschaft und die Kunde der älteren Kirche* 83 (1993): 266–69.

PREFACES

the larger readings. And even with recourse to the lection list, we can't know for sure which part of Matthew the author referenced or which Psalm is quoted in the ninth quotation. The short list drives home the importance of the referential network in Acts, primes readers to identify these texts, and offers a list of works that Acts quotes which we can then read for deeper background. The short quotation list and the lection list are designed to be used in concert, but it is only with the long quotation list that we can begin to gain more specific information on the texts that Acts quotes.

The Long Quotation List

Immediately following the short list of quotations in GA 1162, we encounter another version of the data that runs from 3v to 4v. This Euthalian feature is known as the long quotation list. Its title here is similar to that of the short quotation list, signaling that both lists are intended to offer the same information in different forms.[5] Instead of listing the serial arrangement of quotations against a predetermined sequential list of Jewish, Christian, and classical works, as the short list does, the long list presents quotations as they appear in the Acts narrative, beginning with the first quotation to Matt 3:11 in Acts 1:5 and ending with the final quotation of Isa 6:9–10 in Acts 28:26–27. Each quotation is headed by the title of the work that Acts quotes, followed by the entire text of the quotation itself. For example, the first entry reads "Matthew the Evangelist: John baptized in water, but you will be baptized in the holy spirit" (ματθ εὐαγγελιστοῦ . Ἰωάννης μὲν ἐβάπτισεν ὕδατι. ὑμεῖς δὲ βαπτισθήσεσθε ἐν π̄νι ἁγίῳ). The addition of the entire text of the quotation is the main innovation of the long list, enabling those interested to explore the literature that Acts engages.[6] Unlike the short list, which orders the quotations but without reference to specific locations in Acts, the long list allows read-

---

5. "Summary of the Divine Witnesses of the Book of Acts" (ἀνακεφαλαίωσις θείων μαρτυριῶν τῆς βίβλου τῶν πράξεων).

6. The texts of the quotations in the long list, as far as I have engaged them, appear to always represent the text of the quotation as it's represented in Acts and not any version of the text that can be traced to a different form of the source tradition. This reality enables easier cross-referencing between the list and Acts. It also means

Making Lists Out of Acts

ers to flip between the list and the text itself and to identify the precise boundaries of the quotation, at least as the list presents it. This activity is further supported by annotations in the text that pinpoint the source of quotations. The quotation to Matthew in Acts 1:5 is accompanied by a marginal note that reads "1 Matthew the Evangelist" (ᾱ ματ̄θ εὐαγγλιστού) in GA 1162, and the quotation is preceded by a *vacat* or blank space within the line. Information from the list is cross-referenced in the text, and the text is structured by the scribe to emphasize the presence of the quotation by setting it off from the surrounding material. As you read through this copy of Acts, the marginal notations consistently bring your attention back to the quotation lists at the front of the codex.

Despite some minor differences in the content of the two lists in GA 1162, they are mostly consistent in the information they present. For example, in quotation 27, the reference to Aratus the Astronomer in Acts 17:28, the long list also adds Homer the Poet as a source, since Paul prefaces his quotation with a notice that he's citing multiple poets. Some small differences aside,[7] these complementary lists work together to present a map of the intertextuality of Acts. They do not focus on any criteria for identifying references or assert the theological significance of the quotations, as most modern discussions on the use of Jewish scriptural traditions in the New Testament tend to do. The lists assume the veracity of these quotations and leave it to readers to use their information in whatever way they see fit in their interpretive activities. The lists enable the identification of the quotations in the text, quantify them, and arrange them both against a kind of canonical list and in the order that they appear in the narrative.

Scholars have long argued about which version of the list is "original" to the earliest layers of the Euthalian tradition. J. Armitage Robinson, for example, argued that the short list is essentially useless in light of the information presented in the long list; therefore, the short list must be a later derivation.[8] Instead of focusing on the development of the

---

that these texts in the long list function as additional textual witnesses to key parts of Acts, a reality that has not yet been fully explored or understood.

7. See further Allen, "Early Textual Scholarship."

8. J. Armitage Robinson, *Euthaliana: Studies of Euthalius Codex H of the Pauline*

Euthalian tradition and concerning ourselves with which is "original," the lists help us, more importantly, to imagine how they might affect someone who reads Acts in a manuscript like GA 1162. Together, they draw our attention to the realities of the reuse of antecedent scriptural traditions and similarities in Acts, even to later Christian texts like the Apostolic Constitutions. With these lists prefacing our reading, we are on the lookout for these references; the long list even helps us to locate these texts with greater specificity. Pushing back against Robinson, even the short list is useful as a preface. It doesn't help us to identify particular source texts or even the location of quotations in Acts; instead it does something more fundamental: it instills a greater understanding of Acts and its structure by representing its quotations in conversation with other ancient literature. We learn, at least in a partial way, about the narrative quality of Acts, the location of its main speeches (which tend to be heavy on quotations), and the extent of its author's perceived literary network. We see what Luke may have read, a reality that changes how we approach this text.

The Hypothesis to Acts

The hypothesis to Acts, which follows immediately after the end of the long list (4v–6r), also abstracts information from the narrative and arranges it in new ways as a way to direct readerly attention. Hypotheses are generally prose prefaces that summarize the work and give basic information about them. One exists for each work in the Euthalian tradition, and it is the most prevalent feature across the manuscripts, even though most scholars don't view hypotheses as part of the earliest layers of the Euthalian tradition.[9] The hypothesis to Acts comes after a short introduction that introduces Luke as the author and a brief summary of the narrative, and it is comprised mainly of lists of the apostles and dea-

---

Epistles and the Armenian Version (Cambridge: Cambridge University Press, 1895; Eugene, OR: Wipf & Stock, 2004), 17–18.

9. Hypotheses exist in well over 90 percent of all Greek copies of the Catholic Epistles and Paul. They appear less frequently in connection to Acts but are still prevalent. On the hypotheses and their origins, see Dahl, "Euthalian Apparatus," 253–60.

Making Lists Out of Acts

cons and the miracles they performed.[10] Unlike the hypotheses for the letters, which formulaically offer information on the author, the place that the letter was composed, and the issues it addresses, the hypothesis to Acts is at its core a lengthy list with a short narrative introduction.

The first list in the hypothesis is the lists of apostles and deacons, which enumerates the names of leaders in the early church as presented in Acts, drawn from the list of apostles and the appointment of a new twelfth member (1:13–26) and the appointment of leaders from outside the initial core of Jesus's disciples (6:1–6). After listing these names, we read that "Paul also was called to be a chosen vessel, and he himself was sent with Barnabas to preach the Lord to the Gentiles everywhere." This portion of the hypothesis is constructed directly from the text of Acts and, like the narrative, gives special attention to the activities of Paul and one of his co-workers, even if briefly. The list prepares readers to be familiar with the primary characters in the work and their remits, keying readers to direct their interpretive gazes toward these figures and summarizing their roles as a way to facilitate comprehension in the narrative.

The importance of these characters is further reinforced by the list of miracles that follows (table 10.2).

TABLE 10.2. *List of miracles in the Acts hypothesis*

Number	Text	Actor	Description
1	3:1–10	Peter and John	Healed the man lame from birth at the Beautiful Gate
2	5:1–11	Peter	Reproved Ananias and Sapphira
3	9:32–35	Peter	Raised Aeneas the paralytic
4	9:36–42	Peter	Raised Dorcas from the dead
5	10:10–16	Peter	Saw a vessel being sent down full of animals

10. The summary is very short, describing the action in Acts 9–28 as "the electing of Paul and what he went through, and, finally, his voyage to Rome." Translations of the hypothesis are from Vemund Blomkvist, *Euthalian Traditions: Text, Translation and Commentary* (Berlin: de Gruyter, 2012), 96–99 with minor alterations.

PREFACES

Number	Text	Actor	Description
6	5:15	Peter	His shadow healed the sick
7	12:6–11	Peter	Set free from prison by an angel
8	12:20–23	[angel of the Lord]	Herod dies, eaten by worms
9	6:8	Stephen	Signs and wonders
10	8:26–39	Philip	Baptized the eunuch as he read Isaiah
11	8:6–7	Philip	Cast out demons and healed in Samaria
12	9:1–18	Paul	Vision on the road to Damascus
13	14:8–11	Paul	Cured a man lame from birth in Lystra
14	16:9–10	Paul	Called to Macedonia through a vision
15	16:16–18	Paul	Cleansed a woman with a spirit of divination in Philippi
16	16:25–27	Paul and Silas	Released from prison via earthquake; healing by his clothing
17	20:9–11	Paul	Raised Eutychus from the dead in Troas
18	13:8–11	Paul	Blinded the sorcerer Elymas in Cyprus
19	27:21–26	Paul	Saved by God on the shipwreck en route to Rome
20	28:4–6	Paul	Unharmed by snake bite
21	28:7–8	Paul	Healed the father of Publius of dysentery on Malta
22	28:9	Paul	Healed the sick on Malta

The list enumerates twenty-two miracles (or constellations of miracles) in Acts enacted by six individuals and an angel of the Lord, who is credited for the death of Herod (Acts 12:22–23). The events it describes are varied, including healings, exorcisms, sudden deaths, resurrections, blindings, unusual survivals, and visionary experiences. The number of miracles and their distribution throughout the narrative highlight their centrality to the rhetoric of Acts. That so many different individuals in so many locations participated in these events suggests that their activities were indeed sanctioned by God and that divine support was central to development of early Christian communities throughout the Roman Empire. Some of the miracles are vague, like the description for Stephen, which draws only on Acts 6:8: "Stephen, full of grace and power, did great wonders and signs among the people." But the specificity of the description in this list relies entirely on the level of specificity of the miracle in Acts. The list adheres closely to the textual description, refusing to offer any further information or clarification on the events it describes. The hypothesis ends abruptly at the conclusion of the miracle list, leaving it to the reader to draw their own inferences as to its significance for reading the narrative.

Building on a broader tradition of listing the apostles, disciples, and miracles,[11] the hypothesis directs readers to the configuration of the main characters in Acts and the miracles for which they are responsible, perhaps even having a broader educational function, as Kelsie Rodenbiker has argued.[12] Even though there is a literary significance to the plot of Acts moving from the apostles in Jerusalem to Paul in Rome and covering the spread of the gospel around the majority of the eastern portions of the Roman Empire, the hypothesis does not focus on these particular aspects of the work. Crafting a succinct and compelling plot summary for a work like Acts and its theological or literary significance is no easy task. Instead, the author of the hypothesis opts to highlight supernatural plot points out of narrative order, priming readers to focus on these texts and consider the significance of the supernatural works wrought by the apostles.

---

11. It is somewhat common for lists of apostles, disciples, prophets, or miracles of Jesus to be transmitted with gospel manuscripts and other works. Some of these paratextual works are associated with the work of pseudo-Dorotheus. See D. Theodor Schermann, *Propheten- und Apostellegenden nebst Jüngerkatalogen des Dorotheus und verwandter Texte* (Leipzig: Hinrichs'sche, 1907); and C. H. Turner, "A Primitive Edition of the Apostolic Constitutions and Canons: An Early List of Apostles and Disciples," *Journal of Theological Studies* 15 (1913): 53–65.

12. Kelsie G. Rodenbiker, "Marking Scriptural Figures as Sacred Names," *Religions* 13 (2022), https://doi.org/10.3390/rel13070577.

Conclusion

Acts in GA 1162 is heavily prefaced—there is a lot of material to get through before you come to the text itself. In addition to the prologue, lection list, quotation lists, and hypothesis, there are two different chapter lists that divide Acts up into forty and thirty-six chapters respectively.[13] This complex constellation of paratexts has direct effects on the reader, especially because each in its own way abstracts and is closely devoted to specific aspects of the Acts narrative. They are highly text-immanent, refraining from speculation, extending traditions, or filling gaps. As a group, they invite readers to give special consideration to particular features of Acts: its ability to offer information about the divine (prologue), its multiform divisions and their significance (lection list), its quotations, their distribution, sources (quotation lists), its characters, and their great signs and wonders (*hypothesis*). These are, of course, key aspects of the narrative, but they aren't exhaustive. The Pauline travel narratives sometimes attached to Acts in the Euthalian tradition—the ἀποδημίαι παύλου (Travels of Paul) and πλοῦς παύλου (Voyage of Paul)—represent Paul's geographical peregrinations, for example, but these are attached to the prefaces to the Pauline corpus in GA 1162, not Acts.[14] The inherent selectivity of prefatory traditions is what gives these features the power to shape reading events. They reflect the concerns of the people who crafted them and their own reading contexts, but they continue to have effects as subsequent generations of people read Acts into the era of print. Many Bibles even today include maps of "Paul's Missionary Journeys" that are in the same tradition as these late ancient traditions.

Prefaces are always in conversation with other preface traditions. The hypothesis for Acts, for example, is related to lists of miracles and apostolic era figures attributed to Dorotheus that appear alongside some copies of the gospels. But the key point is not necessarily the history

---

13. See Charles E. Hill, *The First Chapters: Dividing the Text of Scripture in Codex Vaticanus and Its Predecessors* (Oxford: Oxford University Press, 2022), 178–79 and 314–23.

14. The locations of these biographical prefaces are themselves itinerant in the manuscripts, being attached to both Acts and the Pauline corpus.

Making Lists Out of Acts

of the production of these preface traditions but to understand how these texts and lists influence perceptions of what the New Testament works do and mean. Similar prefaces exist also for the Catholic Epistles and Pauline Letters in the Euthalian tradition. This close look at Acts's specific tradition is a brief glance at the framing devices that accompany the ancient and medieval Greek manuscripts of the New Testament. The effects of these features can be wide-ranging, so long as people refuse to flip past them. The effort needed to produce and transmit these complicated lists signals to me that people actually used them and that they were deemed to be important parts of what constitutes the New Testament. The varied ways that they are presented in particular manuscripts and spread unevenly across the tradition is another way that the New Testament is defined by change. The presence or absence of these features has the power to change what readers focus on, the questions they bring to the text, and the way they navigate the narrative. In the way artworks have the power to alter the way we view the world by focusing our attention on particular aspects of our experiences, so too do paratexts have the ability to change the way we view the texts they engage with by directing our gaze to specific aspects of the narrative.

TRACES OF USE

Books are alive. The traces of use that we come across when we read are proof that once released into the world, books absorb experiences, becoming reservoirs of our thoughts and actions. Reading can be active, marking up, correcting, annotating, doodling, and thinking alongside the texts found in books, leaving tangible traces of thoughts and activities.[1] In fact, according to Stephen Orgel, "One of the most commonplace aspects of old books is the fact that people wrote in them."[2] This truism also holds for the New Testament's Greek manuscripts, which often bear the marks of later correctors and readers. Not all paratexts are made by the authors, scribes, or craftspeople responsible for producing a manuscript in the first instance. Margins, flyleaves, and the text itself often become the space where subsequent users leave their imprint, creating their own paratexts that then go on to affect the way that the work communicates to subsequent readers.[3] Man-

---

1. On interested or active readers in manuscript cultures, see Liv Ingeborg Lied, *Invisible Manuscripts: Textual Scholarship and the Survival of 2 Baruch* (Tübingen: Mohr Siebeck, 2021), 113–17. Readers might also actively change the manuscript by adding or excising material or rebinding collections to create composite codices. See Kathryn M. Rudy, *Piety in Pieces: How Medieval Readers Customized Their Manuscripts* (Cambridge: Open Book, 2016), who explores this practice in fifteenth-century Netherlandish prayer books.

2. Stephen Orgel, *The Reader in the Book: A Study of Spaces and Traces* (Oxford: Oxford University Press, 2015), 2.

3. The practice of marking these spaces continued well into the age of print. See

uscripts invite engagement. A blank flyleaf or seductively large margin begs to be written on; a complex text invites readers to think through it via writing and annotation.[4]

One of the first books that I remember writing in, as an active reader myself, was a Bible. The neighborhood church I began attending as a teenager was big on Bible study, and I quickly learned that one way to show piety was to read with a pen and highlighter in hand, making copious annotation on any scrap of text that might speak to your life or reveal your future path. I was making paratexts without knowing what I was doing. They represented my attempt to understand my experiences with the text, to make connections across these diverse works that I was beginning to think about in new ways. I'm sure that most of these notes weren't all that insightful, but they were a snapshot of my thinking at the time, a bit of my learning preserved on the page for anyone to read. My notes were the evidence of my practicing to read in more sophisticated ways and of my burgeoning understanding of how Bibles worked.

I am, of course, not the only person who has ever annotated a book or a sacred text. An entire field of bibliographic research exists that examines the marks made by readers in various times and places, giving us insight into the contemporaneous responses of long-dead, usually anonymous readers.[5] The study of annotation practices is a kind of book archaeology, digging through the

---

William H. Sherman, *Used Books: Marking Readers in Renaissance England* (Philadelphia: University of Pennsylvania Press, 2010), 79; and Ann M. Blair, *Too Much to Know: Managing Scholarly Information before the Modern Age* (New Haven: Yale University Press, 2010), 71.

4. For an overview of the use of margins in medieval western European contexts (not all of which are relevant to Greek New Testament manuscripts that circulated largely in the Byzantine cultural sphere), see Michael Camille, *Image on the Edge: The Margins of Medieval Art* (London: Redaktion Books, 1992).

5. Examples of this type of research are legion, but some of the more compelling examples (for medieval manuscripts generally) include Orgel, *Reader in the Book*; Mariken Teeuwen and Irene van Renswoude, eds., *The Annotated Book in the Early Middle Ages: Practices of Reading and Writing* (Turnhout: Brepols, 2017); and Patrizia Carmassi, "Book Material, Production, and Use from the Point of View of the

pages to trace a book's history and information on its owners, users, and their thoughts.[6] To borrow a phrase from Liv Ingeborg Lied and Hugo Lundhaug, manuscripts and any other type of written-on object are "snapshots of evolving tradition," moments of insight into longer and more complex processes of transmission and reading.[7]

Manuscripts of the New Testament are fertile ground for this type of research, especially because they have until only recently been viewed primarily as textual witnesses, not as physical objects that tell their own stories about the people who made, used, and otherwise valued them.[8] As Jennifer Wright Knust notes, it is the very handwritten-ness of the manuscripts that makes them avenues for understanding the people who made them: "Written out by hand for over a millennium, passed from person to person, and employed in many ways, New Testament manuscripts preserve traces of the assumptions, priorities, and interests of those who produce and preserve them."[9] Preserved within and alongside the text of the New Testament are the reminiscences of times where

---

Paratext," in *Inscribing Knowledge in the Medieval Book: The Power of Paratexts*, ed. R. Brown-Grant et al. (Berlin: de Gruyter, 2019), 304–30.

6. Comparing book analysis and archaeology is the opening metaphor in the classical study by Herbert Hunger on reading and writing in Byzantium, *Schreiben und Lesen in Byzanz: Die byzantinische Buchkultur* (Munich: C. H. Beck, 1989).

7. See Liv Ingeborg Lied and Hugo Lundhaug, eds., *Snapshots of Evolving Tradition: Jewish and Christian Manuscript Culture, Textual Fluidity, and New Philology* (Berlin: de Gruyter, 2017). See also Liv Ingeborg Lied, "Bible as Notepad: Exploring Annotations and Annotation Practices in Biblical Manuscripts," in *Bible as Notepad: Tracing Annotations and Annotation Practices in Late Antique and Medieval Biblical Manuscripts*, ed L. I. Lied and M. Maniaci (Berlin: de Gruyter, 2018), 1–9.

8. I tried to write some of these stories for Revelation's manuscripts in Garrick V. Allen, *Manuscripts of the Book of Revelation: New Philology, Paratexts, Reception* (Oxford: Oxford University Press, 2020). Eldon Jay Epp argues that New Testament textual criticism's "unitary goal" is to establish (1) "the earliest attainable text . . . and at the same time (2) [to assess] the textual variants that emerge . . . so as to hear the narratives of early Christian thought and life." "Note to Readers," in *Perspectives on New Testament Textual Criticism*, vol. 2 (Leiden: Brill, 2021), xxiv. I agree with this twofold goal, but traditionally only the former aspect has been emphasized.

9. Jennifer Wright Knust, "The New Testament Text, Paratexts, and Reception His-

people read their sacred texts, people who utilized this space to leave perhaps the only trace of their existence that we now have. These annotations, set aside for good reason by textual critics who are interested in the transmission of the New Testament's text and in identifying its earliest readings, range from the scholarly to the pious, from the mundane to the silly, made by famous men from intellectual urban hubs and anonymous nobodies from Byzantine backwaters alike.

In his taxonomy of paratexts in Greek gospel manuscripts, Patrick Andrist calls these annotations "post-production paratexts," and he divides them into three categories: readers' paratexts (those that engage the text), book paratexts (those that tell us about the history of the manuscript), and post-production side content (items that tell us nothing about the text or the book, items that are incidental to its content).[10] These paratexts are not the product of the people responsible for making the manuscript in its earliest production layer; they are the work of subsequent readers and users and have various relationships to the main text of the manuscript. Andrist's careful distinctions are further complicated by the fact that manuscripts were often updated, remade, rearranged, rebound, or otherwise reworked multiple times over their working lives.[11] Manuscripts are stratified, and it is not always possible to disentangle these layers with certainty. Nonetheless, there is a distinct set of paratexts—the users' para-

---

tory," in *The Oxford Handbook to the Textual Criticism of the Bible*, ed. T. Wasserman and S. Crawford (Oxford: Oxford University Press, forthcoming).

10. Patrick Andrist, "Toward a Definition of Paratexts and Paratextuality: The Case of Ancient Greek Manuscripts," in *Bible as Notepad: Tracing Annotations and Annotation Practices in Late Antique and Medieval Biblical Manuscripts*, ed. L. I. Lied and M. Maniaci (Berlin: de Gruyter, 2018), 130–49. On other models of understanding annotation in different reading cultures, see Sherman, *Used Books*, 16–18.

11. See Marilena Maniaci, "Miscellaneous Reflections on the Complexity of Medieval Manuscripts," in *Collecting, Organizing and Transmitting Knowledge: Miscellanies in Late Medieval Europe*, ed. S. Corbellini, G. Murano, and G. Signore (Turnhout: Brepols, 2018), 11–22.

texts—that reveal what readers thought about the text, the manuscript as an object, or about themselves as human individuals.

It's these users' paratexts that I explore in the chapters that follow. I want to show the complexity of paratextuality as a phenomenon that extends beyond the scribes and craftspeople who first designed and produced any given manuscript. Paratexts beget paratexts; books gather them like snowballs rolling down a winter hill as they pass from one reader to another. Or, to return to an archaeological metaphor, manuscripts can become unexcavated stratified tells, gathering layer upon layer of detritus over time. Users' paratexts are often overlooked in biblical scholarship or viewed as the incidental extras that good textual critics must set aside to get at the original meaning or initial text of the New Testament. They are perceived, at least implicitly, as hindrances to the unadulterated text, as things that tell us nothing about the New Testament in its first-century context. This longstanding perspective in biblical studies, which is right from a certain oblique angle, is the result of what Orgel calls "our own idealization of the text."[12] Orgel is talking about annotations in early printed books. For him, the error lies in thinking that print culture created fixity as opposed to the instability of manuscripts and even digital texts as media for writing. Something similar persists in the modern imagination when it comes to Bibles, which we view as unchanging, as fixed because they are sacred, as something we can reconstruct by setting aside anything the text has accrued since antiquity. For scholars of the New Testament, some idealizations tend to revolve around theological ideas like inerrancy or infallibility, which shape the way its transmission and the historical realities of its changes, both textual and paratextual, are viewed.

The truth is that regardless of medium—whether manuscript, print, or digital—Bibles are defined by change, even if in subtle ways. This idea comes into focus especially in the paratexts, but also in how manuscript readers engaged with the text in tangible

---

12. Orgel, *Reader in the Book*, 9.

ways, by altering, adding to, and excising things from manuscripts that contain sacred traditions.[13] Their annotations and other interventions reveal their thoughts about the New Testament, their playfulness and absentmindedness, and in some instances their deepest desires. Paratexts are windows onto the lives of these past readers of the New Testament, revealing the embodied and mediated nature of bookwork and reading.

In addition to showing that the New Testament is and has always been an embodied tradition, created and enlivened by the many hands responsible for its composition and transmission, the other thing that users' paratexts do is enable us to see what people have done with these manuscripts once they are made. We can start to identify and trace the residues of reading that made their imprint on the New Testament. I won't create a new taxonomy of users' paratexts because to do so would require a fresh look at nearly every page of every New Testament manuscript to capture the complexity and specificity of these items. Instead, I want to explore the possibilities that manuscripts offer users by telling the story of user's paratexts by exploring some concrete examples and taking a close look at the value of these annotations for multiple questions relating to the transmission of the New Testament.

Speaking again about readerly notes in early printed books, Orgel says, "It is a rare book that remained unmarked in some way, even if only by an owner's name."[14] And I can confirm from experience that I don't think I have yet to come across a manuscript of the Greek New Testament without any markings from

---

13. One example of excising paratexts is in the multiple manuscripts that have their titles cut out or have the first folio of a work missing, like (non-exhaustively) GA 1338, 1421, 2369, and 2376. In these cases the material was likely removed due to the artistic nature of the headpieces or titles, but parchment was reused from old manuscripts for multiple reasons, including the making of new manuscripts (as in the case of GA 015). For more on the history of dismembering and reusing manuscript material (always an ethically fraught exercise in any context, ancient or modern), see Christopher de Hamel, *Cutting Up Manuscripts for Pleasure and Profit* (Charlottesville, VA: Book Arts Press, 1996).

14. Orgel, *Reader in the Book*, 19.

later readers, even if only folio numbers from modern librarians.[15] Each manuscript has something new to tell us if only we pay close attention. Just as the New Testament is replete, continually revealing new realities, so too are the individual manuscripts that transmit its texts.

---

15. The closest I have come to reading a manuscript that contains the Greek New Testament free of paratextual interference is GA 562, which is held across the street from my office at the University of Glasgow Library (Glasgow, Ms. Hunter 170; diktyon 17306). It's a sixteenth-century copy of the Gospel of John and is quite small in dimension. It can almost fit in your pocket. It has only the occasional folio number in the upper right margin of some rectos.

Chapter 11

Corrections and the Curious Case of Codex Montfortianus

The First Letter of John is unusual. It's the longest of the Catholic Epistles, but it has no formal elements of an ancient letter. It's more like an anonymous homily or exhortative discourse, even though it does talk about itself as a written text (5:13). Among all the peculiarities of this work, one passage stands out because of its role in medieval and early modern doctrinal debates on the Trinity.

In my copy of the NRSV, 1 John 5:7–8 reads: "There are three that testify: the Spirit and the water and the blood, and these three agree." A note after the first clause ("there are three that testify") directs me to a footnote, which reads: "A few other authorities read (with variations) There are three that testify *in heaven, the Father, the Word, and the Holy Spirit, and these three are one. And there are three that testify on earth* [the Spirit and the water and the blood, and these three agree]." This paratext in my modern Bible acknowledges the existence in some manuscripts of what scholars have called the Johannine Comma, an expansion of the initial Greek text of 1 John 5:7–8.[1] In the Comma, there are three witnesses in heaven (Father, Word, and Spirit) and three on earth (Spirit, water, blood), all of whom are in concord in their witness to the truth. As Juan Hernández Jr. argues, the Comma is a relic in the text, a reading that, although obviously not original to the earliest text of 1 John, persists in the theological imagination because of its obvious trinitarian

---

1. The KJV preserves the Comma in the main text, as in the Scofield Bible for example. Although Scofield does not comment on this passage.

relevance.[2] The Comma is a possible antidote to the tension that the Trinity became a central Christian doctrine but that it is never explicitly articulated in the New Testament in an unambiguous way. This reality made the Comma a central point of conflict in trinitarian thinking from the sixteenth century onward.[3]

The text of the Comma only came into the Greek tradition by way of the Latin New Testament.[4] Its authenticity and place in the Greek tradition was a hotly debated question as printed editions of the Greek New Testament began to appear. In his 1516 and 1519 editions, the humanist scholar Desiderius Erasmus didn't print the Comma because it was not attested in the Greek manuscripts he had to hand.[5] In the first and second editions of his *Annotationes*, a set of notes on the New Testament, Erasmus records, "In the Greek text I find only this about the threefold testimony: 'because there are three witnesses, spirit, water, and blood.'"[6] This

---

2. See Juan Hernández Jr., "The *Comma Johanneum*: A Relic in the Textual Tradition," *Early Christianity* 11 (2020): 60–70.

3. Grantley McDonald argues that "the Johannine Comma is a keyhole that allows us to peer straight into the heart of the violent struggles over the understanding of the Trinity that took place from the sixteenth to the nineteenth centuries." *Biblical Criticism in Early Modern Europe: Erasmus, the Johannine Comma and Trinitarian Debate* (Cambridge: Cambridge University Press, 2016), 11.

4. See H. A. G. Houghton, *The Latin New Testament: A Guide to Its Early History, Texts, and Manuscripts* (Oxford: Oxford University Press, 2016), 178–81, and Raymond E. Brown, *The Epistles of John* (Garden City, NY: Doubleday, 1982), 781–86, who locates its production in North Africa or Spain; McDonald, *Biblical Criticism*, 4–5. On the variations of the Comma in Greek, see Klaus Watchtel, *Der byzantinische Text der Katholischen Briefe: Eine Untersuchung der Koine des Neuen Testaments* (Berlin: de Gruyter, 1995), 314–15.

5. On the manuscripts used by Erasmus, see Patrick Andrist, "Structure and History of the Biblical Manuscripts Used by Erasmus for His 1516 Edition," in *Basel 1516: Erasmus' Edition of the New Testament*, ed. M. Wallraff, S. S. Menchi, and K. von Greyerz (Tübingen: Mohr Siebeck, 2016), 81–124; and, in the same volume, Andrew J. Brown, "The Manuscript Sources and Textual Character of Erasmus' 1516 Greek New Testament," 125–44.

6. The third note on 1 John 5. See Anne Reeve, ed., *Erasmus' Annotations on the New Testament: Galatians to the Apocalypse* (Leiden: Brill, 1993), 768–71; and Robert D. Sider, *Erasmus on the New Testament: Selections from the* Paraphrases, *the* Annotations,

Corrections and the Curious Case of Codex Montfortianus

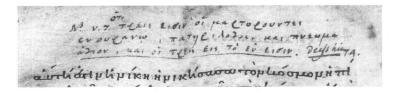

Figure 11.1. Later insertion of the Johannine Comma in the upper margin *(GA 177, Munich, BSB, Cod. graec. 211, 74r)*

note caused uproar. The future archbishop of York, Edward Lee, for example, suggested that Erasmus's omission of the Comma was at best careless scholarship or at worst evidence of heresy.[7] The stakes were high.

Erasmus was right, however, about the lack of witnesses to the Comma in the Greek tradition. Even today, the Comma appears in Greek in only ten copies of 1 John. In five of these manuscripts the passage is a later insertion located in the margins next to the main text (GA 88, 177, 221, 429, and 636; figure 11.1), perhaps copied from printed editions by later hands. It is found in only five Greek manuscripts in the running text (GA 61, 629, 918, 2318, and 2473), dating from the fourteenth (GA 629) to the eighteenth centuries (GA 2318).[8]

Coincidentally, not long after Erasmus's polemical exchanges over the Comma, he came across a manuscript that happened to have the Comma as part of its main text. He first found this text in Codex Montfortianus, a sixteenth-century manuscript of the entire New Testament now held at Trinity College Dublin (figure 11.2; TCD MS 30; diktyon 13584), produced sometime between 1500 and 1520, perhaps in response

---

and the Writings on Biblical Interpretation (London: University of Toronto Press, 2020), 206–9. On the *Annotationes*, see Erika Rummel, *Erasmus' Annotations on the New Testament: From Philologist to Theologian* (London: University of Toronto Press, 1986), esp. 132–34 on the Comma, and a translation in McDonald, *Biblical Criticism*, 315–22.

7. On Lee, see Rummel, *Erasmus' Annotations*, 124–25; and McDonald, *Biblical Criticism*, 16–22.

8. See Hernández, "*Comma Johanneum*," 62–63; and Wachtel, *Der byzantinische Text*, 318–20.

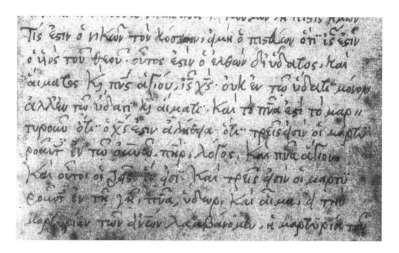

Figure 11.2. The Johannine Comma in Codex Montfortianus *(GA 61, Dublin, TCD MS 30, 439r).* With permission of The Board of Trinity College Dublin

to Erasmus's edition.[9] According to J. Rendel Harris, Codex Montfortianus was copied in Cambridge by the Franciscan Grey Friars from the Leicester Codex (GA 69), with a Greek version of the Comma translated from the Latin Vulgate.[10] The story is more complex than Harris thought, but two users' paratexts do give us hints as to the context of the making

---

9. Houghton notes that Codex Montfortianus is "a sixteenth-century codex into which the Johannine Comma seems to have been incorporated in order to confound Erasmus: the presence of this variant as well, stemming from an internal Latin error, confirms that Latin source lies behind these verses in this manuscript." *Latin New Testament,* 181. Images of the manuscript are available at Trinity College Dublin's digital collections: https://digitalcollections.tcd.ie/concern/works/000004722?locale=en (accessed 14 June 2023).

10. See J. Rendel Harris, *The Origin of the Leicester Codex of the New Testament* (London: Clay, 1887), esp. 46–53. Henk Jan de Jonge dismantles the straightforward idea that Montfortianus was produced to explicitly confound Erasmus and that Erasmus was bound by a promise to Lee to include the reading should a manuscript be furnished. "Erasmus and the *Comma Johanneum*," *Ephemerides Theologicae Lovanienses* 56 (1980): 381–89. See also Andrew J. Brown, "Excursus—Codex 61 (Montfortianus) and 1 *John* 5,7–8," in *Opera omnia Desiderii Erasmi Roterodami* VI-4,

Corrections and the Curious Case of Codex Montfortianus

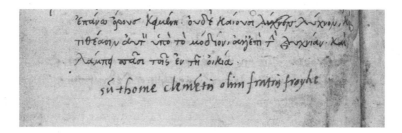

Figure 11.3. Owner's note *(GA 61, Dublin, TCD MS 30, 12v)*. With permission of The Board of Trinity College Dublin

of Montfortianus. The first is an owner's note in the lower margin of 12v that connects Montfortianus to a well-known Franciscan, Frater Froyke, and John Clement, a scholar known to Erasmus (figure 11.3). The second paratext is comprised of two annotations that read "Jesus, Mary, Francis" (ἰησοῦς μαρία φράγκισκος), which reflects a common Franciscan formula.[11] These features suggest that it was produced in England by a Franciscan scribe, and then passed in some capacity to John Clement.

According to Grantley McDonald, Clement likely showed Montfortianus to Erasmus in Leuven in early 1520 (or at least a transcription of 1 John 5:7–9 made from the manuscript).[12] Erasmus subsequently in-

---

ed. A. J. Brown (Leiden: Brill, 2013), 30–41 on this common myth and 68–106 on the manuscript sources for Codex Montfortianus.

11. The note reads "I belong to Thomas Clement, formerly to Friar Froyke" (*su thome clementis olim fratris froyke*). Thomas is the son of John Clement, to whom he bequeathed this book. Another owner's note is located on 471r, which reads *Master Wyllams of corpus ch[ry]sti*, connecting the book to Oxford in the sixteenth century. On the Franciscan connection to Montfortianus, see McDonald, *Biblical Criticism*, 35–41. On Master Williams, see Brown, "Excursus," 51–54.

12. See the nuanced discussion in McDonald, *Biblical Criticism*, 13–41, where he casts doubt on the classical narrative of Erasmus's inclusion of the Comma in his 1522 edition and makes a compelling case that John Clement brought the codex to Erasmus in Leuven. See also de Jonge, "Erasmus," 386–89; Brown, "Excursus," 54–58; and David M. Whitford, "Yielding to the Prejudices of His Times: Erasmus and the Comma Johanneum," *Church History and Religious Culture* 95 (2015): 19–40, who argues that Erasmus added the Comma to avoid accusations of heresy.

cluded the Comma in his 1522 edition, maintaining his suspicions of its authenticity. The textual skullduggery of humanist biblical scholarship, reinforced by personal rivalries, new technologies like print, and the economics of the emerging book trade, created an enduring place for Codex Montfortianus in the imagination of textual scholars for half a millennium now.

The story of Montfortianus's role in early printing of the New Testament and European humanist scholarship is fascinating, and it's what first brought my attention to this manuscript. But I want to change the focus of the discussion surrounding Montfortianus to examine its many users' paratexts which reflect scholarly proclivities of its owners and other readers by focusing on the many corrections to the text.[13] As we have already seen, some users' paratexts, like the owner's note and the Franciscan motto, tell us something about the location where the manuscript was made and who possessed it. Although it is not always possible to identify the individuals who made each annotation, the users' paratexts in Codex Montfortianus show the range of engagement with the New Testament's text that is also visible to some degree in many other manuscripts. The type of users' paratext that I want to focus on here is the *correction*.

A persistent feature of Codex Montfortianus is its copious corrections to the text made by the initial scribe and multiple later readers. It's not unusual to find corrections in manuscripts that contain the New Testament. Corrections are common in some of our earliest manuscripts, like in P46 (Dublin, CBL BP II; Ann Arbor, Inv. Nr. 6238), the oldest copy of Paul's letters bound in one codex, and in Codex Sinaiticus (GA 01, London, British Library, Add. 43725), the earliest Greek pandect Bible, which boasts over 23,000 corrections across the Old and New Testaments.[14] In a time before moveable type and word processing, the only

---

13. On its owners and users, see the detailed work of Brown, "Excursus," 41–68. On owners and later annotators, see also Orlando T. Dobbin, *The Codex Montfortianus* (London: Samuel Bagster, 1854), 6–17. Dobbin identifies at least three annotators, the main scribe, a later hand, and the copyist of Revelation, who also made annotations based on Erasmus's 1516 edition. On users of the codex from the sixteenth to nineteenth centuries, see McDonald, *Biblical Criticism*, 228–41 and 283–87.

14. On corrections in P46, see R. V. G. Tasker, "The Text of the 'Corpus Paulinum,'"

way to fix mistakes in copying was either to recopy the entire page (an expensive and time-consuming option) or to replace the original reading with a new one. Scribes usually opted for the latter option, and most corrections were made by the initial scribe or a corrector who presided over their work as the manuscript was first produced, although this process differed from place to place. In some instances, though, like Codex Sinaiticus (fourth century), Codex Bezae (fourth–fifth centuries), Codex Montfortianus, and others, many later active readers left their mark on the text through correction.[15]

Most corrections in biblical manuscripts are small-scale fixes to unintentional mistakes made by the first scribe: changes of grammatical case, adjustments verb morphology, deletions of repetitions, supplements to the text to fix accidental omissions, *in scribendo* modifications. Copying and other bookwork were arduous and repetitive, and any momentary lapse of focus might lead to the introduction of unintended readings.[16] But some corrections go beyond the simple fixing of error. In Montfortianus, for example, at least one corrector of the book of Revelation altered the text in many places to resemble the text of another copy or edition, in this case Erasmus's 1516 edition or the textual tradition that

---

New Testament Studies 1 (1955): 190–91; and Jacob W. Peterson, "Patterns of Correction as Paratext: A New Approach with Papyrus 46 as a Test Case," in *The Future of New Testament Textual Scholarship: From H. C. Hoskier to the Editio Critica Maior and Beyond*, ed. G. V. Allen (Tübingen: Mohr Siebeck, 2019), 201–29. On corrections in Sinaiticus, see David C. Parker, *Codex Sinaiticus: The Story of the World's Oldest Bible* (London: British Library, 2010), 79–90; and Klaus Wachtel, "The Corrected New Testament Text of Codex Sinaiticus," in *Codex Sinaiticus: New Perspectives on the Ancient Biblical Manuscript*, ed S. McKendrick et al. (London: British Library, 2015), 97–106. Images, transcriptions, and translations of Sinaiticus are available at https://www.codexsinaiticus.org/en/ (accessed 10 August 2023).

15. On the correctors in Codex Bezae, a particularly complicated Greco-Latin diglot, see David C. Parker, *Codex Bezae: An Early Christian Manuscript and Its Text* (Cambridge: Cambridge University Press, 1992), 123–65. See also James R. Royse, "The Corrections in the Freer Gospel Codex," in *The Freer Biblical Manuscripts: Fresh Studies of an American Treasure Trove*, ed. L. W. Hurtado (Atlanta: SBL Press, 2006), 185–226.

16. Alan Mugridge notes that "even the simple matter of 're-inking the pen' could result in a scribe making a mistake due to a break in concentration." *Copying Early Christian Texts: A Study in Scribal Practice* (Tübingen: Mohr Siebeck, 2016), 104.

undergirded it.[17] In most cases, the motivation of the corrector is lost to time, with only the physical manifestation of their textual mania present on the page.

Importantly, corrections are a form of paratext because they usually provide options to readers. Depending on the operation the corrector used to delete the first reading, the original text and the correction may both be legible, giving the later reader a chance to consider the significance of both possibilities. Corrections help us to reconstruct the context of the person who made them, fundamentally altering the interpretive possibilities available to later readers.[18]

Fixing Mistakes

Many corrections in Montfortianus were made by the main scribe in the process of copying, what are called *in scribendo* corrections. For example, in Matt 1:20 (8r) where an angel appears to Joseph, the scribe initially copied out the correct text that describes the heavenly visitor as an "angel of the Lord" (ἄγγελος κυ̅). For some reason, the scribe thought the way he had copied the *nomen sacrum* "Lord" (κυ̅) was incorrect, perhaps influenced by the fact that the next word also begins with kappa (κατ' ὄναρ, "during a dream").[19] So he crossed out the *nomen sacrum*, only to recopy it again, leaving the text as follows: "angel of the Lord of the Lord"

---

17. See Brown, "Excursus," 94–95.

18. Peterson sees the role of corrector as someone who provides "an improved reading experience or clearer understanding of the text as the corrector sees it." "Patterns," 209–10. This may be the goal of some correctors, especially when the corrections are made by the initial scribe, but the effects of some corrections make reading situations more complex, raising interpretive questions that otherwise might not have materialized. Parker adds that studying corrections is useful because it "offers insight into the ways in which readers studied and used biblical manuscripts," is good paleographic training, and informs us about how the text of the New Testament changed over time. *Codex Sinaiticus*, 79–80.

19. On *nomina sacra* (or sacred names)—conventional abbreviations for certain key words in Greek New Testament manuscripts—and their significance, see Larry W. Hurtado, *The Earliest Christian Artifacts: Manuscripts and Christian Origins* (Grand Rapids: Eerdmans, 2006), 95–134.

Corrections and the Curious Case of Codex Montfortianus

(ἄγγελος κυ̅ κυ̅).[20] In this case, we have a correction of a correction that didn't need to be corrected in the first place.

The scribe made many other corrections to clarify his sometimes-illegible handwriting. The last clause in Matt 5:12 (12v, "thus they persecuted the prophets who came before you") begins with the word οὕτω(ς) ("thus"). The scribe's first attempt to copy this word resulted in a tau that is more than twice the normal size for the letter. Crossing out the first ουτ, he then copied ουτω next to it, but this time with a tau with a more normal height. In this case, a paleographical anomaly led the scribe to amend the text.

Similarly, a morphological mistake motivated the scribe to correct a word in the divorce saying in Matt 5:31. The scribe initially wrote δώτω instead of δότω ("give"), which he fixed by crossing out the incorrectly spelled word and inserting the correct reading above the line. Likewise in Matt 6:19 (15r), he began to write the word κλέπται ("thieves") as βλε, accidentally starting the word with a beta. Messily crossing it out after the first three letters, he then copied the word as intended. *In scribendo* corrections are common in Montfortianus, revealing to us the level of scribal skill of the person responsible for the text of this manuscript. While not perfect on every instance, the scribe was usually able to correct mistakes as he worked.

Corrections to Other Known Texts

While many corrections simply fix scribal mishaps or minor errors, some changes reflect comparison with the text of other copies. In Montfortianus, most of these corrections (but not all) were made by the main scribe on a subsequent reading against other manuscripts or

---

20. Similar corrections occur elsewhere, like at Matt 5:15 (12v, λύχνον is copied twice with the first crossed out), 6:4 (14v, ἐλεημοσύνη), and 6:26 (15v, where the *nomen sacrum* ουρανιος is crossed out twice before it is written a third time). Other annotations appear to note textual variation without changing the text itself. For example, an obelus in the right margin at Matt 1:19, connected to three dots above the word "to make an example of" (παραδειγματίσαι) notes that this word has alternatives in other sources. In this case, other witnesses read δειγματίσαι, which carries approximately the same meaning in English.

print editions. These types of corrections are more complex and result in texts known elsewhere in the tradition. For example, in Matthew's genealogy (Matt 1:11, 7v), the text now reads, "And Josiah was the father ~~of Joachim, and Joachim was the father~~ of Jeconiah and his brothers at the time of the deportation to Babylon" (ἰωσίας δὲ ἐγέννησε τὸν ~~ἰωακείμ. ἰωακείμ δὲ ἐγέννησε~~ τὸν ἰεχονίαν καὶ τοὺς ἀδελφοὺς ἀυτοῦ ἐπὶ τῆς μετοικεσίας βαβυλῶνος). The deleted text is crossed out roughly and further noted with an obelus (a siglum similar to a small cross) in the left margin. Joachim is included in some Greek, Syriac, and Latin witnesses to this passage, but only in a sparse handful, and the addition of him here breaks up the symmetry of the genealogy, which notes that there should only be fourteen generations from David until the exile (Matt 1:17). Adding Joachim makes it fifteen. This correction was likely made by the first scribe when he later compared his text against another manuscript or edition.

Another example can be found in Jesus's debate with Satan in the desert in Matt 4:10 (11r). Jesus's final words to Satan in Montfortianus are, "Get behind me (ὀπίσω μου), Satan," a well-known phrase that mirrors Jesus's response to Peter's declaration in Matt 16:23. A later reader wanted to omit the words "behind me," noting this desire by placing cancelation dots under the offending words. The clause now reads, "Get behind me, Satan" (ὕπαγε ὀπίσω μου σατανᾶ). Both readings are preserved in the Greek tradition, but this omission is part of a broader attempt to revise the first form of the text copied in Matthew toward another text. The corrector altered the first text, creating options for readers—they can ignore the original reading, ignore the correction, or, if they are very sophisticated, reflect on the variations preserved in this exemplar. The form of correction here (using underdots as cancellation markers) doesn't appear to be the work of the first scribe, who usually scribbled out the first readings in a messy way.

Another more orderly omission is marked after Matt 7:8 (16r) where the initial scribe copied a form of the text from Luke 11:11–12 in the place of Matt 7:9–10 (figure 11.4). The corrector, using a slightly different ink and messier contemporary hand, underlined the text inserted from Luke and wrote the correction in the lower margin. This change notes a reading that is out of place, gives the "correct" text, and offers access to both possible readings. The red letters above the correction

Corrections and the Curious Case of Codex Montfortianus

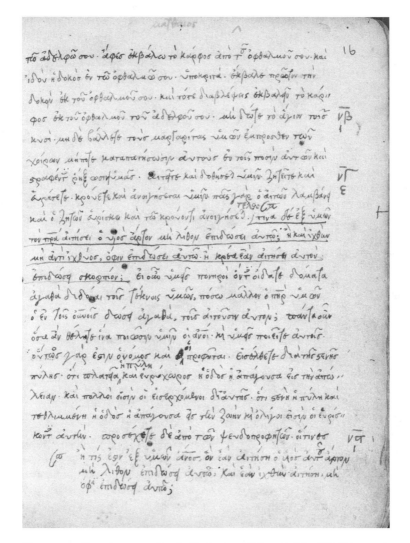

Figure 11.4. Complex correction in Matt 7:8–10 (GA 61, Dublin, TCD MS 30, 16r). With permission of The Board of Trinity College Dublin

in the right margin are the Eusebian chapter and canon table numbers, in this case, 53_5, that is, the fifty-third chapter of Matthew with parallels on the fifth canon table, the one that registers shared readings between Matthew and Luke only. It is unclear how the parallel text in Luke came to be embedded in Matthew, but it is fitting that this correction gives readers access to both parallel sayings about children asking their parents for food without having to flip directly to the Lukan parallel.

Most of these corrections appear to have been made by the main scribe, but multiple examples are the work of other annotators, although likely readers close to the time the manuscript was produced. One example is a corrector who occasionally made small-scale changes to the text in a darker ink and somewhat more skilled hand. For example, this corrector wrote in Matt 9:9 (19r) the word ἐκεῖθεν ("from there") in the right margin next to three dots and an insertion siglum (similar to ^), inserting it between the *nomen sacrum* ι̅ς̅ ("Jesus") and εἶδεν ("he saw") by writing the same three dots and insertion siglum between these words in the text itself. On the same page, this person also made three changes to Matt 9:15 by correcting a spelling error (δύναται] δύνανται), substituting one word for another (νηστεύειν, "to fast"] πενθεῖν, "to mourn"); and adding χρόνον ("time").

The active work of this later corrector is supplemented on the same page by two additional later correctors. One is that same hand responsible for the rubricated *kephalaia* titles, Eusebian material, and liturgical information. In the lower margin, this person wrote in red ink υἱοὶ τοῦ νυμφίως, which was perhaps intended to correct the reading of υἱοὶ τοῦ νυμφῶνος ("sons of the bridegroom") in the main text. Because νυμφιῶς is a rare word, appearing only in a fifth-century CE grammatical text by Orion (roughly meaning "now clothed beautifully"), someone tried to delete this suggested change by scraping off the red text in the lower margin. The final corrector active on 19r offers an unclear Latin reading that appears in the right margin next to Matt 9:15, where our first corrector added χρόνον ("time"). As far as I can tell, this correction is the only place where χρόνον appears in Matt 9:15 in the Greek tradition, and the Latin note here does include the Greek letters χρον. I suggest that this later corrector worked to fix the initial correction here, attempting to show that we should ignore the word χρόνον in this instance.

Conclusion

This description of the correcting activity in the first few chapters of Matthew is highly selective, but it does give the flavor of what it was like to read a manuscript like Montfortianus. To understand the logic and effects of corrections in Montfortianus in greater detail, we would need to systemically catalogue the multiple corrections on each page for the entire manuscript.

Although I haven't presented the full picture here, multiple things become clear for our thinking about corrections as paratexts. First, reading the New Testament in a manuscript culture can be substantially different than reading a printed critical edition or modern English Bible. In many cases, the accretions of use and past reading experiences impact the ways that later readers engage the text. Even before we can interpret the text, we have to decide what words to process; this is more complicated when we are presented with multiple options and corrections of corrections in multiple languages. Manuscript readers only rarely encountered biblical texts that were uncorrected or otherwise highly polished finished products like our modern editions. Working around (and with) corrections is a reality of reading.

Second, corrections highlight to readers the innate similarities of certain New Testament texts. The complex correction in Matthew 7 on 16r is one such example. It corrects a genuine anomaly insofar as part of Luke was copied instead of its Matthean parallel. But it does so in a way that leaves both texts available to the readers, providing opportunities to compare parallels without flipping pages or using the Eusebian system.[21] A similar change was made a few pages later in Matthew 10 (21v–22r). In this case, Matt 10:37–38 and 19:27–30 were written between Matt 10:33 and 10:34. Matthew 10:37 is then added in the lower margin of 22r and inserted in its proper place in the narrative.[22] The logic of this initial inscription is clear: it clusters all of Matthew's sayings on leaving one's

---

21. The Eusebian system is difficult to use in Montfortianus because, although it has marginal annotations, it does not preserve the corresponding tables.

22. For more on this reading, see Garrick V. Allen, *Manuscripts of the Book of Rev-*

family into a single utterance. The correction highlights the unusual nature of this nomadic text but leaves the entire insertion legible, offering readers the choice to make sense of this passage how they so choose by encouraging the connections made by the initial scribe between Jesus's sayings in chapters 10 and 19 to endure.

Overall, corrections show in the most tangible way that the biblical text is a living thing, created in each instance by discerning people. The text is never fixed even after those who initially made the manuscripts thought their work was done. Montfortianus preserves evidence of corrections at multiple stages made by multiple people: *in scribendo* changes by the main scribe to fix mistakes and later text-critical corrections by the main scribe and at least three later readers working in both Greek and Latin, sometimes correcting previous corrections. Corrections are the residues of asynchronic textual conversations across space and time. This manuscript is tangible evidence that change is an essential aspect of what constitutes the New Testament. It is proof that we tend to, care for, and alter the things that we value the most. Montfortianus is more than a monument to the heat of humanist biblical scholarship and sixteenth-century textual polemics; it's a reservoir of tradition, of careful reading, and of the value of looking at even the later New Testament manuscripts for the questions we continue to bring to this tradition.

---

elation: New Philology, Paratexts, Reception (Oxford: Oxford University Press, 2020), 165–70.

Chapter 12

Daydreaming and Learning with the New Testament

Users' paratexts are not always as technical or text-critical as those preserved in Codex Montfortianus. Not every person who read a copy of Matthew was concerned with comparing its text to other copies and traditions. Manuscripts of the Greek New Testament sometimes became the space for both daydreaming and for the basic learning of literacy and scribal craft. Like modern high school textbooks passed from student to student, year by year, manuscripts of the New Testament absorbed interventions that offered insight into the mindset of readers, including their silly scribbles and deep personal thoughts, and into the evidence of their learning. A single manuscript can be an archive of the ways it was handled, albeit a selective one.[1]

Dreaming

GA 1175 (Patmos, Monastery of St. John the Theologian, 16, diktyon 54260) is a copy of Acts, the Catholic Epistles, and Paul's letters made in the tenth century.[2] The manuscript contains multiple Euthalian para-

---

1. This phenomenon is not restricted to the New Testament. See, for example, Joanna Frońska, "Writing in the Margin—Drawing in the Margin: Reading Practices of Medieval Jurists," in *Inscribing Knowledge in the Medieval Book: The Power of Paratexts*, ed. R. Brown-Grant et al. (Berlin: de Gruyter, 2019), 141–59.

2. The text breaks off part way through Titus; Philemon is missing. Images of GA 1175 are available at the New Testament virtual Manuscript Room: https://ntvmr.uni-muenster.de/manuscript-workspace (accessed 5 July 2023). For more on this manu-

texts, including the quotation lists, prologues, hypotheses, Pauline biographical texts, chapter lists, and lection lists. The chapter numbers and titles in the prefatory chapter lists also appear regularly in the margins, and the quotations as enumerated in the lists are marked in the margins of the text as well. GA 1175 is a fulsome version of the Euthalian tradition. As such, it was designed by its initial producers to be replete with paratexts and to shape reading experiences through these items.

But not all paratexts in GA 1175 are so serious. You can find doodles of what I have been privately calling "weird little guys" hidden among the Euthalian material.[3] These images are hard to describe, but include what appear to be angels, perhaps crucified characters, and a triangle fellow with a couple little friends (e.g., figure 12.1). A more developed sketch occurs in the long quotation list to the Pauline Letters on 98r, where a battle plays out in the right margin next to the text of quotation from Exodus (figure 12.2). These racialized doodles depict a figure in Eastern dress shooting arrows at a figure in Western garb holding a firearm.[4] The quality of the illustration is much higher than the triangle man, and it may reflect cultural perceptions of conflict between the Byzantine empire and Islamic adversaries from the tenth century onward. A perceived adversarial relationship with Islam and Islamic rulers found its way into multiple Greek New Testament manuscripts in the late and post-Byzantine period, most notably through marginal notes that identify the number of the beast in Rev 13:18 as Muhammad or some related figure.[5]

---

script, see Kirsopp Lake and Silva New, *Six Collations of New Testament Manuscripts* (Cambridge, MA: Harvard University Press, 1932), 220–43.

3. I define doodles, following Sharat Gupta, as "aimless scribbles or drawings that are usually done when the person's primary attention is otherwise occupied by some other task." See "Doodling: The Artistry of the Roving Metaphysical Mind," *Journal of Mental Health and Human Behaviour* 21 (2016): 16–19. According to Gupta, doodles are by definition unique and unrelated to the primary task at hand.

4. Stratis Papaioannou identifies the doodle as a "post-Byzantine scribble" describing a battle between a "Westerner" and "a black pirate." "Readers and Their Pleasures," in *The Oxford Handbook of Byzantine Literature*, ed. S. Papaioannou (Oxford: Oxford University Press, 2021), 546–47.

5. On this tradition, see Garrick V. Allen, "Monks, Manuscripts, Muhammad, and the Future of the Critical Edition," in *From Scrolls to Scrolling: Sacred Texts, Materiality, and Dynamic Media Cultures*, ed. B. A. Anderson (Berlin: de Gruyter, 2020), 181–211;

Daydreaming and Learning with the New Testament

Although possibly reflecting a broader ideology of cultural stereotypes in the contested space of the Eastern Mediterranean, this sketch also reveals the idealized fantasy of foreign lands, different people, and perhaps even the heroics of battle. The sketches are the result of imagination, of daydreams of other lives and places.

It's not surprising that we regularly find doodles and other types of informal images in the manuscripts. In many cases, doodling is a physical response to daydreaming triggered by boredom. Scribbling around on a blank margin or flyleaf is one possible way for a reader to combat everyday tedium in whatever situation necessitated them having the manuscript before them. Social scientific and healthcare literature abounds with studies that examine this practice in high school or medical students, and there is even some evidence that the practice of doodling is a cognitively effective way to maintain attention under certain circumstances and may even improve memory.[6]

Regardless of the possible benefits of the practice, these annotations in GA 1175 allow us to imagine a scenario where a monk, sitting in the library on the remote Aegean island of Patmos tasked with adding in the ἀρχή ("beginning") and τέλος ("end") notations in the biblical text, demarcating the lections for the liturgical year, became distracted in the face of the scope of his mechanistic but demanding labor.[7] When he reached the liminal spaces in the manuscript that didn't require him to work with exacting accuracy—in this case, the Euthalian prefatory material—he used it to offload the mental strain of his work. Instead of paying close attention to the liturgical units and textual segmentation, he took a moment to scrib-

---

and Garrick V. Allen, "An Anti-Islamic Marginal Comment in the Apocalypse of 'Codex Reuchlin' (GA 2814) and Its Tradition," in *Der Codex Reuchlins zur Apokalypse: Byzanz—Basler Konzil —Erasmus*, ed. M. Karrer (Berlin: de Gruyter, 2020), 193–98. Images in other Greek New Testament manuscripts portray Eastern or Muslim figures in stereotyped ways. See, for example, GA 603 (65r) and 1686 (341v).

6. E.g., Karen Wilson and James H. Korn, "Attention During Lecture: Beyond Ten Minutes," *Teaching Psychology* 2 (2007): 85–89; and Jackie Andrade, "What Does Doodling Do?," *Applied Cognitive Psychology* 24 (2009): 100–106.

7. The ἀρχή and τέλος divisions were added by a much later hand; the Euthalian material is not primarily oriented toward liturgical usage, but manuscripts with Euthalian annotations are often presented alongside liturgical information.

TRACES OF USE

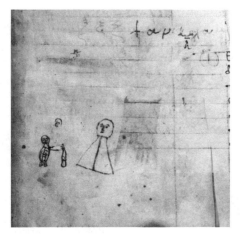

Figure 12.1. Triangle guy with two little friends in the lower left margin *(GA 1175, Patmos, St. John the Theologian Monastery, 16, 6r)*

Figure 12.2. A battle in the margins *(GA 1175, Patmos, St. John the Theologian Monastery, 16, 98r)*

ble, to imagine himself as someone else doing some kind of other activity, to imagine ridiculous creatures and silly things. He can do all of this without standing up from his writing table, looking like he's still working.

These sketches bear no relationship to the texts to which they are juxtaposed; they simply represent the playfulness of someone who used the manuscript at some point after it was produced in the tenth century, perhaps someone who worked to recontextualize the Euthalian material and these biblical texts into a liturgical cycle. The doodles are not examples of elite artwork or of a tradition of manuscript illumination or decoration. The fact that they exist only in the Euthalian prefatory material to Acts and Paul shows that their creator saw these parts of the manuscript as a liminal space, as a place where it was safe to intervene, as a place to imagine other worlds, other creatures, and other people, even if in stereotype. This complex manuscript became a place to imagine and to record these imaginings.

Daydreaming and Learning with the New Testament

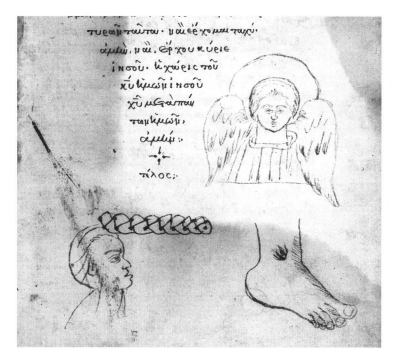

Figure 12.3. Angel, foot, underbite man in profile *(GA 2049, Athens, Hellenic Parliament Library, 45, 254r). Courtesy of the Library of the Hellenic Parliament.*

Imaginative amateur artwork is widespread in the tradition, and this phenomenon has not yet been mapped or sufficiently understood by scholars when it comes to their presence in Greek copies of the New Testament.[8] Based on my recent experience of reading widely in the

---

8. Annotations along these lines exist in multiple manuscript and typographic cultures, across works, language, and time. Doodles in the New Testament are part of a much broader tradition, and research in this area has focused on late medieval and early modern books and manuscripts. See, for example, Eleanor Chan, "Scrollwork: Visual Cultures of Musical Notation and Graphic Materiality in the English Renaissance," *Journal of Medieval and Early Modern Studies* 53 (2023): 347–77; William H. Sherman, *Used Books: Marking Readers in Renaissance England* (Philadelphia: University of Pennsylvania Press, 2010); Helen Smith and Louise Wilson, eds., *Renais-*

149

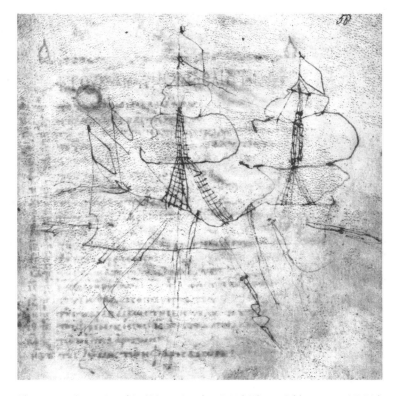

Figure 12.4. Sea-going ship *(GA 497, London, British Library, Add. 16943, 58r).* British Library Board.

manuscripts, these images run the gamut, including things like a cluster of sketches at the end of Revelation (figure 12.3), an image of the monastery where a manuscript was produced (GA 2459), a seagoing ship (figure 12.4), a ghostly portrait of Paul in the margins (GA 325), a little scorpion (GA 375), a sad fish (GA 596), a sketchy Mark the evangelist (GA 1451), and an image of Jesus with tiny little hands (figure 12.5).[9] It

---

sance Paratexts (Cambridge: Cambridge University Press, 2011); and H. J. Jackson, *Marginalia: Readers Writing in Books* (New Haven: Yale University Press, 2001).

9. For these images, see, respectively, GA 2049, Athens, Hellenic Parliament Li-

Daydreaming and Learning with the New Testament

Figure 12.5. Jesus with tiny little hands *(GA 1735, Mt. Athos, Great Lavra Monastery, B42, 192v). With the kind permission of the Synaxis of the Great Lavra Monastery. Library of Congress Collection of Manuscripts from the Monasteries of Mt. Athos.*

brary, 45, diktyon 1141, sixteenth century, which has multiple drawings of figures and anatomy in the flyleaves; Almyros, Archaeological Museum, 2, diktyon 32296, twelfth century, 1943r; GA 497 (London, British Library, Add. 16943, diktn 38919, eleventh century (see also GA 013 [Hamburg, Staats- und Universitätsbibliothek, In Scrin. 91, diktyon 32376, ninth century], f. 286; Oxford, Bodleian, Ms. Auct. E.5.9, diktyon 47061, would take many years to create a complete catalog of amateur images located in the manuscripts, but this sample shows the diversity of topics, artistic skill, and the lived reality of manuscripts as objects.

These images usually tell us very little about the texts they adorn. Instead, they are valuable because they are one of the rare ways that we can access anything about the many anonymous people who made and used these objects. We get a sliver of access into the things that populated their thoughts as they read the New Testament: images of Jesus and other biblical figures, representations of the places they were sitting as they read, body parts, and the like. These images show us how imaginings of far-off people and places collided in tangible ways with Bibles as important everyday objects, as collective spaces where small parts of human lives were deposited.[10]

The dreams of readers also manifested in other, more serious ways. Alongside doodles, we find examples of heartfelt acclimations of faith and the tangible residues of prayer. Like my grandmother's family Bible, manuscripts became spaces to record memories and devotions.

Many of these more pious notations consist of standardized formulations wishing grace or peace to Christ in some form or another. One example can be found at the end of 2 Corinthians in Codex Montfortianus (265v). In the lower margin, directly below the large ἀμήν ("amen") at the end of the letter, a different hand has written "grace to God in Christ Jesus our Lord" (τῷ θεῷ χάρις ἐν χῷ ἰῦ τῷ κῷ | ἡμῶν). Similar texts are found regularly in the Greek manuscripts, particularly at the start and end of works and as parts of colophons, or scribal notes that sometimes appear at the end of the codex.

Later readers also used the margins of manuscripts as places to record prayers and other family events of importance. One example is found in

---

28v; Vatican City, BAV, Vat. Gr. 1533, diktyon 68164, eleventh century, end flyleaves; Venice, Biblioteca Nazionale Marciana, Gr. I,57, diktyon 70153, eleventh century, 1r; Mt. Athos, Great Lavra Monastery, A 18, diktyon 26946, thirteenth century, 69r; GA 1735, Mt. Athos, Great Lavra Monastery, B 42, diktyon 27094, tenth century.

10. Chan, "Scrollwork," 357, referring to annotated Renaissance English musical manuscripts, argues that doodling and other marks are a kind of collective practice, mediating between music, text, and the physicality of singing.

Daydreaming and Learning with the New Testament

Figure 12.6. Prayer by Peter the shoemaker *(GA 2604, Dublin, CBL W 139, 310v).*
© The Trustees of the Chester Beatty Library, Dublin

the lower margin of the Gospel of Luke in GA 2604 (figure 12.6), a twelfth-century deluxe gospel book in Dublin that I've already mentioned.[11]

Written in a later hand, a one-time reader scrawled, "Remember, Lord, the soul of your servant Peter the shoemaker, and his partner Anastasia and their children" (μνήσθητ[ι)] κ[υρι]έ τήν ψυχήν τοῦ δούλ[ο]υ σου πέτρ[ου] τζαγκάρη. καὶ τῆς συμβίου ἀυτ[οῦ] ἀναστασιας καὶ των τεκνῶν ἀυτῶν). We don't learn anything about what Peter the shoemaker thought about the Gospel of Luke, but we learn that he and his family existed and what his trade was. The tangible remains of his prayer give us the space to begin to imagine the circumstances by which he came to this book, the cares that led him to mark it up, and what he thought about the efficacy of the gospel book as a sacred space, a place where God could surely read and respond to his basic desires for his family.[12]

---

11. I've written about this manuscript and briefly about this annotation in other places. See Garrick V. Allen, "The Possibilities of a Gospel Codex: GA 2604 (Dublin, CBL W 139), Digital Editing, and Reading in a Manuscript Culture," *Journal of Biblical Literature* 140 (2021): 430; Garrick V. Allen, "Digital Tools for Working with New Testament Manuscripts," *Open Theology* 5 (2019): 13–28; and Anthony P. Royle and Garrick V. Allen, "Framing Mark: Reading Mark 16 in a Catena Manuscript," *Comparative Oriental Manuscript Studies Bulletin* 8 (2022): 385–400.

12. Gospel books in particular were viewed as tangible manifestations of the body of Christ in some Byzantine contexts, making them ideal locations for efficacious prayer and other forms of devotion. See Filippo Ronconi and Stratis Papaioannou, "Book Culture," in *The Oxford Handbook of Byzantine Literature*, ed. S. Papaioannou (Oxford: Oxford University Press, 2021), 64–65; and Robert S. Nelson, "Image and Inscription: Pleas for Salvation in Spaces of Devotion," in *Art and Text in Byzantine Culture*, ed. L. James (Cambridge: Cambridge University Press, 2007), 100–119. See

Peter the shoemaker's graphic prayer is connected to the broader Byzantine view of history as present in concrete ways through items like statues, relics, icons, and holy books, as something that individuals could participate in on a daily basis. One way that people in Byzantium created spaces of memory for their own personal histories was through book annotation, making notes of contemporary events and personal affairs, like the death and birth of children.[13] Peter's prayer is part of a larger tradition, found in manuscripts of the New Testament and many other kinds of Byzantine books, where the lives of individuals now lost to time make themselves known to us even if we can only perceive them through a glass darkly.

Learning with the New Testament

The final type of users' paratext I want to explore is the evidence of basic learning found in many of the New Testament's manuscripts. The process of producing a manuscript was complex, requiring multiple individuals with their own set of highly specialized skills to collaborate over an extended period. Setting aside the manufacturing of parchment, inks, writing implements, and the skilled production of covers and bindings, scribal work required practice, time, and a level of mastery of letter forms, ligatures, abbreviations, and (at least) basic literacy. Scribal training in most contexts where Greek New Testament manuscripts were produced was likely informal, organized by local institutions like churches, monasteries, or local government administration, a reality witnessed in the colophons we possess.[14] One way that scribes learned the basic

---

also a prayer written by a certain Theodosios in the lower margin at the end of John in GA 1138 (Mt. Athos, Chelandari Monastery, 5, diktyon 19810), 257r.

13. Stratis Papaioannou, "Byzantine *historia*," in *Thinking, Recording, and Writing History in the Ancient World*, ed. K. A. Raaflaub (London: Wiley, 2014), 297–313, esp. 306–8.

14. Colophons are scribal notes that give information on the name of the scribe, the date the manuscript was completed, and sometimes other information. They are surprisingly infrequent in Greek New Testament manuscripts compared to other traditions. See Kirsopp Lake and Silva Lake, *Dated Greek Minuscule Manuscripts to the Year 1200*, 10 vols. (Boston: American Academy of Arts and Sciences, 1934–1945);

Daydreaming and Learning with the New Testament

tasks of their craft—reading and writing—was to copy letter forms and phrases from existing manuscripts, including copies of the New Testament. These penmanship exercises are found in dozens (at least) of our copies of the Greek New Testament.[15]

For example, consider GA 1277 (Cambridge, Cambridge University Library, Ms. Add. 3046, diktyon 12109), a damaged eleventh-century copy of Acts, the Catholic Epistles, and Paul with commentary. On the first page of Acts (1r), a later hand has written a clumsier version of the Greek alphabet in the lower margin. A few pages later, on 4v, a person practiced copying the distinctive form of the alpha that the main scribe of the text had used three times on that folio at the end of the line, in addition to some difficult to decipher notations in the left margin. Further down still, on 122r, yet another hand wrote an alphabet in the lower margin, followed by abbreviations for articles and prepositions, all in the midst of the text of 2 Peter (figure 12.7).

The history of GA 1277 is unclear, but at multiple points in its working life, it served not only as a set of sacred texts to be read, but as an educational space where scribes or students could begin to learn their craft in a way that would enable the propagation of the New Testament and other texts.[16] In this way, GA 1277 and the many other manuscripts with similar interventions show the complex social lives of these objects and the roles they played in various communities. They give a glimpse into a broader practice, one that we have only begun to think about seriously in biblical studies.[17]

---

and Jeremiah Coogan, "Byzantine Manuscript Colophons and the Prosopography of Scribal Activity," in *From Constantinople to the Frontier: The City and the Cities*, ed. N. S. M. Matheo, T. Kampianaki, and L. M. Bondioli (Leiden: Brill, 2016), 297–310.

15. Penmanship exercises are also common in early printed Bibles and many other manuscript cultures. See Sherman, *Used Books*, 80–83.

16. In many contexts learning the alphabet was the first building block in literacy education from late antiquity onward. See Raffaella Cribiore, *Writing, Teachers, and Students in Graeco-Roman Egypt* (Atlanta: Scholars, 1996), 8–11.

17. These alphabet exercises resemble manuscripts, tablets, and potsherds that preserve school exercises, mostly from late ancient Egypt. See, for example, Roger Bagnall, "The Educational and Cultural Background of Egyptian Monks," in *Monastic Education in Late Antiquity: The Transformation of Classical Paideia*, ed. L. I. Larsen and S. Rubenson (Cambridge: Cambridge University Press, 2018), 75–100. This list is

TRACES OF USE

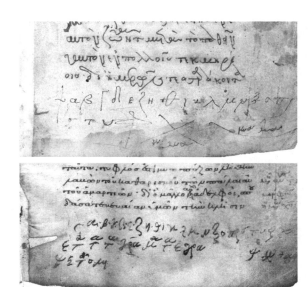

Figure 12.7. Practice writing in the lower margin at start of Acts *(GA 1277, Cambridge, Cambridge University Library, Ms. Add. 3046)*, in the lower margin at start of Acts (1r), practice alphas (4v), and alphabet and abbreviations (114r). *Reproduced by kind permission of the Syndics of Cambridge University Library.*

Daydreaming and Learning with the New Testament

A final example of this type of annotation is found in GA 1270 (Modena, Biblioteca Estense Universitaria, α.W.2.07, diktyon 43529), another eleventh-century copy of the Praxapostolos and Paul's letters. Located between the list of the liturgical readings and the start of the Euthalian prologue to Paul is a blank page that has been filled in by at least two later hands (figure 12.8).

Among other items, like repeated phrases about the "book(s) of Per-agios" near the top of the page and some repeated letters (epsilons and taus mainly), the opening words of the Euthalian prologue to Paul are visibly scrawled nine times along with the same opening: "Prologue affixed to the book" (πρόλογος προτασσόμενος τῆς βίβλιου). Near the top of the page, the scribe worked hard to repeat the opening lines of the prologue, even including the punctuation at the end of the line. Some mistakes were made—spelling πρόλογος as πρόλωγως, for example—but the person responsible was copying the text on the page to the right as a way to learn the letter forms or title of this part of the Euthalian system. As we move down the page, however, the script becomes significantly larger, more cartoonish, perhaps becoming a physical manifestation of the scribe's boredom or inattentiveness to the task.[18] Regardless of our ability to reconstruct the scribe's mental processes here, it's key to note that, again, the liminal spaces in the manuscripts—the blank folio between content sections in this instance—become areas of learning, human activity, and reading. GA 1270 and the many other manuscripts that preserve similar material are some of the most tangible evidence that we have for particular reading experiences. In most cases, we must

---

not exhaustive, but I have encountered alphabet exercises in multiple New Testament manuscripts at various locations (margins or flyleaves), including in GA 015, 045, 27, 59, 83, 172, 216, 223, 321, 325, 433, 450, 458, 502, 632, 639, 644, 677, 1015, 1020, 1116, 1410, 1413, 1526, 1702, 1717, 1721, 1735, 1737, 1742, 1743, 1746, 2049, 2321, 2358, 2434, and 2893.

18. There are multiple examples of later users copying the first words of a work and its special characters on a blank folio. See, for example, the start of Mark in GA 2369 (Baltimore, Walters Art Museum, W. 523, diktyon 8845, 98v–99r; images available for download at: https://www.thedigitalwalters.org/Data/WaltersManuscripts/html/W523/ [accessed 10 July 2023]) or the subscription to Mark in GA 2418 (Zagora, Public Historical Library, 2, diktyon 27488), 87v, where the scribe has taken an entire page to copy out the subscription in different iterations.

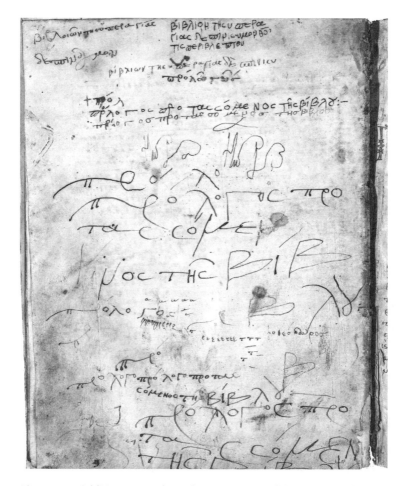

Figure 12.8. Additions to an eleventh-century copy of the Praxapostolos and Paul's letters *(GA 1270, Modena, Biblioteca Estense Universitaria, a. W. 2. 07, 7v)*. *Su concessione del Ministero della Cultura – Gallerie Estensi, Biblioteca Estense Universitaria*

imagine what a reader might have done with the text before them under whatever circumstance. But here, we know that a person learning to write or practicing their letters actually read the Euthalian prologue to Paul, or its title at the very least. Their motivations, goals, and larger situation remain unclear, but this type of evidence helps us to locate ourselves with humility in the larger arc of scriptural engagement, most of which remains intangible and inaccessible to modern scholars, even when we pay close attention to the peculiarities of the manuscripts.

Conclusion

The users' paratext is a broad category that covers several features and underlying impulses, ranging from the text-critical to the daydreamy. These idiosyncratic annotations and more coherent evidences of use reveal what William Sherman has called "both the large-scale patterns of use and extraordinary encounters of individuals and their books."[19] It is impossible in this context to give a full overview of this class of paratext for the Greek New Testament because users' paratexts can be highly context specific and because the New Testament has been transmitted in multiple different locations and timeframes, spanning ancient Egypt to the Renaissance British Isles. Nonetheless, exploring the manuscripts for these kinds of annotations and interventions by later readers gives us unique insight into individuals and into larger culturally conditioned ways of reading.

On the one hand, through amateur artworks we see ourselves in human individuals of the past. Exploring this same phenomenon, Stratis Papaioannou argues that "in this protean, heterogeneous art, often defying expectations, we encounter the desire on the part of readers (in their many guises) of Byzantine texts to play or to pray, to express themselves, and also to communicate their very real, human need for pleasure, beyond utility or norm."[20] On the other hand, through corrections and the concerns for textual accuracy in a manuscript like Codex Montfortianus, we see the nascent concerns of modern textual criticism. In examples like this, we witness a combination of past readers comparing texts and fixing their own quotidian mistakes as they write, all the while working

---

19. Sherman, *Used Books*, xvi.
20. Papaioannou, "Readers," 547.

to navigate an emerging world of European scholarship at the outset of a massive technological revolution in media and religious change.

Users' paratexts offer something for multiple scholarly questions: the transmission of the New Testament, its production and use in specific contexts, perception of its textual change and approaches to dealing with textual pluriformity, reception history, social history, art history, and more. There is a famous dictum articulated by the nineteenth-century editors of the New Testament, Westcott and Hort, that "knowledge of the documents should precede final judgement upon readings,"[21] meaning that textual critics must first know something about the manuscripts before they make decisions about which form of the text was original. Westcott and Hort were thinking about things like date, paleography, place of production, and the accuracy of scribal performance. But I think this statement has a broader valence, especially now that digital manuscript images are more readily available to many people. Scholars and students who work with these manuscripts for whatever reason must not so quickly set aside the accidental evidence of later readers. Not only do users' paratexts tell us about the life of the manuscript, but they tell us something about the way the book was used. Some of this information has little bearing on making textual decisions. But if we want to understand in greater detail the history and transmission of the New Testament's texts and its manuscripts, we must begin to think more carefully about the things that textual scholars have largely set aside since the outset of critical scholarship.

---

21. B. F. Westcott and F. J. A. Hort, *The New Testament in the Original Greek*, vol. 1 (Cambridge: Cambridge University Press, 1881), 31.

Chapter 13

THE MARGINS AND BIBLICAL SCHOLARSHIP

A main argument that runs through this book is that manuscripts are not just witnesses to the text of the New Testament, but they are also physical spaces that contextualize our interactions with these literary traditions. Like modern commentaries or other tools we use to learn about the New Testament, paratexts supplement and shape the way we read and understand these traditions. The margins are generative spaces that create opportunities for scholars, scribes, and readers to grapple with and frame their sacred traditions. When we change our framework and start by looking at the margins, working from the outside in toward the text, we gain new interlocutors, new evidence for how the New Testament was construed and interpreted, and new questions to ask the text and the people responsible for both idiosyncratic paratexts and larger systems. Paratexts help us to achieve new vantage points on the text and its interpretation, altering our basic assumptions of what constitutes the New Testament. We achieve a more captious understanding, one that reinforces the idea that the New Testament, and sacred traditions more generally, have never been static even in situations where texts are not wildly divergent from one another.

Far from undermining the reliability of sacred texts, the realities of paratexts and their many functions emphasize the innate value of the New Testament. Paratexts demonstrate that thousands of anonymous scholars, careful readers, and anonymous craftspeople expended significant energy to initially craft, transmit, and use these features in their many configurations from the second century onward. The amount of effort, time, and resources to include the Eusebian system in a gospel codex or the Euthalian lists and annotations in a copy of Paul's letters is substantial. Paratexts reflect the inherent value of Bibles in the many contexts that transmitted them and in the ways the people worked to maintain its relevance across the centuries. If the New Testament is something that is divinely ordained, something that offers access to divine revelation, then the many forms that we have it in are how it was meant to come down to us—through the hands of many anonymous annotators, thinkers, and scribes. Regardless of what we ultimately think the New Testament is, and whatever theological beliefs we hold about it, paratexts are a large part of its story that we must consider if we are to seriously grapple with what the text communicates.

The material that we've worked through to this point, including titles, cross-reference systems, corrections, eccentric annotations, and various prefaces, have shown the critical value for thinking more broadly about the New Testament's transmission and reception, and for underlying conceptualizations of scripture. But even these areas have only scratched the surface on the New Testament's paratextuality. I haven't, for example, said very much about the commentary traditions that are often found in the manuscripts alongside or embedded among the texts they comment upon. For instance, the commentary by Andrew of Caesarea on the book of Revelation played a major role in the work's transmission, structuring, and interpretation, with its features appearing in over 40 percent of Revelation's extant Greek manuscripts.[1] Recent research has also attended to catena traditions—extracts from various early Christian authors arranged as commentary on each New Testament work (apart from Revelation). Building on research from the early twentieth century, Hugh Houghton and his team in Birmingham have drawn attention to the ubiquity, importance, and origins of the catena traditions and their connections to Byzantine intellectual and book cultures.[2]

---

1. See Garrick V. Allen, *Manuscripts of the Book of Revelation: New Philology, Paratexts, Reception* (Oxford: Oxford University Press, 2020), 74–120.

2. See, for example H. A. G. Houghton and D. C. Parker, eds., *Codex Zacynthius: Catena, Palimpsest, Lectionary* (Piscataway, NJ: Gorgias, 2020); Georgi R. Parpulov, *Catena Manuscripts of the Greek New Testament: A Catalogue* (Piscataway, NJ: Gorgias, 2021); H. A. G. Houghton, ed., *Commentaries, Catenae and Biblical Traditions* (Piscataway, NJ: Gorgias: 2016); and Panagiotis Manafis, *(Re)writing History in Byzantium: A Critical Study of Collection of Historical Excerpts* (London: Routledge, 2020). For

The Margins and Biblical Scholarship

Commentary and catenae quite overtly shape interpretive practices by attaching explicit interpretations of the scriptural text.

I've also not examined the paratextual value of the material aspects of books in any detail. In chapter 2, I briefly mentioned the materiality and layout as features that have significance in shaping readerly encounters and the social value of a manuscript book. But in recent years, manuscript scholars have paid close attention to the significance of writing supports (parchment, papyrus, paper, etc.), textual layout, practices of punctuation, and paleography or the handwriting used to make a manuscript.[3] These unavoidable aspects of reading the New Testament in a manuscript culture are closely tied to the mechanics and technology of book production, the economic context in which the manuscript was produced, and the skill of those who made it. Although they are essential parts of what make up a reading experience, they are not usually tools used to shape interpretation or to represent knowledge of the text in the same way that, say, prefaces are. Nonetheless, there is much more to explore when it comes to the paratextual valency of these material aspects of manuscript production. We have only begun to understand the significance of materiality when it comes to the New Testament's manuscripts.

Another ingrained part of most manuscripts that I've not explored here is the liturgical apparatus. In addition to the many lectionary manuscripts, which extract and reorder the texts of the New Testament according to the Orthodox liturgical calendar, many of the continuous text manuscripts that we've considered in this book have liturgical items that

---

the larger context of biblical commentary in Greek, see Baukje van den Berg, Divna Manolova, and Przemysław Marciniak, eds., *Byzantine Commentaries on Ancient Greek Texts, 12th–15th Centuries* (Cambridge: Cambridge University Press, 2022); and Franco Montanari and Lara Pagani, eds., *From Scholars to Scholia: Chapters in the History of Ancient Greek Scholarship* (Berlin: de Gruyter, 2011).

3. See, e.g., Bruce Holsinger, *Animals, Archives, and the Making of Culture from Herodotus to the Digital Age* (New Haven: Yale University Press, 2022); Maria Luisa Agati, *The Manuscript Book: A Compendium of Codicology*, trans. C. W. Swift (Rome: Bretschneider, 2017); Pasquale Orsini, *Studies on Greek and Coptic Majuscule Scripts and Books* (Berlin: de Gruyter, 2019); and Georgios Boudalis, *The Codex and Crafts in Late Antiquity* (New York: Bard Graduate Center, 2018).

show readers when the text is to be read and where to start and stop their lections. I mentioned some of these features at the beginning of the section "Traces of Use" in reference to GA 2604, but we didn't explore the many extensive lists of readings (for example, *menologia* and *synaxaria*) that order the liturgical year or their effects on people who read these manuscripts for reasons other than liturgical performance. The liturgical lists are often cross-referenced, as in GA 2604, with marginal annotations that give the date for the reading or the feast day to which it's attached. There is much more to say about the liturgical paratexts connected to most of the New Testament's manuscripts.[4]

This book has also focused exclusively on the Greek manuscript tradition (and Bibles in English). Manuscripts of the New Testament are preserved in many other languages, including Latin, Coptic, Armenian, Slavonic, Syriac, Ethiopic, Georgian, Arabic, Gothic, and more. Multiple manuscripts are polyglottal, containing texts in multiple languages.[5] Each of these traditions has their own paratextual proclivities, some of which are unique to their context and some of which are connected to the Greek tradition. Scholars are beginning to explore these traditions with interesting results. For example, Claire Clivaz's Mark16 project has collected full transcriptions of Mark 16 in various traditions and languages, including an interest in the paratextuality of these traditions.[6] If we are to understand the New Testament more fully, we must consider the many languages and context in which it was produced and used.

4. For insight on this area, see the essays in Klaas Spronk, Gerard Rouwhorst, and Stefan Royé, eds., *Catalogue of Byzantine Manuscripts in Their Liturgical Context* (Turnhout: Brepols, 2013).

5. For an introduction to these traditions, see the essays in Bart D. Ehrman and Michael W. Holmes, eds., *The Text of the New Testament in Contemporary Research: Essays on the Status Quaestionis* (Leiden: Brill, 2013); and David C. Parker, *An Introduction to the New Testament Manuscripts and Their Texts* (Cambridge: Cambridge University Press, 2008), 57–81.

6. https://mark16.sib.swiss/ (accessed 9 August 2023). See Claire Clivaz, "A Multilingual Turn: Introducing the Mark16 COMSt Bulletin," *Comparative Oriental Manuscript Studies Bulletin* 8 (2022): 7–15; and Mina Monier, "Mark's Endings in Context: Paratexts and Codicological Remarks," *Religions* 13 (2022), https://doi.org/10.3390/rel13060548.

The Margins and Biblical Scholarship

Moreover, although we've touched on the odd doodles that sometimes materialize in the margins, I've not explored the more highly artistic illumination traditions of author portraits, headpieces, or the aesthetics of Eusebian canon tables that often appear in medieval Greek manuscripts. Most of these illuminations are part of a highly stylized tradition that functioned, in concert with the Orthodox liturgy, as a way to access the life of the saints and the heavenly realm, as pathways to the spiritual world, or as inspired in their own right.[7] The artistic images present in some deluxe manuscripts reinforce the message of many of the prologues that present the texts as pathways to spiritual realities and divine communion. These features have often been studied for their art historical value or as ways to identify the timeframe in which the manuscript was produced.[8] Although they are not substantially textual, like prefaces, they do have a paratextual valence insofar as they shape how readers approach the text since they bolster the idea that the New Testament is an avenue to divine revelation.[9] In illuminated manuscripts, as Leslie Brubaker argues, "Art and text produce parallel streams of com-

---

7. See Karin Krause, *Divine Inspiration in Byzantium: Notions of Authenticity in Art and Theology* (Cambridge: Cambridge University Press, 2022), 88–131 and 232–72.

8. E.g., Kurt Weitzmann, *Studies in Classical and Byzantine Manuscript Illumination* (Chicago: University of Chicago Press, 1971); Annemarie Weyl Carr, *Byzantine Illumination 1150–1250: The Study of a Provincial Tradition* (Chicago: University of Chicago Press, 1987); Annemarie Weyl Carr, "New Testament Imagery," in *A Companion to Byzantine Illuminated Manuscripts*, ed. V. Tsamakda (Leiden: Brill, 2017), 261–69; and Kathleen Maxwell, "Illuminated Byzantine Gospel Books," 270–83 in the same volume.

9. For example, Patrick Andrist argues against viewing non-textual items, like illuminations, as paratextual since they are visual, not textual. "Toward a Definition of Paratexts and Paratextuality: The Case of Ancient Greek Manuscripts," in *Bible as Notepad: Tracing Annotations and Annotation Practices in Late Antique and Medieval Biblical Manuscripts*, ed. L. I. Lied and M. Maniaci (Berlin: de Gruyter, 2018), 136–37. I take the point, but they do often maintain paratextual functions and are in many cases (like in GA 2604) surrounded by epigrammic texts that are surely paratextual in nature. For one take on the value of manuscript images as knowledge transmission, see John Lowden, "The Transmission of 'Visual Knowledge' in Byzantium through Illuminated Manuscripts: Approaches and Conjectures," in *Literacy, Education and Manuscript Transmission in Byzantium and Beyond*, ed. C. Holmes and J. Waring (Leiden: Brill, 2002), 59–80. On epigrams, see Bissera V. Pentcheva, "Epigrams on

munication that create a dialogue between what words can describe and what pictures can show."[10] The visual and textual coalesce to make meaning and offer access to revelatory experiences.

Commentary, catena, liturgy, and illumination aside, another thing is missing from this book: an overarching or universal theory about paratextuality and its consequences. As William H. Sherman noted over a decade ago, speaking about Renaissance English book culture, "Anyone who turns to marginalia with high hopes of easy answers quickly discovers that the evidence they contain turns out to be (if not always thin, scattered, and ambiguous) peculiarly difficult to locate, decipher, and interpret."[11] Paratexts are simultaneously universal and highly specific. They exist in some form across literatures, languages, and mediums from the ancient world through to modern printing, as my appeal to my own experience with modern Bibles throughout has shown. But paratextual traditions also developed in highly individual ways in response to specific texts. The Eusebian system only works for the gospels; the Euthalian apparatus was crafted especially for Acts and the New Testament's letters. This tension, the universal and specific, makes the study of paratextuality and its effects necessarily fragmentary. It is difficult to craft a master narrative, especially one that can be explained by the political or theological movements that we know influenced the history of the Bible. Paratexts help us to get behind the grand narratives and big stories we tell about the Bible and its interpretation, the parts of its history that are so easily lost in plain sight, getting us to the aspects of change that we cannot so easily set aside to keep the stories we tell ourselves about Bibles in place. In this way they are subversive to the normal practices of biblical scholarship, which often seeks to synthesize large bodies of evidence into linear stories about the past. But I think that they help us to see the Bible for what it is: a highly contingent set of works that have their own histories, maintained by thousands of people we know

---

Icons," in *Art and Text in Byzantine Culture*, ed. L. James (Cambridge: Cambridge University Press, 2007), 120–38.

10. Leslie Brubaker, "Every Cliché in the Book: The Linguistic Turn and the Text-Image Discourse in Byzantine Manuscripts," in James, *Art and Text in Byzantine Culture*, 58.

11. William H. Sherman, *Used Books: Marking Readers in Renaissance England* (Philadelphia: University of Pennsylvania Press, 2010), xiii.

The Margins and Biblical Scholarship

nothing about because they viewed it as a source of divine revelation to be studied, used in liturgy, and understood. The New Testament is a composite artwork, crafted from the ancient literary remains of the earliest Christian authors. Paratexts too, as ingrained parts of the tradition that impinge on, reframe, and interrupt the biblical texts, have revelatory potential insofar as they direct our attention to parts of the text that we might be apt to overlook.

Exploring visual arts and the ways that the perceived meanings of biblical stories shift over time (even when their words stay the same), theologian David Brown has argued that tradition and change are agents of divine revelation.[12] Instead of being diluted by changes after the first century, Christianity has been "hugely enriched" by subsequent developments.[13] From this perspective, the New Testament is not something that existed in a perfected state as it left the authors' hands, something that biblical scholarship must recover as its main goal by stripping away all succeeding elements that have been added to the text, something that we must save from the wiles of time. Instead of working to sideline paratexts as unoriginal and unnecessary human additions to the divine tradition, in Brown's scheme, these items are deeply enriching to the biblical texts they engage with, perhaps even revelatory. When we view tradition as a source of revelation on equal footing with the Bible itself, paratexts become a central point of evidence for understanding the potential of the New Testament as a transhistorical, multifaceted, and ever-changing set of sacred traditions presented to us in many languages, mediums, layouts, and materials.[14] Scripture and tradition rely on one another for their ongoing existence and both have generative potential for understanding ourselves, God, and the world.[15]

---

12. For a capacious perspective on divine revelation that extends beyond the Bible, see David Brown, *Tradition and Imagination: Revelation and Change* (Oxford: Oxford University Press, 1999).

13. Brown, *Tradition and Imagination*, 1.

14. See further my response to Brown's work in the area of textual criticism in Garrick V. Allen, "Text and Tradition: David Brown and New Testament Textual Criticism," in *The Moving Text: Interdisciplinary Perspectives on David Brown and the Bible*, ed. G. V. Allen, C. R. Brewer, and D. F. Kinlaw III (London: SCM, 2018), 3–16.

15. David C. Parker notes that "the character of all manuscript copying meant that there was a continuing interplay between Scripture—the text copied—and the

When we think about the New Testament in this way, paratexts become aesthetic objects, small-scale artworks that are derived from and engage with the texts they frame. In his introduction to aesthetics, Gordon Graham argues the main value in works of art lies not in their ability to instill pleasure, create beauty, or evoke emotion, but in the way they create new forms of knowledge and understanding in the people who engage them.[16] In other words, we tend to value artworks more highly, be they paintings, sculptures, musical performances, or even immaterial conceptual pieces, if we gain new propositions or perspectives on the world in which we live.[17] It's not that art imitates life, but that good art changes the way we see the world.

Something similar happens when it comes to paratexts. Rarely would someone turn to the Euthalian quotation lists for their ability to evoke emotion or for the pleasure of their listical beauty. To most they probably inspire some kind of existential dread. But if we can get past this feeling, paratexts offer us knowledge and understanding of the texts they are crafted from and engage with. They have the power to alter the ways we see the text, to direct our attention to certain aspects of its narrative, characters, intertextual relationships, and underlying structures. It's not that paratexts imitate text, but that paratexts change the way we see text itself. Because they mold the way we see the text, paratexts are an essential ingredient in making the New Testament accessible to readers, in making its letters and narratives into literary works that can be read in community and passed down to later generations. Paratexts make scripture into literature, an artistic form that is able to relay complex ideas and concepts.[18] Paratextuality is key to literary communication

---

tradition—the person engaged in the process of copying in and for the church." *The Living Text of the Gospels* (Cambridge: Cambridge University Press, 1997), 204.

16. Gordon Graham, *Philosophy of the Arts: An Introduction to Aesthetics*, 3rd ed. (London: Routledge, 2005); and Gordon Graham, "Learning from Art," *British Journal of Aesthetics* 35 (1995): 26–37.

17. This philosophical theory on art is known as aesthetic cognitivism. It argues (1) that we can learn from art and (2) that our ability to learn from a piece is one reason we tend to value some works more highly than others. See Christoph Baumberger, "Art Seeking Understanding: In Defence of Aesthetic Cognitivism," in *Bilder Sehen: Perspektiven der Bildwissenschaft*, ed. M. Greenlee et al. (Regensburg: Schnell & Steiner, 2013), 41–57. On the cognitive value of conceptual art, see Peter Goldie and Elisabeth Schellekens, *Who's Afraid of Conceptual Art?* (London: Routledge, 2010).

18. See further, Garrick V. Allen and Anthony P. Royle, "Paratexts Seeking Under-

The Margins and Biblical Scholarship

and, as such, is an indivisible part of what makes scripture sacred. There is no Bible, no New Testament, without paratexts.

This reality is why the margins matter. Since the European Enlightenment, biblical scholarship has been concerned to understand the texts of the works themselves, usually in how the initial authors or receivers understood them.[19] This critical goal endures as it continues to serve as the basis for theological education, especially in the United States. Even though novel approaches to the New Testament continue to emerge, one area that has yet to receive sufficient attention is the manuscripts themselves, an area of New Testament study that has primarily belonged to textual critics.[20] By ceding the study of the New Testament's manuscripts to textual critics, we have unintentionally set aside many questions and any evidence that the manuscripts offer beyond the purely textual.[21] The making of critical editions and refining of textual hypotheses, too, will endure. Editions are, after all, "tools for understanding the work."[22] But there is now space to begin to examine in greater detail other aspects of these artifacts, as I have tried to demonstrate in this book.

Paratexts, materials, scribal habits, and other features shed light not only on the origins of the New Testament but on its subsequent transmission, illuminating spaces of reading and production that contribute to the Bible as we know it today on the bookshelf in your grandmother's

---

standing: Manuscripts and Aesthetic Cognitivism," *Religions* 11 (2020), https://doi.org/10.3390/rel11100523.

19. A good overview of the historical-critical method was articulated by C. H. Dodd in his inaugural lecture at the University of Cambridge in 1936. See Dodd, *The Present Task of New Testament Studies* (Cambridge: Cambridge University Press, 1936).

20. Larry W. Hurtado writes that "the manuscripts that constitute our earliest artifacts of Christianity are so widely ignored." *The Earliest Christian Artifacts: Manuscripts and Christian Origins* (Grand Rapids: Eerdmans, 2006), 1. More work is being done on the manuscripts today than earlier in the century, but this area remains a largely untapped source for many scholarly questions.

21. Parker, *Living Text*, 2 notes that not only study of the manuscripts but also textual criticism itself has been "damaged by the notion that [textual criticism] is best left in the hands of experts. . . . Certainly, this particular branch of knowledge is frequently treated as so recherché as to be beyond the comprehension of all but a very few people, devotees who bring rare gifts to a secret god."

22. David C. Parker, *Textual Scholarship and the Making of the New Testament* (Oxford: Oxford University Press, 2012), 105.

basement, the church pew, or the bedside table. The features that I have explored here are hidden in plain sight, obscured in modern reading by the supposed consistency of printed vernacular Bibles and critical editions. They reveal the complexity of the New Testament as a set of ancient texts that have been touched by each successive generation of readers and producers. This complexity is fundamental to what constitutes the New Testament, and it is something scholars and other careful readers will continue to grapple with in the coming generations. What excites me most about the future of research on the New Testament is that, even after years of serious study, I still have more questions about the Bible today than I did when I first picked up my huge family Bible and began to wonder what this thing was all about. The more we turn to overlooked parts of the tradition, like manuscripts and their paratexts, the more we will begin to discover what it is we do not yet know, to pose new questions to these old sacred traditions, and to see that the New Testament does not exist apart from the manuscripts that we have overlooked for far too long.

Taking account of the vast body of material represented by manuscript copies of the New Testament helps us to begin to tell new stories about the significance, relevance, and import of this collection of literary works. As the studies in this book demonstrate, these new stories are not simple, nor do they have linear plots or clear character arcs. But the manuscripts give us raw material to say something new about the past, about ourselves, and about the people who used these artifacts, stories that have the potential to reshape how we think about sacred traditions and what we choose to do with them.

Bibliography

Abbot, Ezra. *The Authorship of the Fourth Gospel and Other Critical Essays.* Boston: Ellis, 1888.
Agati, Maria Luisa. *The Manuscript Book: A Compendium of Codicology.* Translated by C. W. Swift. Rome: Bretschneider, 2017.
Aland, Barbara, Kurt Aland, Gerd Mink, Holger Strutwolf, and Klaus Wachtel, eds. *Novum Testamentum Graecum Editio Critica Maior.* IV/1. 2nd ed. Stuttgart: Deutsche Bibelgesellschaft, 2013.
Aland, Kurt, ed. *Kurzgefasste Liste der griechischen Handschriften des Neuen Testaments.* Berlin: de Gruyter, 1994.
———, ed. *Synopsis of the Four Gospels.* United Bible Societies, 1972.
Alexander, Loveday. *The Preface to Luke's Gospel: Literary Convention and Social Context in Luke 1:1–4 and Acts 1:1.* Cambridge: Cambridge University Press, 1993.
Allen, Garrick V. "An Anti-Islamic Marginal Comment in the Apocalypse of 'Codex Reuchlin' (GA 2814) and Its Tradition." Pages 193–98 in *Der Codex Reuchlins zur Apokalypse: Byzanz—Basler Konzil—Erasmus.* Edited by M. Karrer. Berlin: de Gruyter, 2020.
———. "The Apocalypse in Codex Alexandrinus: Exegetical Reasoning and Singular Readings in New Testament Greek Manuscripts." *Journal of Biblical Literature* 135 (2016): 859–80.
———. "Are There Ancient Editions of Paul's Letters? The Euthalian Apparatus as a Storehouse of Tradition." *Studia Theologica* 77 (2023): 1–31.
———. *The Book of Revelation and Early Jewish Textual Culture.* Cambridge: Cambridge University Press, 2017.
———. "Digital Tools for Working with New Testament Manuscripts." *Open Theology* 5 (2019): 13–28.

BIBLIOGRAPHY

———. "Early Textual Scholarship on Acts: Observations from the Euthalian Quotation Lists." *Religions* 13 (2022). https://doi.org/10.3390/rel13050435.

———. *Manuscripts of the Book of Revelation: New Philology, Paratexts, Reception.* Oxford: Oxford University Press, 2020.

———. "Monks, Manuscripts, Muhammad, and the Future of the Critical Edition." Pages 181–211 in *From Scrolls to Scrolling: Sacred Texts, Materiality, and Dynamic Media Cultures.* Edited by B. A. Anderson. Berlin: de Gruyter, 2020.

———. "Paratexts and the Reception History of the Apocalypse." *Journal of Theological Studies* 70 (2019): 600–632.

———. "The Possibilities of a Gospel Codex: GA 2604 (Dublin, CBL W 139), Digital Editing, and Reading in a Manuscript Culture." *Journal of Biblical Literature* 140 (2021): 409–34.

———. "Text and Tradition: David Brown and New Testament Textual Criticism." Pages 3–16 in *The Moving Text: Interdisciplinary Perspectives on David Brown and Bible.* Edited by G. V. Allen, C. R. Brewer, and D. F. Kinlaw III. London: SCM Press, 2018.

———. "Titles in the New Testament Papyri." *New Testament Studies* 68 (2022): 156–71.

Allen, Garrick V., and Anthony P. Royle. "Paratexts Seeking Understanding: Manuscripts and Aesthetic Cognitivism." *Religions* 11 (2020). https://doi.org/10.3390/rel11100523.

Allen, Garrick V., and Kelsie G. Rodenbiker. "Titles of the New Testament (TiNT): A New Approach to Manuscripts and the History of Interpretation." *Early Christianity* 11 (2020): 265–80.

Allison, Dale C., Jr. *James.* London: Bloomsbury, 2013.

Andrade, Jackie. "What Does Doodling Do?" *Applied Cognitive Psychology* 24 (2009): 100–106.

Andrist, Patrick. "Structure and History of the Biblical Manuscripts Used by Erasmus for His 1516 Edition." Pages 81–124 in *Basel 1516: Erasmus' Edition of the New Testament.* Edited by M. Wallraff, S. S. Menchi, and K. von Greyerz. Tübingen: Mohr Siebeck, 2016.

———. "Toward a Definition of Paratexts and Paratextuality: The Case of Ancient Greek Manuscripts." Pages 130–49 in *Bible as Notepad: Tracing Annotations and Annotation Practices in Late Antique and Medieval*

Bibliography

Biblical Manuscripts. Edited by L. I. Lied and M. Maniaci. Berlin: de Gruyter, 2018.

Askin, Lindsey A. "Scribal Production and Literacy at Qumran: Considerations of Page Layout and Style." Pages 23–36 in *Material Aspects of Reading in Ancient and Medieval Cultures: Materiality, Presence and Performance.* Edited by A. Krauß, J. Leipziger, and F. Schücking-Jungblut. Berlin: de Gruyter, 2020.

Avrin, Leila. *Scribes, Script and Books: The Book Arts from Antiquity to the Renaissance.* London: British Library, 1991.

Badley, Graham Francis. "Un-doing a Title." *Qualitative Inquiry* 20 (2014): 287–95.

Bagnall, Roger. "The Educational and Cultural Background of Egyptian Monks." Pages 75–100 in *Monastic Education in Late Antiquity: The Transformation of Classical Paideia.* Edited by L. I. Larsen and S. Rubenson. Cambridge: Cambridge University Press, 2018.

Balbanski, Vicky. "Mission in Matthew against the Horizon of Matthew 24." *New Testament Studies* 54 (2008): 161–75.

Balicka-Witakowska, Ewa. "Carl Nordenfalk." Pages 1–16 in *Canones: The Art of Harmony.* Edited by A. Bausi, B. Reudenbach, and H. Wimmer. Berlin: de Gruyter, 2020.

Barclay, John. "Mirror-Reading a Polemical Letter: Galatians as a Test Case." *Journal for the Study of the New Testament* 10 (1987): 73–93.

Barr, James. "Why the World Was Created in 4004 B.C.: Archbishop Ussher and Biblical Chronology." *Bulletin of the John Rylands Library* 67 (1985): 575–608.

Barth, John. *The Friday Book, or, Book-titles Should Be Straightforward and Subtitles Avoided: Essays and Other Nonfiction.* New York: Putnam, 1984.

Baumberger, Christoph. "Art Seeking Understanding: In Defence of Aesthetic Cognitivism." Pages 41–67 in *Bilder Sehen: Perspektiven der Bildwissenschaft.* Edited by M. Greenlee et al. Regensburg: Schnell & Steiner, 2013.

Bausi, Alessandro, Bruno Reudenbach, and Hanna Wimmer, eds. *Canones: The Art of Harmony.* Berlin: de Gruyter, 2020.

Bendoratis, Kristian. "Apocalypticism, Angels, and Matthew." Pages 31–51 in *The Jewish Apocalyptic Tradition and the Shaping of New Testament*

BIBLIOGRAPHY

Thought. Edited by B. E. Reynolds and L. T. Stuckenbruck. Minneapolis: Fortress, 2017.

Berg, Baukje van den, Divna Manolova, and Przemysław Marciniak, eds. *Byzantine Commentaries on Ancient Greek Texts, 12th–15th Centuries.* Cambridge: Cambridge University Press, 2022.

Binggeli, André, and Matthieu Cassin. "Le project *Diktyon*: Mettre en lien les ressources électroniques sur les manuscrits grecs." Pages 202–6 in *Greek Manuscript Cataloguing: Past, Present and Future.* Edited by P. Degni, P. Eleuteri, and M. Maniaci. Turnhout: Brepols, 2018.

Birdsall, Neville. *Collected Papers in Greek and Georgian Textual Criticism.* Piscataway, NJ: Gorgias, 2013.

Blair, Ann M. *Too Much to Know: Managing Scholarly Information before the Modern Age.* New Haven: Yale University Press, 2010.

Blomkvist, Vemund. *Euthalian Traditions: Text, Translation and Commentary.* Berlin: de Gruyter, 2012.

Bottigheimer, Ruth B. "Family Bibles." Pages 313–19 in *The Oxford Encyclopedia of the Bible and the Arts.* Edited by T. Beal. Oxford: Oxford University Press, 2015.

Boudalis, Georgios. *The Codex and Crafts in Late Antiquity.* New York: Bard Graduate Center, 2018.

———. "Straps, Tabs and Strings: Book-Marks in the Codices of the St. Catherine's Monastery in Sinai." *Journal of Paper Conservation* 20 (2019): 81–105.

Boxall, Ian. *Matthew through the Centuries.* Oxford: Wiley Blackwell, 2019.

Brown, Andrew J. "Excursus—Codex 61 (Montfortianus) and 1 *John* 5,7–8." Pages 30–41 in *Opera omnia Desiderii Erasmi Roterodami.* VI/4. Edited by A. J. Brown. Leiden: Brill, 2013.

———. "The Manuscript Sources and Textual Character of Erasmus' 1516 Greek New Testament." Pages 125–44 in *Basel 1516: Erasmus' Edition of the New Testament.* Edited by M. Wallraff, S. S. Menchi, and K. von Greyerz. Tübingen: Mohr Siebeck, 2016.

Brown, David. *Tradition and Imagination: Revelation and Change.* Oxford: Oxford University Press, 1999.

Brown, Raymond E. *The Epistles of John.* Garden City, NY: Doubleday, 1982.

Brown-Grant, Rosalind, Patrizia Carmassi, Gisela Drossbach, Anne D. Hedeman, Victoria Turner, and Iolanda Ventura, eds. *Inscribing Knowledge in the Medieval Book: The Power of Paratexts*. Berlin: de Gruyter, 2019.

Brownsmith, Esther, Liv Ingeborg Lied, and Marianne Bjelland Kartzow. "A Jubilee of Fifty Books Known Only by Title." *Journal for the Study of the Pseudepigrapha* 32 (2023): 376–98.

Brubaker, Leslie. "Every Cliché in the Book: The Linguistic Turn and the Text-Image Discourse in Byzantine Manuscripts." Pages 58–82 in *Art and Text in Byzantine Culture*. Edited by L. James. Cambridge: Cambridge University Press, 2007.

Bruyne, Donatien de. *Prefaces to the Latin Bible*. 2 vols. Turnhout: Brepols, 2015.

Buzi, Paola. "New Testament Titles in the Coptic Manuscript Tradition: An Overview." *Religions* 13 (2022). https://doi.org/10.3390/rel13060476.

Camille, Michael. *Image on the Edge: The Margins of Medieval Art*. London: Redaktion Books, 1992.

Campbell, Gordon. *Bible: The Story of the King James Versions 1611–2011*. Oxford: Oxford University Press, 2010.

Carmassi, Patrizia. "Book Material, Production, and Use from the Point of View of the Paratext." Pages 304–30 in *Inscribing Knowledge in the Medieval Book: The Power of Paratexts*. Edited by R. Brown-Grant, P. Carmassi, G. Drossbach, A. D. Hedeman, V. Turner, and I. Ventura. Berlin: de Gruyter, 2019.

Caroli, Menico. *Il titolo iniziale nel rotolo librario Greco-egizio*. Bari: Levante, 2007.

Carpenter, Mary Wilson. *Imperial Bibles, Domestic Bodies: Women, Sexuality, and Religion in the Victorian Market*. Athens: Ohio University Press, 2003.

Carr, Annemarie Weyl. *Byzantine Illumination 1150–1250: The Study of a Provincial Tradition*. Chicago: University of Chicago Press, 1987.

———. "New Testament Imagery." Pages 261–69 in *A Companion to Byzantine Illuminated Manuscripts*. Edited by V. Tsamakda. Leiden: Brill, 2017.

Carriker, Andrew. *The Library of Eusebius of Caesarea*. Leiden: Brill, 2003.

Chan, Eleanor. "Scrollwork: Visual Cultures of Musical Notation and Graphic Materiality in the English Renaissance." *Journal of Medieval and Early Modern Studies* 53 (2023): 347–77.

Clivaz, Claire. "Mk 16 im Codex Bobbiensis. Neue Materialien zur *conclusion* brevior des Markusevangeliums." *Zeitschrift für Neues Testament* 47 (2021): 59–85.

———. "A Multilingual Turn: Introducing the Mark16 COMSt. Bulletin." *Comparative Oriental Manuscript Studies Bulletin* 8 (2022): 7–15.

Constantinou, Eugenia Scarvelis. *Andrew of Caesarea: Commentary on the Apocalypse*. Washington, DC: Catholic University of America Press, 2011.

———. *Guiding to a Blessed End: Andrew of Caesarea and His Commentary in the Ancient Church*. Washington, DC: Catholic University of America Press, 2013.

Constas, Nicholas. *On Difficulties in the Church Fathers: The Ambigua*. 2 vols. London: Harvard University Press, 2014.

Coogan, Jeremiah. "Byzantine Manuscript Colophons and the Prosopography of Scribal Activity." Pages 297–310 in *From Constantinople to the Frontier: The City and the Cities*. Edited by N. S. M. Matheo, T. Kampianaki, and L. M. Bondioli. Leiden: Brill, 2016.

———. *Eusebius the Evangelist: Rewriting the Fourfold Gospel in Late Antiquity*. Oxford: Oxford University Press, 2022.

———. "Mapping the Fourfold Gospel: Textual Geography in the Eusebian Apparatus." *Journal of Early Christian Studies* 25 (2017): 337–57.

Cramer, John Anthony. *Catenae graecorum partum in Novum Testamentum*. Vol. 1. Catenae in evangelia s. Matthaei et s. Marci ad fidem codd. Mss. Hildesheim: Georg Olms, 1967.

Crawford, Matthew R. "Ammonius of Alexandria, Eusebius of Caesarea and the Origins of Gospels Scholarship." *New Testament Studies* 61 (2015): 1–29.

———. "Do the Eusebian Canon Tables Represent the Closure or the Opening of the Biblical Text? Considering the Case of Codex Fuldensis." Pages 17–27 in *Canones: The Art of Harmony*. Edited by A. Baussi, B. Reudenbach, and H. Wimmer. Berlin: de Gruyter, 2020.

———. *The Eusebian Canon Tables: Ordering Textual Knowledge in Late Antiquity*. Oxford: Oxford University Press, 2019.

Cribiore, Raffaella. *Writing, Teachers, and Students in Graeco-Roman Egypt*. Atlanta: Scholars, 1996.

Cummings, Brian. "The Book as Symbol." Pages 93–96 in *The Book: A Global*

Bibliography

History. Edited by Michael F. Suarez, SJ, and H. R. Woudhuysen. Oxford: Oxford University Press, 2013.

Dahl, Nils Alstrup. "The 'Euthalian Apparatus' and 'Affiliated Argumenta.'" Pages 231–75 in *Studies in Ephesians*. Edited by D. Hellholm, V. Blomkvist, and T. Fornberg. Tübingen: Mohr Siebeck, 2000.

Darby, Peter. "The Codex Amiatinus *Maiestas Domini* and the Gospel Prefaces of Jerome." *Speculum* 92 (2017): 343–71.

Davies, W. D., and D. C. Allison. *Matthew 1–7*. London: T&T Clark, 1988.

Dobbin, Orlando T. *The Codex Montfortianus*. London: Samuel Bagster, 1854.

Dobrynina, Elina. "On the Dating of Codex H (Epistles of the Apostle Paul)." Pages 137–49 in *Le livre manuscrit grec: Écritures, matériaux, histoire*. Edited by M. Cronier and B. Mondrain. Paris: Centre d'Histoire et Civilisation de Byzance, 2020.

Dodd, C. H. *The Present Task of New Testament Studies*. Cambridge: Cambridge University Press, 1936.

Du Toit, Philip La Grange. "'This Generation' in Matthew 24:34 as a Timeless, Spiritual Generation akin to Genesis 3:15." *Verbum et ecclesia* 39 (2018): e1–e9. https://doi.org/10.4102/ve/v39i1.1850.

Duchet, Claude. "La Fille abandonée et la bête humaine, Eléments de titrologie Romanesque." *Littérature* 12 (1973): 49–73.

Duncan, Dennis, and Adam Smyth. "Introductions." Pages 3–10 in *Book Parts*. Edited by D. Duncan and A. Smyth. Oxford: Oxford University Press, 2019.

Edwards, Mark. "Quoting Aratus: Acts 17,28." *Zeitschrift für die neutestamentliche Wissenschaft und die Kunde der älteren Kirche* 83 (1993): 266–69.

Ehrman, Bart D., and Michael W. Holmes, eds. *The Text of the New Testament in Contemporary Research: Essays on the Status Quaestionis*. Leiden: Brill, 2013.

Epp, Eldon Jay. "Note to Readers." Pages xxiii–xxiv in *Perspectives on New Testament Textual Criticism*. Vol. 2. Leiden: Brill, 2021.

Evans, Craig A. *Word and Glory: On the Exegetical and Theological Background of John's Prologue*. Sheffield: Sheffield Academic Press, 1993.

Feldt, Laura, and Christian Høgel. "Reframing Authority—the Role of Media and Materiality." Pages 1–13 in *Reframing Authority: The Role of Media and Materiality*. Edited by L. Feldt and C. Høgel. Sheffield: Equinox, 2018.

BIBLIOGRAPHY

Fernández Marcos, Natalio. *The Septuagint in Context: Introduction to the Greek Version of the Bible*. Translated by W. G. E. Watson. Atlanta: SBL Press, 2000.

Fewster, Gregory Peter. "Finding Your Place: Developing Cross-Reference Systems in Late Antique Biblical Codices." Pages 155–79 in *The Future of New Testament Textual Scholarship: From H. C. Hoskier to the Editio Critica Maior and Beyond*. Edited by G. V. Allen. Tübingen: Mohr Siebeck, 2019.

Fischer, John. "Entitling." *Critical Inquiry* 11 (1984): 286–98.

Ford, Alan. *James Ussher: Theology, History, and Politics in Early-Modern Ireland and England*. Oxford: Oxford University Press, 2007.

Frenschkowski, Marko. "Studien zur Geschichte der Bibliothek von Cäsarea." Pages 53–104 in *New Testament Manuscripts: Their Texts and Their World*. Edited by T. J. Kraus and T. Nicklas. Leiden: Brill, 2006.

Frońska, Joanna. "Writing in the Margin—Drawing in the Margin: Reading Practices of Medieval Jurists." Pages 141–59 in *Inscribing Knowledge in the Medieval Book: The Power of Paratexts*. Edited by R. Brown-Grant, P. Carmassi, G. Drossbach, A. D. Hedeman, V. Turner, and I. Ventura. Berlin: de Gruyter, 2019.

Gaebelein, Arno C. *The History of the Scofield Reference Bible*. Spokane, WA: Living Word Edition, 1991. First published 1943 by Our Hope Publications.

Galavaris, George. *The Illustrations of the Prefaces in Byzantine Gospels*. Vienna: Verlag der Österreichischen Akademie der Wissenschaften, 1979.

Gamble, Harry Y. *Books and Readers in the Early Church: A History of Early Christian Texts*. New Haven: Yale University Press, 1995.

Ganz, David, and Barbara Schellewald, eds. *Clothing Sacred Scriptures: Book Art and Book Religion in Christian, Islamic, and Jewish Cultures*. Berlin: de Gruyter, 2019.

Gathercole, Simon J. "The Titles of the Gospels in the Earliest New Testament Manuscripts." *Zeitschrift für die neutestamentliche Wissenschaft und die Kunde der älteren Kirche* 104 (2013): 33–76.

Genette, Gérard. *Palimpsests: Literature in the Second Degree*. Translated by C. Newman and G. Prince. Lincoln: University of Nebraska Press, 1997.

Bibliography

———. *Paratexts: Thresholds of Interpretation*. Translated by J. E. Lewin. Cambridge: Cambridge University Press, 1997.
Gentry, Peter J. "The Septuagint and Origen's Hexapla." Pages 191–206 in *The T&T Clark Handbook of Septuagint Research*. Edited by W. A. Ross and W. E. Glenny. London: T&T Clark, 2021.
Gibbons, Victoria Louise. "The Manuscript Titles of *Truth*: Titology and the Medieval Gap." *Journal of the Early Book Society* 11 (2008): 197–206.
Goldie, Peter, and Elisabeth Schellekens. *Who's Afraid of Conceptual Art?* London: Routledge, 2010.
Grafton, Anthony, and Megan Williams. *Christianity and the Transformation of the Book: Origen, Eusebius, and the Library of Caesarea*. London: Harvard University Press, 2006.
Graham, Gordon. "Learning from Art." *British Journal of Aesthetics* 35 (1995): 26–37.
———. *Philosophy of the Arts: An Introduction to Aesthetics*. 3rd ed. London: Routledge, 2005.
Gray, Alasdair. *The Book of Prefaces*. London: Bloomsbury, 2000.
Gupta, Sharat. "Doodling: The Artistry of the Roving Metaphysical Mind." *Journal of Mental Health and Human Behaviour* 21 (2016): 16–19.
Hall, Isaac H. "Note on Early Verse-Divisions of the New Testament." *Journal of Biblical Literature* 10 (1891): 65–69.
Hamel, Christopher de. *The Book: A History of the Bible*. London: Phaidon, 2001.
———. *Cutting Up Manuscripts for Pleasure and Profit*. Charlottesville, VA: Book Arts Press, 1996.
Harris, J. Rendel. *The Origin of the Leicester Codex of the New Testament*. London: Clay, 1887.
Hartog, Paul. "Pamphilus the Librarian and the Institutional Legacy of Origen's Library in Caesarea." *Theological Librarianship* 14 (2021): 22–34.
Head, Peter M. "Named Letter-Carriers among the Oxyrhynchus Papyri." *Journal for the Study of the New Testament* 31 (2009): 279–99.
———. "Punctuation and Paragraphs in P66 (P.Bod.II): Insights into Scribal Behavior." Pages 3–29 in *Studies on the Intersection of Text, Paratext, and Reception*. Edited by G. R. Lanier and J. N. Reid. Leiden: Brill, 2021.
Hellholm, David, and Vemund Blomkvist. "Paraenesis as an Ancient Genre-

Designation: The Case of the 'Euthalian Apparatus' and the 'Affiliated Argumenta.'" Pages 467–519 in *Early Christian Paraenesis in Context*. Edited by J. Starr and T. Engberg-Pedersen. Berlin: de Gruyter, 2004.

Hengel, Martin. *Die Evangelienüberschriften*. Heidelberg: Universitätsverlag, 1984.

Hernández, Juan, Jr. "Andrew of Caesarea and His Reading of Revelation: Catechesis and Paranesis." Pages 755–74 in *Die Johannesapokalypse: Kontexte—Konzepte—Rezeption*. Edited by J. Frey, J. A. Kelhoffer, and F. Tóth. Tübingen: Mohr Siebeck, 2012.

———. "The *Comma Johanneum*: A Relic in the Textual Tradition." *Early Christianity* 11 (2020): 60–70.

Hill, Charles E. *The First Chapters: Dividing the Text of Scripture in Codex Vaticanus and Its Predecessors*. Oxford: Oxford University Press, 2022.

Hoek, Leo H. *La marque du titre: Dispositifs sémiotiques d'une pratique textuelle*. Paris: Mouton, 1981.

Holsinger, Bruce. *Animals, Archives, and the Making of Culture from Herodotus to the Digital Age*. New Haven: Yale University Press, 2022.

Houghton, H. A. G., ed. *Commentaries, Catenae and Biblical Traditions*. Piscataway, NJ: Gorgias: 2016.

———. *The Latin New Testament: A Guide to Its Early History, Texts, and Manuscripts*. Oxford: Oxford University Press, 2016.

Houghton, H. A. G., and D. C. Parker, eds. *Codex Zacynthius: Catena, Palimpsest, Lectionary*. Piscataway, NJ: Gorgias, 2020.

———. "An Introduction to Greek New Testament Commentaries with a Preliminary Checklist of New Testament Catena Manuscripts." Pages 1–35 in *Commentaries, Catenae and Biblical Tradition*. Edited by H. A. G. Houghton. Piscataway, NJ: Gorgias, 2016.

Howley, Joseph A. "Tables of Contents." Pages 65–79 in *Book Parts*. Edited by D. Duncan and A. Smyth. Oxford: Oxford University Press, 2019.

Hunger, Herbert. *Schreiben und Lesen in Byzanz: Die byzantinische Buchkultur*. Munich: C. H. Beck, 1989.

Hurtado, Larry W. *The Earliest Christian Artifacts: Manuscripts and Christian Origins*. Grand Rapids: Eerdmans, 2006.

Irigoin, Jean. "Titres, sous-titres et sommaires dans les œvres des historiens grecs du Ier siècle avant J.-C. au Ve siècle après J.-C." Pages 127–34

Bibliography

in *Titres et articulations du texte dans les œvres antiques*. Edited by J.-C. Fredouille, M.-O. Goulet-Cazé, P. Hoffman, P. Petitmengin, and S. Deléani. Paris: Institut d'Études Augustiniennes, 1997.

Jackson, H. J. *Marginalia: Readers Writing in Books*. New Haven: Yale University Press, 2001.

Jansen, Laura, ed. *The Roman Paratext: Frame, Texts, Readers*. Cambridge: Cambridge University Press, 2014.

Johnson, Luke Timothy. *Brother of Jesus and Friend of God: Studies in the Letter of James*. Grand Rapids: Eerdmans, 2004.

Jonge, Henk Jan de. "Erasmus and the *Comma Johanneum*." *Ephemerides Theologicae Lovanienses* 56 (1980): 381–89.

Kavrus-Hoffmann, Nadezhda. "Producing New Testament Manuscripts in Byzantium: Scribes, Scriptoria, Patrons." Pages 117–45 in *The New Testament in Byzantium*. Edited by D. Krueger and R. S. Nelson. Washington, DC: Dumbarton Oaks, 2016.

Kitzinger, Beatrice. "Eusebian Reading and Early Medieval Gospel Illumination." Pages 133–171 in *Canones: The Art of Harmony*. Edited by A. Baussi, B. Reudenbach, and H. Wimmer. Berlin: de Gruyter, 2020.

Klinghardt, Matthias. "Wie und warum ist der Jakobusbrief ins Neue Testament gekommen? Der Jakobusbrief als kanonisches Pseudepigraph." *Zeitschrift für Neues Testament* 25 (2022): 85–95.

Knust, Jennifer Wright. "The New Testament Text, Paratexts, and Reception History." In *The Oxford Handbook to the Textual Criticism of the Bible*. Edited by T. Wasserman and S. Crawford. Oxford: Oxford University Press, forthcoming.

Knust, Jennifer Wright, and Tommy Wasserman. *To Cast the First Stone: The Transmission of a Gospel Story*. Princeton: Princeton University Press, 2018.

Korpel, Marjo. "Unit Delimitation as a Guide to Interpretation: A *Status Quaestionis*." Pages 3–33 in *Les delimitations éditoriales des Écritures—Editorial Delimitations of the Scriptures*. Edited by G. Bady and M. Korpel. Leuven: Peeters, 2020.

Krause, Karin. *Divine Inspiration in Byzantium: Notions of Authenticity in Art and Theology*. Cambridge: Cambridge University Press, 2022.

Kwakkel, Erik. "Decoding the Material Book: Cultural Residue in Medieval

Manuscripts." Pages 60–76 in *The Medieval Manuscript Book: Cultural Approaches*. Edited by M. Johnston and M. van Dussen. Cambridge: Cambridge University Press, 2015.

Lake, Kirsopp, and Silva Lake. *Dated Greek Minuscule Manuscripts to the Year 1200*. 10 vols. Boston: American Academy of Arts and Sciences, 1934–1945.

Lake, Kirsopp, and Silva New. *Six Collations of New Testament Manuscripts*. Cambridge, MA: Harvard University Press, 1932.

Lamb, William R. S. *The* Catena in Marcum: *A Byzantine Anthology of Early Commentary on Mark*. Leiden: Brill, 2012.

Lang, T. J. "Arts of Memory, Ancient Manuscript Technologies, and the Aims of Theology." *Religions* 13 (2022). https://doi.org/10.3390/rel13050426.

Lang, T. J., and Matthew R. Crawford. "The Origins of Pauline Theology: Paratexts and Priscillian of Avila's *Canons on the Letters of the Apostle Paul*." *New Testament Studies* 63 (2017): 125–45.

Larsen, Matthew D. C. "Correcting the Gospel: Putting the Titles of the Gospels into Historical Perspective." Pages 78–103 in *Rethinking Authority in Late Antiquity: Authorship, Law, and Transmission in Jewish and Christian Tradition*. Edited by A. J. Berkovitz and M. Letteney. New York: Routledge, 2018.

Leder, H., C.-C. Carbon, and A.-L. Ripsas. "Entitling Art: Influences of the Title Information on Understanding and Appreciation of Paintings." *Acta Psychologica* 121 (2006): 176–98.

Levinson, Jerrold. "Titles." *Journal of Aesthetics and Art Criticism* 44 (1985): 29–39.

Lied, Liv Ingeborg. "Bible as Notepad: Exploring Annotations and Annotation Practices in Biblical Manuscripts." Pages 1–9 in *Bible as Notepad: Tracing Annotations and Annotation Practices in Late Antique and Medieval Biblical Manuscripts*. Edited by L. I. Lied and M. Maniaci. Berlin: de Gruyter, 2018.

———. "Epistles from Jerusalem: The Paratexts of Syriac 2 Baruch and the Peshitta Jeremiah Corpus." *Religions* 13 (2022). https://doi.org/10.3390/rel13070591.

———. *Invisible Manuscripts: Textual Scholarship and the Survival of 2 Baruch*. Tübingen: Mohr Siebeck, 2021.

Bibliography

Lied, Liv Ingeborg, and Brent Nongbri. *Working with Manuscripts: A Guide for Textual Scholars*. New Haven: Yale University Press, 2024.

Lied, Liv Ingeborg, and Hugo Lundhaug, eds. *Snapshots of Evolving Tradition: Jewish and Christian Manuscript Culture, Textual Fluidity, and New Philology*. Berlin: de Gruyter, 2017.

Lied, Liv Ingeborg, and Marilena Maniaci, eds. *Bible as Notepad: Tracing Annotations and Annotation Practices in Late Antique and Medieval Biblical Manuscripts*. Berlin: de Gruyter, 2018.

Lincicum, David. "The Paratextual Invention of the Term 'Apostolic Fathers.'" *Journal of Theological Studies* 66 (2015): 139–48.

Lippmann, Marie, Neil H. Schwartz, Neil G. Jacobson, and Susanne Narciss. "The Concreteness of Titles Affects Metacognition and Study Motivation." *Instructional Science* 47 (2019): 257–77.

Lockett, Darian R. *Letters from the Pillar Apostles*. Eugene, OR: Pickwick, 2017.

Lowden, John. "The Transmission of 'Visual Knowledge' in Byzantium through Illuminated Manuscripts: Approaches and Conjectures." Pages 59–80 in *Literacy, Education and Manuscript Transmission in Byzantium and Beyond*. Edited by C. Holmes and J. Waring. Leiden: Brill, 2002.

Mainberger, Sabine. "Musing about a Table of Contents: Some Theoretical Questions Concerning Lists and Catalogues." Pages 19–34 in *Lists and Catalogues in Ancient Literature and Beyond: Toward Poetics of Enumeration*. Edited by R. Laemmle, C. S. Laemmle, and K. Wesselmann. Berlin: de Gruyter, 2021.

Maiorino, Giancarlo. *First Pages: A Poetics of Titles*. University Park: Pennsylvania State University Press, 2008.

Manafis, Panagiotis. *(Re)writing History in Byzantium: A Critical Study of Collection of Historical Excerpts*. London: Routledge, 2020.

Mangum, Todd R., and Mark S. Sweetnam. *The Scofield Bible: Its History and Impact on the Evangelical Church*. Milton Keynes: Paternoster, 2009.

Maniaci, Marilena. "Miscellaneous Reflections on the Complexity of Medieval Manuscripts." Pages 11–22 in *Collecting, Organizing and Transmitting Knowledge: Miscellanies in Late Medieval Europe*. Edited by S. Corbellini, G. Murano, and G. Signore. Turnhout: Brepols, 2018.

Maniaci, Marilena, and Giulia Orofino. "Making, Writing and Decorating the Bible: Montecassino, a Case Study." Pages 61–93 in *Scribes and the Presentation of Texts*. Edited by B. A. Shailor and C. W. Dutschke. Turnhout: Brepols, 2021.

Martin, H.-J., and J. Vezin, eds. *Mise en page et mise en text du livre manuscrit*. Geneva: Cercle de la Librarie, 1990.

Maxwell, Kathleen. "Illuminated Byzantine Gospel Books." Pages 270–83 in *A Companion to Byzantine Illuminated Manuscripts*. Edited by V. Tsamakda. Leiden: Brill, 2017.

McDonald, Grantley. *Biblical Criticism in Early Modern Europe: Erasmus, the Johannine Comma and Trinitarian Debate*. Cambridge: Cambridge University Press, 2016.

McKenzie, Judith S., and Francis Watson. *The Garima Gospels: Early Illuminated Gospel Books from Ethiopia*. Oxford: Manar al-Athar, 2016.

Metzger, Bruce M. *The Canon of the New Testament: Its Origin, Development, and Significance*. Oxford: Clarendon, 1987.

———. *Manuscripts of the Greek Bible: An Introduction to Palaeography*. Oxford: Oxford University Press, 1981.

———. *The Text of the New Testament: Its Transmission, Corruption, and Restoration*. 2nd ed. Oxford: Oxford University Press, 1968.

Monier, Mina. "Mark's Endings in Context: Paratexts and Codicological Remarks." *Religions* 13 (2022). https://doi.org/10.3390/rel13060548.

Montanari, Franco, and Lara Pagani, eds. *From Scholars to Scholia: Chapters in the History of Ancient Greek Scholarship*. Berlin: de Gruyter, 2011.

Mroczek, Eva. *The Literary Imagination in Jewish Antiquity*. Oxford: Oxford University Press, 2016.

Mugridge, Alan. *Copying Early Christian Texts: A Study in Scribal Practice*. Tübingen: Mohr Siebeck, 2016.

Müller, Darius. "Abschriften des Erasmischen Textes im Handschriftenmaterial der Johannesapokalypse." Pages 165–269 in *Studien zum Text der Apokalypse*. Edited by M. Sigismund, M. Karrer, and U. Schmid. Berlin: de Gruyter, 2015.

Myrvold, Kristina, and Dorina Miller Parmenter. "Religious Miniature Books: Introduction and Overview." Pages 1–11 in *Miniature Books: The Format and Function of Tiny Religious Texts*. Edited by K. Myrvold and D. M. Parmenter. Sheffield: Equinox, 2019.

Bibliography

Nelson, Robert S. *The Iconography of Preface and Miniature in the Byzantine Gospel Book.* New York: New York University Press, 1980.

———. "Image and Inscription: Pleas for Salvation in Spaces of Devotion." Pages 100–119 in *Art and Text in Byzantine Culture.* Edited by L. James. Cambridge: Cambridge University Press, 2007.

Nestle, E. "Die Eusebianische Evangeliensynopse." *Neue kirchliche Zeitschrift* 19 (1908): 50–51, 93–114, 219–32.

Nicklas, Tobias. "Retelling Origins: Stories of the Apostolic Past in Late Antiquity." Pages 1–20 in *The Apostles Peter, Paul, John, Thomas and Philip with Their Companions in Late Antiquity.* Edited by T. Nicklas, J. E. Spittler, and J. N. Bremmer. Leuven: Peeters, 2021.

Nienhuis, David R. *Not by Paul Alone: The Formation of the Catholic Epistle Collection and the Christian Canon.* Waco, TX: Baylor University Press, 2007.

Nordenfalk, Carl. *Die spätantiken Kanontafeln.* 2 vols. Göteborg: Isacsons, 1938.

Numbers, Ronald L. "'The Most Important Biblical Discovery of Our Time': William Hebry Green and the Demise of Ussher's Chronology." *Church History* 69 (2000): 257–76.

Omont, Henri. *Notices sur un très ancient manuscrit grec en oncialtes des Épîtres de saint Paul.* Paris: Imprimerie nationale, 1889.

Orgel, Stephen. *The Reader in the Book: A Study of Spaces and Traces.* Oxford: Oxford University Press, 2015.

Orsini, Pasquale. *Studies on Greek and Coptic Majuscule Scripts and Books.* Berlin: de Gruyter, 2019.

Papaioannou, Stratis. "Byzantine *historia*." Pages 297–313 in *Thinking, Recording, and Writing History in the Ancient World.* Edited by K. A. Raaflaub. London: Wiley, 2014.

———. "Readers and Their Pleasures." Pages 525–58 in *The Oxford Handbook of Byzantine Literature.* Edited by S. Papaioannou. Oxford: Oxford University Press, 2021.

Parker, David C. *Codex Bezae: An Early Christian Manuscript and Its Text.* Cambridge: Cambridge University Press, 1992.

———. *Codex Sinaiticus: The Story of the World's Oldest Bible.* London: British Library, 2010.

BIBLIOGRAPHY

———. *An Introduction to the New Testament Manuscripts and Their Texts.* Cambridge: Cambridge University Press, 2008.

———. *The Living Text of the Gospels.* Cambridge: Cambridge University Press, 1997.

———. *Textual Scholarship and the Making of the New Testament.* Oxford: Oxford University Press, 2012.

Parpulov, Georgi R. *Catena Manuscripts of the Greek New Testament: A Catalogue.* Piscataway, NJ: Gorgias, 2021.

Penn, Michael Philip. "Know Thy Enemy: The Materialization of Orthodoxy in Syriac Manuscripts." Pages 221–41 in *Snapshots of Evolving Traditions: Jewish and Christian Manuscript Culture, Textual Fluidity, and New Philology.* Edited by L. I. Lied and H. Lundhaug. Berlin: de Gruyter, 2017.

Pentcheva, Bissera V. "Epigrams on Icons." Pages 120–38 in *Art and Text in Byzantine Culture.* Edited by L. James. Cambridge: Cambridge University Press, 2007.

Petersen, Silke. "Die Evangelienüberschriften und die Entstehung des neutestamentlichen Kanons." *Zeitschrift für die neutestamentliche Wissenschaft und die Kunde der älteren Kirche* 97 (2006): 250–74.

Peterson, Jacob W. "Patterns of Correction as Paratext: A New Approach with Papyrus 46 as a Test Case." Pages 201–29 in *The Future of New Testament Textual Scholarship: From H. C. Hoskier to the Editio Critica Maior and Beyond.* Edited by G. V. Allen. Tübingen: Mohr Siebeck, 2019.

Poleg, Eyal. *The Material History of the Bible: England 1200–1553.* London: British Academy, 2020.

Reeve, Anne, ed. *Erasmus' Annotations on the New Testament: Galatians to the Apocalypse.* Leiden: Brill, 1993.

Reynolds, Benjamin E., and Loren T. Stuckenbruck, eds. *The Jewish Apocalyptic Tradition and the Shaping of New Testament Thought.* Minneapolis: Fortress, 2017.

Ritter-Schmalz, Cornelia, and Raphael Schwitter, eds. *Antike Texte und ihre Materialität: alltägliche Präsenz, mediale Semantik, literarische Reflexion.* Berlin: de Gruyter, 2019.

Robinson, J. Armitage. *Euthaliana: Studies of Euthalius Codex H of the Pauline*

Bibliography

Epistles and the Armenian Version. Eugene, OR: Wipf & Stock, 2004. First published 1895 by Cambridge University Press.

Rodenbiker, Kelsie G. "Marking Scriptural Figures as Sacred Names." *Religions* 13 (2022). https://doi.org/10.3390/rel13070577.

———. "The Second Peter: Pseudepigraphy as Exemplarity in the Second Canonical Petrine Epistle." *Novum Testamentum* 65 (2023): 109–31.

Ronconi, Filippo, and Stratis Papaioannou. "Book Culture." Pages 44–75 in *The Oxford Handbook of Byzantine Literature*. Edited by S. Papaioannou. Oxford: Oxford University Press, 2021.

Royé, Stefan. "The Cohesion between the Ammonian-Eusebian Apparatus and the Byzantine Liturgical Pericope System in Tetraevangelion Codices." Pages 55–116 in *Catalogue of Byzantine Manuscripts in the Liturgical Context*. Edited by K. Spronk, G. Rouwhorst, and S. Royé. Turnhout: Brepols, 2013.

Royle, Anthony P., and Garrick V. Allen, "Framing Mark: Reading Mark 16 in a Catena Manuscript." *Comparative Oriental Manuscript Studies Bulletin* 8 (2022): 385–400.

Royse, James R. "The Corrections in the Freer Gospel Codex." Pages 185–226 in *The Freer Biblical Manuscripts: Fresh Studies of an American Treasure Trove*. Edited by L. W. Hurtado. Atlanta: SBL Press, 2006.

Rudy, Kathryn M. *Piety in Pieces: How Medieval Readers Customized Their Manuscripts*. Cambridge: Open Book, 2016.

Rummel, Erika. *Erasmus' Annotations on the New Testament: From Philologist to Theologian*. London: University of Toronto Press, 1986.

Ruzzier, Chiara. *Entre université et ordre mendiants: La production des bibles portatives latines au XIIIe siècle*. Berlin: de Gruyter, 2022.

Schermann, D. Theodor. *Propheten- und Apostellegenden nebst Jüngerkatalogen des Dorotheus und verwandter Texte*. Leipzig: Hinrichs'sche, 1907.

Schironi, Francesca. TO ΜΕΓΑ ΒΙΒΛΙΟΝ: *Book-Ends, End-Titles, and Coronides in Papyri with Hexametric Poetry*. Durham: American Society of Papyrologists, 2010.

Schmid, Josef. *Studien zur Geschichte des griechischen Apokalypse-Textes*. Part 1, Der Apokalypse-Kommentar des Andreas von Kaisareia. Munich: Karl Zink, 1956.

Schmid, Ulrich. "Die Apokalypse, überliefert mit anderen neutestament-

BIBLIOGRAPHY

lichen Schriften—eapr-Handschriften." Pages 421–41 in *Studien zum Text der Apokalypse*. Edited by M. Sigismund, M. Karrer, and U. Schmid. Berlin: de Gruyter, 2015.

Scofield, C. I. *Rightly Dividing the Word of Truth, Being Ten Outline Studies of the More Important Divisions of Scripture*. 1896.

Sherman, William H. *Used Books: Marking Readers in Renaissance England*. Philadelphia: University of Pennsylvania Press, 2010.

Shoemaker, Stephen. *Ancient Traditions of the Virgin Mary's Dormition and Assumption*. Oxford: Oxford University Press, 2002.

Shuger, Debora. *Paratexts of the English Bible, 1525–1611*. Oxford: Oxford University Press, 2022.

Sider, Robert D. *Erasmus on the New Testament: Selections from the Paraphrases, the Annotations, and the Writings on Biblical Interpretation*. London: University of Toronto Press, 2020.

Smith, Helen, and Louise Wilson, eds. *Renaissance Paratexts*. Cambridge: Cambridge University Press, 2011.

Smith, W. Andrew. *A Study of the Gospels in Codex Alexandrinus: Codicology, Palaeography, and Scribal Hands*. Leiden: Brill, 2014.

Soden, Hermann von. *Die Schriften des Neuen Testaments in ihrer ältesten erreichbaren Textgestalt hergestellt auf Grund ihrer Textgeschichte*. 1/1. Göttingen: Vandenhoeck & Ruprecht, 1911.

Spronk, Klass, Gerard Rouwhorst, and Stefan Royé, eds. *Catalogue of Byzantine Manuscripts in Their Liturgical Context*. Turnhout: Brepols, 2013.

Strøm-Olsen, Rolf. "The Propylaic Function of the Eusebian Canon Tables in Late Antiquity." *Journal of Early Christian Studies* 26 (2018): 403–31.

Tasker, R. V. G. "The Text of the 'Corpus Paulinum.'" *New Testament Studies* 1 (1955): 180–91.

Teeuwen, Mariken, and Irene van Renswoude, eds. *The Annotated Book in the Early Middle Ages: Practices of Reading and Writing*. Turnhout: Brepols, 2017.

Turner, C. H. "A Primitive Edition of the Apostolic Constitutions and Canons: An Early List of Apostles and Disciples." *Journal of Theological Studies* 15 (1913): 53–65.

Wachtel, Klaus. "The Corrected New Testament Text of Codex Sinaiticus." Pages 97–106 in *Codex Sinaiticus: New Perspectives on the Ancient Bib-*

Bibliography

lical Manuscript. Edited S. McKendrick, D. Parker, A. Myshrall, and C. O'Hogan. London: British Library, 2015.
———. *Der byzantinische Text der Katholischen Briefe: Eine Untersuchung der Koine des Neuen Testaments*. Berlin: de Gruyter, 1995.
Wall, Robert W. "A Unifying Theology of the Catholic Epistles: A Canonical Approach." Pages 13–40 in *The Catholic Epistles and Apostolic Tradition*. Edited by K. W. Niebuhr and R. W. Wall. Waco, TX: Baylor University Press, 2009.
Wallraff, Martin. "The Canon Tables on the Psalms: An Unknown Work of Eusebius of Caesarea." *Dumbarton Oaks Papers* 67 (2013): 1–14.
———. *Die Kanontafeln des Euseb von Kaisareia: Untersuchung und kritische Edition*. Berlin: de Gruyter, 2021.
———. *Kodex und Kanon: Das Buch im frühen Christentum*. Berlin: de Gruyter, 2013.
Watson, Francis. *The Fourfold Gospel: A Theological Reading of the New Testament Portraits of Jesus*. Grand Rapids: Baker, 2016.
Watts, James W. "Three Dimensions of Scriptures." Pages 9–32 in *Iconic Books and Texts*. Edited by J. W. Watts. Sheffield: Equinox, 2013.
Weavers, William. "The Verse Divisions of the New Testament and the Literary Culture of the Reformation." *Reformation* 16 (2011): 161–77.
Weitzmann, Kurt. *Studies in Classical and Byzantine Manuscript Illumination*. Chicago: University of Chicago Press, 1971.
Wellesley, Mary. *Hidden Hands: The Lives of Manuscripts and Their Makers*. London: Riverrun, 2021.
Westcott, B. F., and F. J. A. Hort, *The New Testament in the Original Greek*. Vol. 1. Cambridge: Cambridge University Press, 1881.
Whitford, David M. "Yielding to the Prejudices of His Times: Erasmus and the Comma Johanneum." *Church History and Religious Culture* 95 (2015): 19–40.
Wiley, Jennifer, and Keith Rayner. "Effects of Titles on the Processing of Text and Lexically Ambiguous Words: Evidence from Eye Movements." *Memory & Cognition* 28 (2000): 1011–21.
Willard, Louis Charles. *A Critical Study of the Euthalian Apparatus*. Berlin: de Gruyter, 2009.
Willson, Justin. "The Terminus in Late Byzantine Literature and Aesthetics." *Word & Image* 38 (2022): 435–47.

Wilson, Karen, and James H. Korn, "Attention During Lecture: Beyond Ten Minutes." *Teaching Psychology* 2 (2007): 85–89.

Zacagni, Alessandro. *Collectanea monumentorum veterum ecclesiae graecae, ac latine quae hactenus in Vaticana Bibliotheca delituerunt.* Rome: Typis Sacra, 1698.

Zuntz, Günther. *The Ancestry of the Harklean New Testament.* London: British Academy, 1945.

———. "Euthalius = Euzoius?" *Vigiliae Christianae* 7 (1953): 16–22.

Index of Subjects

aesthetic cognitivism, 167–68
Alexander, Loveday, 91n2
Ammonius of Alexandria, 71–72, 74, 77n4
Andrew of Caesarea, 12n5, 48, 93n6, 162
Andrist, Patrick, 126, 165n9
Annotation practices, 123–29
Apostolic Constitutions, 111, 113, 116
Aratus the Astronomer, 111, 113, 115
Askin, Lindsey A., 10n3
authorship, 41n5, 43, 45, 49, 55, 77n3

baseball, 1
Bendoratis, Kristian, 18n3
Bernstein, Ellen, 28
Bible(s): *Adventure Bible*, 32; American Patriot's Bible, 32; and change, 2, 5–8, 16, 26, 33–34, 43–44, 98–99, 109, 127–28, 144; English, 6, 10, 16, 24n14, 33, 44–45, 49, 54, 58, 143; English Standard Bible (ESV), 44; family Bibles, 2, 152, 170; King James Version (KJV), 19–20, 24, 131n1; modern, 3, 10, 16, 33, 54, 58–60, 88, 131, 143; New Revised Standard Version (NRSV), 17n2, 27, 44, 131; Orthodox Study Bible, 32, 44, 74; *She Reads Truth*, 32. *See also* Green Bible; Scofield Reference Bible
Blomkvist, Vemund, 81, 103
book archaeology, 124–27
Bookless, Dave, 28, 33
bookmark, 8, 59
book technology, 9, 58, 64–65, 163
boredom, 147

Brown, David, 167
Brownsmith, Esther, 38
Brubaker, Leslie, 165
Buzi, Paola, 36

Cambridge University Press, 59
canon, 40, 43, 48–53, 89
Clement, John, 135
Clement, Thomas, 135n11
Clivaz, Claire, 164
Coogan, Jeremiah, 64, 65n8, 73n19
Crawford, Matthew, 64n7, 66n11
Cummings, Brian, 9

Dahl, Nils Alstrup, 77n5
Defoe, Daniel, 43n11
Diatessaron-Gospel, 71–72, 74
dictionaries, 9
Dobbin, Orlando T., 136n13
Dobrynina, Elina, 78n9
doodles, 145–60
dormition traditions, 97–98
Dorotheus (pseudo), 119n11, 120
Duncan, Dennis, 91
dust jacket, 13n6, 39

epigrams, 165n9
Epp, Eldon Jay, 125n8
Erasmus, Desiderius, 132–35, 137
Estienne, Robert, 60n4
Eusebian apparatus, 29–31, 63–76, 79, 87–89, 143, 161; canon tables, 31, 64–71, 87, 141–42; *kephalaia* (text divisions), 66–71; *Letter to Carpianus*, 64, 71–73, 94

INDEX OF SUBJECTS

Eusebius, 48, 61, 63–64, 67–69, 71, 74, 79
Euthalian apparatus, 25, 76–89, 94, 101–21, 145–46, 148, 157, 161; chapter lists (*kephalaia*), 78–87, 120; *hypotheses*, 78, 101, 116–21; *Journey of Paul to Rome*, 102, 120; lection list, 79n11, 102, 105–10, 113–14, 120; *Martyrdom of Paul*, 102; prologues, 83, 102–5, 120, 157–58; quotation lists, 102, 110–16, 168; *Travels of Paul*, 83, 102, 120
Euzoius of Caesarea, 77n3
Evagrius of Antioch, 77n3
Evagrius of Pontus, 77n3
Everett, Washington, 57
excision, 128n13

Feldt, Laura, 9n2
Fewster, Gregory, xviii
Fischer, John, 37n7, 39n11, 40n3
flyleaves, 123–24, 147
format. *See* layout
Fowler, Kimberley, xv
Franciscan Grey Friars, 134–35
Frater Froyke, 135

Galilee, 95
Genette, Gérard, 12, 40
genre, 41, 43, 58, 81, 98
Graham, Gordon, 168
Gray, Alasdair, 91
Green Bible, 19, 27–34
Gregory of Nazianzus, 96
Gupta, Sharat, 146n3

Harris, J. Rendel, 134
Hellholm, David, 81
Hengel, Martin, 42
Hernández, Juan, Jr., 131
Hexapla, 72
Høgel, Christian, 9n2
home Bible study movement, 20
Homer, 115
Hort, F. J. A., 160
Houghton, H. A. G., 134n9, 162
Hunger, Herbert, 125n6
Hurtado, Larry W., 169

illumination, 165–66
injustice, 57

Johannine Comma, 131–36
John Paul II, 27
Jonge, Henk Jan de, 134n10

Kartzow, Marianne Bjelland, 38
Kephalaia text division system (gospels), 66n10, 71, 142
Kintzinger, Beatrice, 73
Klinghardt, Matthias, 48n6
Knust, Jennifer Wright, xviii, 6, 11, 125
Kwakkel, Erik, 54n20

Langton, Stephen, 60n4
Larsen, Matthew D. C., 43n10
layout, 9n1, 10–11, 21, 163
Lee, Edward, 133
Letter to Carpianus. *See* Eusebian apparatus
library of Caesarea, 61, 76, 88
Lied, Liv Ingeborg, 38, 125
Lundhaug, Hugo, xviii, 125

Maiorino, Giancarlo, 37
Maniaci, Marilena, 9
Mark16 project, 164
Mary, 96
materiality, 8–10, 59, 163
Maximus the Confessor, 96–97, 103–4
McDonald, Grantley, 132n3, 135
menologion, 94, 164
Metzger, Bruce M., 42n6
Mill Creek, Washington, 35
mise-en-page. *See* layout
Montecassino, 9
Mugridge, Alan, 137n16
Muhammad, 146

Nicklas, Tobias, 52n15

Oecumenius, 77n4
Olivet Discourse, 17–20, 22–23, 28–29
Omont, Henri, 105
Orgel, Stephen, 123, 127–28

Index of Subjects

Origen, 61, 72
Orion, 142
Orofino, Giulia, 9
Oxford University Press, 20
Pagninus, Sanctes, 60n4
paleography, 160, 163
Papaioannou, Stratis, 146n4, 159
parables, spicy, 17
paraenesis, 81
paratexts: alternative readings, 25n16, 139n20; catenae, 12n5, 15, 23n14, 26n18, 93n6, 103, 162; chapters and verses, 59–60, 74, 77, 88; colophons, 152, 154; commentary, 23n14, 26, 29, 93n6, 162; corrections, 16n8, 131–44; cross-references, 13, 25n16, 26, 28–30, 61, 83–86; epilogues, 93n6; footnotes, 20, 23–24; foreword, 93; indexes, 19, 28, 60; lists, 78, 93, 97, 106–21; liturgical traditions, 13, 15, 58n1, 71, 75, 94, 147–49, 163–64; *nomina sacra*, 138–39, 142; page numbers, 11, 14, 16n8, 60; *paragraphoi*, 14; prefaces, 20–23, 25–25, 27, 78, 88, 91–99, 101–9; prologues, 12, 25–26, 91–93; stichometric notations, 14, 16n8; tables of contents, 12, 60. *See also* Eusebian apparatus; Euthalian apparatus; titles
Parker, David C., xvi, 7, 9n1, 58n1, 167n15, 169n21
Petersen, Silke, 42
Peter the shoemaker, 153–54
Phoebe the deacon, 41
prayer, 152–54
Priscillian of Avila, 87

readers, 5, 25, 40, 48, 54
reading: front to back, 74, 88; hypertextual, 69–70; nonlinear, 69, 87–88
Renaissance, 159, 166
Robinson, J. Armitage, 115–16
Rodenbiker, Kelsie, xv, xviii, 119

Royle, Anthony, xiv
Ruzzier, Chiara, 58

Scieri, Emanuele, xv
Scofield, Cyrus Ingerson, 20–26, 29, 32, 131n1
Scofield Reference Bible, 19–26, 32, 44, 92–93, 131n1
scribbles. *See* doodles
scripture and tradition, 13, 98–99, 167–68
Sherman, William H., 34n5, 159, 166
Smyth, Adam, 91
Stefaniw, Blossom, xviii
Stephanus. *See* Estienne, Robert
Stevens, Andrea, xviii
Su, Lily, xv, xviii
Swift, Jonathan, 37n7
synaxarion, 94, 164

Theophilus, 91, 107
thumb index, 59
title page, 40
titles, 16n8, 35–55; inscriptions, 47; *kephalaia* (subtitles), 47, 59–60, 142; running titles, 39, 47, 60; subscriptions, 23n13, 41n5, 47, 50–52, 53n18
titology, 35–37, 48
Tutu, Desmond, 27–28

Ussher, James, 21

Vacation Bible School, 57–59
Venetskov, Maxim, xv, xviii
Vercesi, Martina, xiv, xviii

Wallraff, Martin, 63–64
Watts, James W., 10n2
weird little guys, 146–60
Wellesley, Mary, xiv
Westcott, B. F., 160
Willard-Kyle, Christopher, xviii
Wright, N. T., 28
writing practices, 154–60

Zacagni, Alessandro, 103

193

Index of Manuscripts

Papyri		223	157n17	832	83n16
P46	14, 16n8, 136	250	82–85	909	83n16
		307	51–52	912	103n3
Majuscule Manuscripts		312	49	918	83n16, 133
01 (Codex Sinaiticus)		321	157n17	921	83n16
	136–37	325	150, 157n17	1015	157n17
02 (Codex Alexandrinus)		330	53n17	1020	157n17
	50–51	368	50n10	1067	83n16
05 (Codex Bezae)	137	412	51n14	1116	157n17
013	151n9	429	133	1127	51n14
015 (Codex H)	76n2,	433	157n17	1138	154n12
	78–79, 105, 157n17	450	157n17	1162	102–3, 105–7,
045	157n17	458	157n17		109–16, 120
049	51n14	467	51n13	1175	145–48
056	50, 101n2	497	150	1243	51n13
		502	157n17	1270	103n3, 156–58
Minuscule Manuscripts		526	129n15	1277	155–56
27	157n17	577	51n14	1297	103n3
59	157n17	596	150	1405	103n3
61 (Codex Montfor-		603	147n5	1410	157n17
tianus)	133–45, 152,	621	51n13	1413	157n17
	159	627	83n16	1451	150
83	157n17	629	133	1501	52
88	53n18, 133	632	157n17	1526	157n17
94	53	633	83n16	1594	103n3
101	83n16	636	133	1598	103n3
172	157n17	639	157n17	1686	147n5
177	133	644	83n16, 157n17	1702	157n17
216	157n17	677	157n17	1717	157n17
221	133	796	83n16	1721	157n17

Index of Manuscripts

1733	103n3	2049	149, 157n17	2418		157n18
1735	51n14, 151, 157n17	2055	46	2434		157n17
1737	157n17	2064	46	2459		150
1739	53	2067	46	2473		133
1742	157n17	2197	50n10	2604		15, 29–31, 65,
1743	157n17	2318	133			70–71, 94–98, 101,
1746	157n17	2321	157n17			153, 164
1775	47	2358	157n17	2893		157n17
1838	52n14	2369	157n18	2963		103n3

195

Index of Scripture and Other Ancient Sources

Old Testament / Hebrew Bible

Genesis
1:1 — 27
6–9 — 18

Exodus
22:28 — 108n8

Leviticus
23:29 — 113n3

Deuteronomy
18:15–16 — 113n3
18:19 — 113n3

Isaiah
6:9–10 — 114
13:10 — 29
34:4 — 29

Daniel
7:13 — 29

Zechariah
12:10 — 29
12:14 — 29

New Testament

Matthew
1–3 — 96
1:1–17 — 95
1:11 — 140
1:17 — 140
1:18–2:23 — 95
1:19 — 139n20
1:20 — 138
3:11 — 107, 114
4:10 — 140
5–7 — 66
5:1–7:29 — 66n10
5:12 — 139
5:15 — 139n20
5:31 — 139
6:19 — 139
6:26 — 139n20
7:8 — 140
7:8–10 — 141
7:9–10 — 140
9:9 — 95, 142
9:15 — 142
10:33 — 143
10:34 — 143
10:37 — 143
10:37–38 — 143
13:55 — 52
16:12–20 — 68
16:13 — 74n24
16:23 — 140
19:27–30 — 143
24 — 17, 22–24, 28–29, 32
24:3 — 28
24:5 — 19
24:7–8 — 28
24:11 — 19
24:15 — 17, 24
24:29 — 29
24:29–30 — 28
24:29–32 — 30
24:32 — 24
24:33 — 24
24:34 — 24
24:36 — 19
24:42 — 18
25:15 — 19
27:52–53 — 19
28:16–20 — 18n4

Mark
1:10 — 15
6:3 — 52

196

Index of Scripture and Other Ancient Sources

8:27–30	68, 74n24	9–28	117n10	**Galatians**		
13	57	9:1–18	118	2:9	52	
13:35–37	66	9:1–31	108	3:7–9	85	
		9:32–35	117	4:21–5:1	85	
Luke		9:32–11:26	108			
1:1–4	91	9:36–42	117	**Ephesians**		
9:18–20	68	10:10–16	117	2:1–22	85	
9:18–21	74n24	11:27–14:28	108	4:1–16	86	
11:11–12	140	12:6–11	118			
		12:17	52	**1 Timothy**		
John		12:20–23	118	1:3	79	
1:1–18	91	12:22–23	118	1:12	79	
1:41–42	68, 72n24	13	109	1:12–17	86	
3:16	88	13:8–11	118	2:1	79	
6:68–69	69	14:8–11	118	2:11	79	
		15:1–16:40	108			
Acts		16:9–10	118			
1:1	107	16:16–18	118	**Titus**		
1:1–14	107	16:25–27	118	2:9–15	86	
1:5	107, 114–115	17:1–18:28	108			
1:13–26	117	17:28	113, 115	**Hebrews**		
1:15	107	19:1–21:14	108	4:11–5:10	86	
1:15–26	107	20:9–11	118	7:6–10	86	
1:23–26	86	21:15–25:26	108			
2–4	109	23:5	108n8	**James**		
2:1–47	107	25:27–26:32	108	1:1–2	49	
3:1–10	117	27:1–26	118	3:13	81	
3:1–4:31	107	27:1–28:31	108	3:17	81	
4:5–14	86	28:4–6	118	4:1	81	
4:32–5:42	108	28:7–8	118	4:8	81	
5:1–11	117	28:9	118			
5:15	118	28:26–27	114	**1 John**		
6:1–6	117			2:12–17	86	
6:1–8:1	108	**Romans**		5:7–8	131	
6:8	118–119	3:9–4:25	84–85	5:7–9	135	
7	109	3:24	85	5:13	131	
7:37	113n3	4:1–25	84			
7:40	113	6:1–23	85	**Revelation**		
8:2–40	108			1:1	46	
8:6–7	118	**2 Corinthians**		13:18	147	
8:26–39	118	10:1–18	85			

INDEX OF SCRIPTURE AND OTHER ANCIENT SOURCES

Early Christian Literature	Gregory of Nazianzus	Other Ancient Literature
Eusebius	*Ambigua*	**Herodotus**
	21.4–12 96	
Hist. eccl.		*Hist.*
2.23.1 52		1.116 93
2.28.24–25 48		